How Other Children Learn

RELATED PUBLICATIONS BY CORNELIUS N. GROVE

Communication Across Cultures: A Report on Cross-Cultural Research. National Education Association, 1976.

Cross-Cultural and Other Problems Affecting the Education of Immigrant Portuguese Students in a Program of Transitional Bilingual Education: A Descriptive Case Study. Ed.D. dissertation, Teachers College, Columbia University, 1977.

The Culture of the Classroom in Portugal and the United States. *The Bridge*, 1978.

U.S. Schooling through Chinese Eyes. *Phi Delta Kappan*, Vol. 65 (7), 1984.

Secondary Education in the United States: An Overview for Educators from Abroad. Council on International Educational Exchange, 1990.

How People from Different Cultures *Expect* to Learn. GROVEWELL, 2003.

Understanding the Two Instructional Style Prototypes: Pathways to Success in Internationally Diverse Classrooms. *International Communication Competencies in Higher Education and Management*, Marshall Cavendish Academic (Singapore), 2006.

Encountering the Chinese: A Modern Country, An Ancient Culture, 3rd Ed. Intercultural Press, 2010 (1st Ed., 1999). With co-authors Hu Wenzhong & Zhuang Enping.

The Aptitude Myth: How an Ancient Belief Came to Undermine Children's Learning Today. Rowman & Littlefield, 2013.

Culturally Responsive Pedagogy. *Encyclopedia of Intercultural Competence*, Sage, 2015.

Pedagogy Across Cultures. *International Encyclopedia of Intercultural Communication*. Wiley-Blackwell, 2017.

The Drive to Learn: What the East Asian Experience Tells Us about Raising Students Who Excel. Rowman & Littlefield, 2017.

How 'Weird' Societies Think about Children's Learning. *School Administrator*, 2018.

A Mirror for Americans: What the East Asian Experience Tells Us about Teaching Students Who Excel. Rowman & Littlefield, 2020.Where Children Learn How to Learn. *USA Today Magazine* [formerly, *School and Society*], 2021.

How Other Children Learn

What Five Traditional Societies Tell Us about Parenting and Children's Learning

Cornelius N. Grove

Cornelius N Grove (signature)

ROWMAN & LITTLEFIELD
Lanham • Boulder • New York • London

Published by Rowman & Littlefield
An imprint of The Rowman & Littlefield Publishing Group, Inc.
4501 Forbes Boulevard, Suite 200, Lanham, Maryland 20706
www.rowman.com

86-90 Paul Street, London EC2A 4NE, United Kingdom

British Library Cataloguing in Publication Information Available

Library of Congress Cataloging-in-Publication Data

Names: Grove, Cornelius N., author.
Title: How other children learn : what five traditional societies tell us about parenting
    and children's learning / Cornelius N. Grove.
Description: Lanham, Maryland : Rowman & Littlefield, [2023] | Includes
    bibliographical references. | Summary: "Grove takes a comprehensive look at
    parenting and children's learning in five traditional societies: Aka hunter-gatherers of
    Africa, Quechua of highland Peru, Navajo of the U.S. Southwest, village Arabs of the
    Levant, and Hindu villagers of India"—Provided by publisher.
Identifiers: LCCN 2022049316 (print) | LCCN 2022049317 (ebook) | ISBN
    9781475862898 (Cloth : acid-free paper) | ISBN 9781475871180 (Paperback : acid-
    free paper) | ISBN 9781475862904 (epub)
Subjects: LCSH: Learning—Cross-cultural studies. | Education—Parent participation—
    Cross-cultural studies. | Child rearing—Cross-cultural studies. | Home and school—
    Cross-cultural studies. | Parent and child—Cross-cultural studies.
Classification: LCC LB1060 .G77 2023 (print) | LCC LB1060 (ebook) | DDC
    370.15/23—dc23/eng/20221110
LC record available at https://lccn.loc.gov/2022049316
LC ebook record available at https://lccn.loc.gov/2022049317

This book is dedicated to **Dr. David F. Lancy** *of Utah State University*

Those who know David F. Lancy's work will not be surprised that his name appears in this book's endnotes far more often than that of any other anthropologist, even though his areas of specialty do not include any of the five societies that are examined herein.

Dr. Lancy has done fieldwork in, and published findings about, several traditional societies. For me and many others, even more valuable have been his contributions that inform our grasp of children's socialization and learning. That's because he has collected, studied, and cataloged the works of both historians and anthropologists who have done research on children in societies worldwide. The third edition of his magnum opus, The Anthropology of Childhood, *includes an index that lists some 530 societies in which children have been studied—some you've heard of, some you probably haven't (Kwara'ae, Iñupiaq, Pirahã, !Kung, etc.). So if you are seeking an overview of how children learn to become contributing members of their societies, no one is better prepared than David Lancy to help you gain the broadest of perspectives.*

David, this dedication expresses my gratitude to you for being my principal guide in my own quest to understand children's learning and parents' parenting. And thank you again for welcoming me and discussing our mutual interests when I visited you in 2016, and for the parting gift of plums from the tree in your yard.

Contents

Contents

Preface

Ever since my days as a doctoral candidate, I have regarded anthropologists' contributions to social scientific knowledge as uniquely perceptive and useful.

My doctorate is in international education. Its program of study permitted me to attend courses in social/cultural anthropology, and I took every one I could squeeze in. During my dissertation research, I use anthropologists' key investigative method, participant observation.

What drew me to anthropology was its resolve to gain a comprehensive understanding of how people go about their daily lives within their various groups (families, villages, teams, etc.). Equally important to anthropologists is to fully grasp the background and context that historically gave rise to, and currently provides the stage for, the characteristic behavior of group members. Anthropologists pursue this goal with groups everywhere.

Suppose you were determined to achieve those same goals with a group of people about which, at first, you knew little. How would you proceed? There are those who visit the group and ask its members lots of questions about their daily lives. Nowadays, some stay home and query the group's members electronically. How well would this work?

Anthropologists do it the hard way. After making a strong start in learning the group's language, they travel to one of the group's settlements *and live there full time for months on end*. Gradually, they gain fluency, adapt to the group's patterns of behavior, build relationships, observe everything going on, take copious notes and, yes, ask lots of questions.

This undertaking yields a highly nuanced grasp of that group's values and ways of life, which provides a foil against which you and I can compare our own values and ways of life. In so doing, we come to understand ourselves more fully. We see aspects of our lives that are worth rethinking and others to cherish and keep.

If you regard yourself as a member of that broadly inclusive group, the American middle class, and are a parent, a parent-to-be, or an educator or other professional specializing in early childhood, I am confident that, through this book, you will gain fresh perspectives on both the learning of young children and your ways of dealing with them.

Acknowledgments

It is not lost on me that I am exceptionally fortunate in the outpouring of support I've been receiving ever since I began writing books during the decade of the 2000s.

My private editor has remained the same throughout: Kay M. Jones, whom I met decades ago when we were both fledgling interculturalists, and who later revealed herself to also be a diligent fact-checker, copyreader, and general editor (not to mention a multilingual authority on China and Japan). Kay also regaled me with reminisces of her time growing up on a farm with animals. Thank you, Kay!

Deeply appreciated because they all are volunteering their time are my "readers," friends who read my drafts and alert me to passages that need to be written more clearly. Two have been with me throughout all four of my book projects: Willa Zakin Hallowell, my business partner between 1990 and 2020, and Kathy Molloy. Readers who have contributed to this project include Jo Ann Ross, Laila Williamson, John Gillespie, Lisa Watkins, and Desiree Dymond. One way I express my thanks to these folks is to pay attention to their suggestions.

For *How Other Children Learn*, I was also fortunate to have four specialized readers. For the chapter on the Quechua, I am grateful for the assistance I received from Inge Bolin, the anthropologist on whose fieldwork the chapter is largely based. In the case of the chapter on the village Arabs, I was delighted to have it read by the founder and executive director of The Islamic Speakers Bureau of Atlanta, Soumaya Khalifa, and by Reem Al Rasheed. Finally, the chapter on the village Indians is accurate on several complex points as a direct outcome of the contributions of Dr. Bidhan Chandra. For all ten of my readers, a big thank you!

This book is based on the published findings of dozens of anthropologists of childhood, each of whom devoted months, often years, to participant observation among children and their parents in far-away places. I have come to deeply respect their perseverance and commitment to accuracy. Also consulted were insider accounts of people who were raised in, or who lived for years in, one of the five societies discussed herein. They all made this book possible, but it is impractical to acknowledge them all here. Instead, they're all listed in my six bibliographies.

Introduction

As a lad growing up in Englewood, New Jersey, during the early 1940s, Bob LeVine was a studious child, known to his junior high classmates as "the professor." Next door to his school was the public library, where Bob read at least part of Sigmund Freud's *General Introduction to Psychoanalysis*. (This was not a school assignment.) His reaction was, "Would Freud's generalizations hold among the exotic peoples portrayed in my grandfather's *National Geographic Magazines*?" Bob would grow up to become Professor Robert A. LeVine of Harvard University, now one of the world's leading authorities in the field of the anthropology of childhood.[1]

The question animating my writing of this book parallels the one asked by young Bob when he compared the views of Freud with the on-the-ground facts about people's lives in societies beyond the fringes of the European-American West. My question went something like this:

> To what extent do American truths about children and parenting hold among people who live in societies not nearly as modern as ours?

To uncover answers to that question, I'll be taking a comprehensive look at parenting and children's learning in five traditional societies: Aka hunter-gatherers of Africa, Quechua of highland Peru, Navajo of the U.S. Southwest, village Arabs of the Levant, and Hindu villagers of India. Then, in two summary chapters, I will provide answers by drawing not only on what is known about those five societies but also on what anthropologists have been discovering about parenting and children's learning in dozens of other traditional societies around the world.

WHY EXAMINE CHILDREN AND PARENTS IN
TRADITIONAL SOCIETIES?

We will fully explore the meaning of "traditional society" in the following section. For now, it's enough to know that "traditional" societies are those that have not been affected (so far) by "modern"—urban, industrial—values and ways of life. Traditional societies always have been, and still are, found in small villages and camps where people engage daily with their natural surroundings, where families must put time and effort into coaxing their sustenance from the land, and where virtually no one has had any experience with classroom learning.

Now why would modern people like us seek fresh insights in societies like *that*?

One reason is that doing so expands our understanding of how young children go about learning. Most Americans care a great deal about children's learning, but we've grown accustomed to caring about the types of learning that occurs in classrooms. That's appropriate. But our focus on classroom learning diverts our attention from the learning that, over millennia, countless children in traditional societies do in the absence of formal schooling. Surely we would agree that traditional children also are learning. But what are they learning? How are they learning it? Understanding their learning experiences will sharpen our grasp of the effect of classroom instruction on the mindsets, values, and self-concepts of modern students—and the adults they'll eventually become. For us parents, it will offer an eye-opening counterpoint to our routine ways of thinking about our own children's learning.

For example, an American-based website exhorts parents to "Talk with your toddler about everything! Tell each other stories. Singing with your child is also a terrific way to teach new words and ideas."[2] Sound familiar? We Americans think that it is vitally important to rapidly expand a young child's vocabulary, a belief grounded in the high importance we place on classroom success.[3] But what you're about to discover in this book is that, in at least five traditional societies, no one believes that talking with toddlers hastens or heightens their mental capacities.

Don't worry; this book will not argue that it's useless to talk to toddlers. (On the contrary, I will say in Chapter 8 that I think it's a very good idea.) But do be aware that, whenever you do, you are aligning yourself with a tiny minority of all parents who ever lived. Conscientiously talking with your children confirms you as a member in good standing of an industrial, urban, modern society.

Additional realizations you'll gain as you read further will likely derive from characteristics of traditional children's learning such as these:

- Traditional children learn most of what they need to know to become good adults even though adults rarely take any time to deliberately instruct them.
- They learn by engaging their conscious and subconscious mental abilities, precisely the same abilities that modern children engage to do *their* learning.
- They pay attention to whatever is going on in their vicinity in a way that is fundamentally different from the way modern children pay attention.
- The processes by which they learn are via observation of adults, trial-and-error imitation and practice, and gradually increasing participation in adult activities.
- Alone and together with other children, they have daily opportunities to learn in these ways—exactly the types of opportunities that most modern children lack.

A second reason why people like us study traditional societies is because it's insightful for modern parents to find out how traditional parents deal with their children. I think you'll be astounded by how *uninvolved* they are. The term I will often use in this book is "laissez-faire." With few exceptions, the paraphernalia, experiences, and anxious commitment we routinely associate with child-rearing are absent. You might wonder whether they care how their children will turn out.

Like us, they care. But the background and context in which they do their caring is unlike ours in myriad ways. Family dynamics are quite different from what many of us in the United States are accustomed to. The ways they sustain their families' lives are unlike ours. And formal education is wholly or largely absent from their experience. As we will see later in this book, a consequence of these differences is that it makes sense for traditional parents to be relatively uninvolved with their children. But that does *not* mean that their children are uninvolved with adults.

Traditional children grow up to become well-socialized, contributing, and responsible members of their societies. How does that happen? And because it happens in circumstances that sharply contrast with ours, can we really gather useful new ideas for our child-rearing by examining traditional parenting?

Consider this example: American parents frequently voice concern about the challenge of getting their children to shoulder responsibilities—"chores"—around the house. Frustrated parents sometimes exclaim, "Honestly, it's easier to do the chores myself than to get my kids to do them!" Well, it turns out that children in most traditional societies[4] contribute often, and willingly, to the completion of household and other family-related tasks. Despite the significant differences between the circumstances of their lives and ours, it is entirely possible to gain fresh ideas from a comparison of how traditional and modern parents introduce their children to family responsibilities. In fact, this is the topic of Chapter 7.

Additional insights you'll attain as you continue reading will likely result from characteristics of traditional parents' child-rearing such as these:

- When not nursing or sleeping, infants and very young children are positioned in such a way that they can watch and listen to everyone in their surroundings.
- After weaning, parents cease trying to shield their child from danger and stress, and they have no concept similar to our "age-inappropriate experience."
- In dealing with children, parents consistently remain their competent, mature selves; they do not adopt child-like behavior in an effort to appeal to children.
- Parents never imagine that they are solely responsible for raising their child; they share this responsibility with others, notably including older children.
- They assume that a child who attains puberty—the ability to reproduce—also attains social maturity, the freedom to make decisions affecting him- or herself.

I cannot guarantee you an "aha moment" as you read this book. But I do think you'll come away with a better grasp of the nature and processes of your children's learning, the reasons why we raise our children as we do, and which features of our child-raising repertoire could benefit from a little tweaking. You might wonder, as I have, whether we've overthought this whole child-rearing thing. And you might go so far as to question whether some of our modern American ways with children are undermining their natural capacities for learning, socialization, and progress toward responsible and productive maturity.

WHAT IS A "TRADITIONAL" SOCIETY?

As promised, here is a fuller exploration of the meaning of "traditional society."

A traditional society,[5] for the purposes of this book, is one that is not western, not educated, not industrialized, not rich, and not democratic. The initial letters of those five attributes are W, E, I, R, and D, which spell WEIRD, which has become an often-used acronym among social scientists. The archetypal WEIRD society is our own modern one, that is, not merely middle-class

American society but also other industrialized societies, plus the major urbanized areas of still others.[6]

WEIRD became an acronym during 2010, after three social scientists from Canada published a journal article, "The weirdest people in the world?" It gained wide attention almost overnight.[7] In it, they put forward the observation—the accusation, really—that their fellow social scientists had been routinely publishing sweeping conclusions about the behavior of *all* human beings based on research carried out largely, often entirely, with subjects in societies that were western, educated, industrialized, rich, and democratic. For example, they noted that

> 67 percent of the American samples (and 80 percent of the samples from other countries) were composed solely of undergraduates in psychology courses. In other words, a randomly selected American undergraduate is more than 4,000 times more likely to be a research participant than is a randomly selected person from outside of the West.[8]

This fact need not concern us if we are certain that all human beings in every corner of the Earth over thousands of years have been, and are, identical in their psychosocial and behavioral characteristics. But for anyone who cares to look, it soon becomes obvious that while humans are highly similar in their *physiological* makeup, they differ in myriad other ways large and small including the values they hold, the emotions they express, the behavior they exhibit, the patterns of their thinking, and the regularities of daily life in the societies they have created.

Back in 1948, two eminent anthropologists published a book that included this dictum: "Every human is in certain respects (a) like all other humans, (b) like some other humans, and (c) like no other human."[9] The like-*all*-other category is our inherited physiology; the like-*some*-other category is our society and culture; the like-*no*-other category is the unique style and disposition of each individual.

The focus of anthropology is on the like-*some*-other category. For example, at the level of society and culture, I am similar in *some* ways with inhabitants of both the United Kingdom and of India (but I share more similarities with those in the United Kingdom).

A disadvantage of living out all or most of our lives in a WEIRD society is that we develop a narrow range of expectations about what living on this Earth includes and ought to include. We lose sight of alternative ways of living and learning—ways that enabled our own forebears as well as millions of people in traditional societies past and present to live what, for them, are fulfilling lives.

Here's an example of an expectation about what living on this Earth includes. Within American society, there's a widespread expectation that a good way for fathers to develop close relationships with their infants is via rough-and-tumble play.[10] Our assumption is that the mother-infant bond is formed via her ongoing sensitive care, whereas because fathers are with the infant less often, they take an energetic approach to forming a positive bond. Studies in WEIRD societies in other parts of the world have shown that there, like here, vigorous play is often a feature of fathers' styles. So rough-and-tumble is the "natural" fatherly way, right?

Wrong. In the anthropological record so far, the fathers of one society stand above all others as being the most closely bonded with their children: the fathers of the Aka hunter-gatherers of Central Africa, the focus of Chapter 2. The anthropologist who has devoted the most years—40!—to studying the Aka reports that, during 264 hours of observing fathers, he saw a father playing rough-and-tumble with his infant exactly once. It takes just one example of a society in which fathers are not rough-and-tumble to show that rough-and-tumble is not "natural."

Earlier, I defined a traditional society by saying what it's not. Speaking positively, among the observable characteristics of most traditional societies, past and present, are these eight:

1. Settlement size (e.g., villages or camps) is small;
2. Literacy is nonexistent or narrowly limited to an elite;
3. Change occurs slowly due to conformity with past ways;
4. Geographical mobility is limited (nomads are an exception);
5. Social mobility is low (except for upward mobility via advancing age);
6. Individuals are loyal to extended family members and wary of outsiders;
7. Extended family members live nearby and are paramount in one's social life;
8. Families sustain themselves largely if not entirely through direct reliance on the land (or sea): agriculture, animal husbandry, and/or hunting and gathering.[11]

Absent from this list is any item about decision-making. This is because there is marked variability among traditional societies in terms of hierarchy and leadership. Among the five societies discussed in this book, three are egalitarian (Aka, Quechua, and Navajo) while two are hierarchical (village Arab and village Indian.)

MORE ABOUT THIS BOOK

Since 2010, at least seven books for the general reader have been published about parenting in societies other than that of the United States. Four were written by authors who are not anthropologists, three by professional anthropologists of childhood.

Six of these books proceed by considering one or more problems typically experienced by American parents—for example, toilet training—and, for each problem, explaining how parents in another society deal successfully with it.[12] The pattern goes like this: "We've got a problem; *they've* got a solution! Go and do likewise."

For example, one journalist solves our challenge about bedtimes with a solution from Argentina and our challenge about children's fighting with a solution from Japan. But while we're being told all about the solution, we learn very little about the background and context of the society where that solution is found. Can a solution in Country A be transplanted straight into Country B? Don't bet on it.[13]

The seventh book is a meditation on the ways in which we Americans raise children, written by David F. Lancy, another leading anthropologist of childhood. In *Raising Children*, Dr. Lancy has amassed encyclopedic knowledge of the contrasting ways in which children learn and parents parent down through history and in all corners of the world. Citing countless examples from dozens of societies, he shows that Americans' ideas about children are starkly different from those of almost all other humans.[14]

I believe that it's not helpful to describe an isolated child-rearing practice in a society that is unfamiliar to the reader. In any society, the values and practices of child-rearing, and the expectations about children's learning, all emerged over centuries as adaptations to a blend of historical, ecological, social, economic, political, and spiritual factors. The raising and socializing of children are central events of each society's culture. To be understood, they need to be informed by a holistic overview of that society's background, context, values, and patterns of daily life, for this is the milieu within which each parent parents and each child learns.

How Other Children Learn is not driven by a closed-ended search for isolated solutions to American parents' specific problems. Rather, this book is driven by an open-ended quest to explore the background and context of five traditional societies and only then, within each, to reveal details about its values and expectations with respect to children's learning and parents' caretaking.

About this Book's Time Frame

As discussed in Appendix B, "Sources of Information for the Five Main Chapters," I was able to write this book because I relied heavily on books and journal articles by anthropologists and other researchers who primarily used the data-gathering method known as participant observation.

Relatively few of all those books and journal articles were published after 2000. To have a wide range of anthropological accounts of each of the five societies, I had to rely largely on sources published during the past 75 years. Two exceptions are that much, but not all, of the research among the Aka hunter-gatherers and the Quechua highlanders occurred during the early 2000s.

So if you were hoping to read accounts of present-day child-raising and children's learning in traditional societies, this is not the book for you.

The purpose of this book is to provide, for comparison with our beliefs and practices in U.S. society today, accounts of child-raising and children's learning in five traditional societies between roughly the 1940s and the early 2000s. The five societies were chosen because anthropologists of childhood had published many accounts of their participant observation fieldwork within each of those societies.

About the Participant Observation Research Method

With few exceptions, the facts reported in this book were all revealed by the participant observation method of research (also known as ethnography). Let me put this into context.

When it's deemed worthwhile to do the work of understanding an unfamiliar group of people, two basic approaches are available. One method puts value on getting the work done efficiently. The other puts value on understanding the group from the perspectives of its insiders, that is, the group's own members.

Researchers who prefer efficiency use *survey* methods. They contact as many of the group's members as possible, asking each one to respond to questions about their lives. The contact may be face-to-face, but it often isn't; either way, a questionnaire is involved. Questions concern the frequency of certain activities, for example, "How often did you give your child a full-body bath during the past week?" After responses are collected, the answers are counted and statistically analyzed. The survey method is "quantitative" in that it relies on counting people's responses; survey reports are laden with numbers, graphs, charts, and statistics.

Though the survey method has many uses, it is vulnerable to the criticisms that its findings (a) portray the group based on outsiders' questions, not its members' own lived experiences; (b) reveal little about *why* activities occur; and (c) report not objective facts but what respondents want strangers to believe about their lives.

For anthropologists, that's not good enough. To comprehend an unfamiliar group, they must experience its day-to-day realities and emotions in their natural settings, learning not just *what* is done, but *why* and *how* it's done that way. Such in-depth insight can be gained only by living with the group for a long time.

This research method is called *participant observation* because the researcher observes the group's day-to-day activities while also participating in them. The researcher's goal is to build trust with group members so that, eventually, they will share their motivations and emotions, their "insiders' perspectives" on their lives.

Participant observation is a "qualitative" or "holistic" method. It requires huge effort from the researcher (including gaining fluency in a new language) and years of time to live with the group and compile the research report. It is not an efficient method. (Participant observation is discussed further in Chapter 1.)

One more point: Throughout this book I refer to "anthropologists." This is a shorthand way for me to refer to *researchers who use qualitative methods such as participant observation*. Not only anthropologists use these methods,[15] but anthropologists are more likely to use them than researchers who identify with any other social science.

About the Focus on Values

This book is about the *values* shared by groups of individuals. "Value" refers to an individual or group's preference for, or dislike of, a certain state of affairs regarding events, objects, activities, ideas, intentions, personal characteristics, and so forth.

For example, in traditional societies where formal education is beginning to be available, girls' parents encounter a choice between alternative courses of action: to send their daughters to school or not. It's complicated! A middle-ground option is to send the girl to school just a little bit, that is, part-time (when she's not needed at home) or for only a few years (until she becomes slightly literate). For each girl in the family, a fresh choice must be made, often turning on factors such as how much the girl helps her mother run the household and whether the girl herself seems capable of gaining literacy. Another question in parents' minds is the extent to which literacy will make their daughter marriageable—not marriageable in the abstract but to the type of young man they hope will be interested in her.

Dilemmas always are about conflicting values, although we often talk about dilemmas without mentioning values. In the foregoing example, the dilemma is support mom vs. attend school: *Which will have greater value for this family?* How much support does mom need for the family to function well? How much literacy does the girl need to bring joy to herself and her family by being attractive to a guy with a high school diploma earning a steady salary in the city? But take care! She mustn't have too much literacy; that would be a major turn-off for many guys.

Values influence behavior minute by minute, year after year. We make small choices; we make life-defining choices. Why this, not that? *Values explain why.*

To grasp why a traditional family selects one course of action over another, we must be aware of its constellation of values. In turn, that requires us to be familiar with the background and context of this family's life. This is the main reason why I discuss the background and context that prevails in each of the five societies.

About the Background and Context Discussions

For each of the five societies, my discussion of its background and context is found at the beginning of each of the five main chapters—Chapters 2 through 6. In each of those chapters, the background and context discussion ends at the beginning of the section entitled "How Newborns Arrive and Receive Care."

In the spirit of full disclosure, I have not visited any of the five societies. None of the discussions are based on my own experience.[16] Virtually all of the facts, like everything else in this book, come from (a) the reports of anthropologists and other scholars who lived and worked in these societies with the objective of better understanding their ways, and (b) participating members of these societies, not scholars, who have described and reflected on their insider experiences.

The word "virtually" appears above because there are a few exceptions. For example, a woman from New Zealand married an Arab, lived with him in one of the caves at Petra, Jordan, and bore and raised their three children there. She wrote a book about her experiences. I made use of passages from her book.

The background-and-context sections at the beginning of the five main chapters are far from exhaustive. They don't paint a complete picture; whole books do that. I have had to make choices about what I relate. I've tried to focus on background features that are relevant mainly to families with children.

At the end of each main chapter is a list of at least three suggested further readings. Each of those suggested readings is profiled on this book's website at howotherchildrenlearn.info/profiles. At the end of each chapter in which I discuss a traditional society is a bibliography of the sources I relied on. At the end of the book is a bibliography that covers this Introduction, Chapters 1, 7, 8, and both Appendices. If your curiosity is piqued by anything that I've written, please consult these sources.

About the Apparent Tendency to Idealize

Each time I finish drafting a chapter of one of my books, I send it to several of my friends, my "readers," asking them to alert me about any passage that they find difficult to readily understand. One reader of this book's Quechua chapter replied by exclaiming that "nothing is ever wrong in their lives. So much equilibrium! Where are the rebels? Where are the ones who run away?"

I know that my seeming idealization of my subjects' lives can leave a mistaken impression; indeed, in my previous book I addressed this concern in the Introduction under the same heading as above (*A Mirror for Americans*, xxxiii). I'm fully aware that sooner or later every society, every social group, and every family will endure at least a moderate amount of tension, disharmony, and grief. However, I have chosen to write my books without dwelling on those realities. Here's why:

- My purpose is to share a sense of how other societies and their respective cultures work when they are working well. To include dramatic accounts of each society's conflicts and griefs would eclipse the basic facts about how *most* people within that society get along with each other *most* of the time.
- I deliberately write books, and book chapters, that are short. Delving extensively into a society's dark side would add complexity and length.

As previously stated, readers whose curiosity is stimulated by anything written herein may consult the suggested readings at the end of each chapter as well as the six bibliographies near the back of this book.

About the Films Listed at the Beginning of Each Chapter

Whenever we read any type of descriptive account, our minds supply mental images. If we have no prior personal experience of what's being described, our minds' images are likely to be inaccurate. But what if we had an opportunity to supply our minds with a collection of accurate images before we start reading?

At the beginning of each of the five main chapters, you'll find a list of films and videos that "will enable you to more accurately imagine [this society's] families as you read this chapter." All can be viewed on your computer at no charge (though some have intrusive ads). In length, they range from two minutes to 50 minutes.

I am suggesting these films and videos not for their content—though that might be useful—but rather for the real-life images they provide of people and places that are similar to the ones whose lives and living spaces are described in each chapter. For example, one thing that's stayed with me after viewing all these films is the speed and dexterity with which an Aka woman constructs a new hut. Another is the nonchalance with which Indian women fashion cow dung patties. And a third is the naked barrenness of the high Andes where the Quechua live out their daily lives. I encourage you to view one or more of the films before or soon after you begin reading each of the five main chapters. Hot links to all films and videos are available at howotherchildrenlearn.info/films.

THE PLAN OF THIS BOOK

The five main chapters of this book, each one focused on a traditional culture, are surrounded by three other chapters and two appendices that I hope will aid your grasp of the facts presented herein. Following this Introduction, the chapters are:

1. What Do Anthropologists of Childhood Actually *Do*? This book is anchored in the published research of anthropologists of childhood. Their academic field has been coalescing and growing during the past hundred years. What is the nature of the work of anthropologists of childhood? What do they talk about among themselves? With which academic discipline are they frequently at loggerheads? And what are the conclusions they've reached so far? Chapter 1 will give you a more secure perspective for understanding the five main chapters.

Chapters 2, 3, 4, 5, 6: The Main Chapters. Please feel free to read the five main chapters—about the Aka, Quechua, Navajo, Village Arabs, and Village Indians—in any order. Yes, I did put them in their existing order for a reason. Frankly, though, it doesn't matter that much.

2. Raising Oneself in the Forest: Growing Up among the Aka Hunter-Gatherers of Africa

3. Nothing Special for the Children: Growing Up among the Quechua of Highland Peru

4. Parenting by Persuasion: Growing Up Among the Navajos of the U.S. Southwest

5. According to Nomads' Values: Growing Up Among the Village Arabs of the Levant

6. The Total-Immersion Family: Growing Up Among the Hindu Villagers of India

Each of these five chapters begins by discussing the background and context of the featured society under three or four section headings. When this discussion ends, the chapter continues under six uniform section headings, listed below. "[Name]" is the name of the featured society.

- How Newborns Arrive and Receive Care
- Learning to Be [Name]: The Early Childhood Years
- Learning to Be [Name]: The Later Childhood Years[17]
- Informal Learning by [Name] Children
- Formal Learning by [Name] Children
- From an Anthropologist's Perspective

7. How Do Other Children Learn Responsibility? In this initial, short summary chapter, I look for an explanation for the fact that most children in traditional societies willingly carry out responsibilities beginning at an early age, whereas most children in modern societies resist responsibilities. (Responsibility refers to one's intention to complete a task, usually one repeated on a daily or weekly basis, that benefits the entire group to which one belongs.) Traditional peoples most definitely have something useful—and applicable—to tell us modern folks about how their children become responsible very early in their lives, and remain so.

8. How Do Other Children Learn? And How Do Other Parents Parent? In this main summary chapter, I will first review two of the crucial background and context factors to which traditional parents adapted eons ago. Then I'll consider the role of education—formal instruction—in the millennia-long transition made by some human groups from traditional-agrarian to modern-industrial (WEIRD). Finally, I will draw on anthropologists' findings about traditional societies in general, with examples from this book's five main chapters, to reveal what those societies tell us Americans about, first, children's learning, and then parenting. I am confident that you will find that at least some of my conclusions aren't quite what you expected.

Appendix A. Tables of Anthropological Findings about Children. These five tables will be helpful as you read Chapter 7. The subjects of the five tables are:

1. Background and Context of Other Children and Our Own
2. Contrasting Models of Parenting and Families
3. How Traditional and U.S. Parents THINK about Childrearing
4. What Traditional and U.S. Parents DO about Childrearing
5. Learning and Schooling in Traditional and U.S. Societies

Appendix B. Sources of Information for the Five Main Chapters. Some readers will be curious about how I, who never visited any of this book's five featured societies, acquired the books and journal articles upon which this book is based, and which ones I found especially valuable. The answers are here in this appendix.

Postscript. This is a brief meditation on a fundamental contrast between the mindsets of Aka and American young people as they approach their adult lives.

Bibliography. The Bibliography offers full citations of all the books and journal articles that I consulted as I wrote this Introduction as well as Chapters 1, 7, 8, and both Appendices. Chapters 2 through 6 each ends with its own bibliography.

ABOUT THIS BOOK'S WEBSITE

This book has its own website, found at howotherchildrenlearn.info. More than just a marketing tool, the website provides useful information for you, the reader.

Informative films and videos are listed at the beginning of Chapters 1 through 6, and for each one the complete URL is provided. Such URLs are composed of random numbers and letters, making them laborious to copy. But you don't need to do that because hotlinks are available at howotherchildrenlearn.info/films.

Suggested readings are listed at the end of Chapters 1 through 8, and for each the title, author, date, and text length are provided. (Text length is the number of pages of the text, not including notes and bibliography.) If you think you might be interested in acquiring a reading, you can start by finding out much more about it by consulting my profile of that reading at howotherchildrenlearn.info/profiles.

Also at howotherchildrenlearn.info are published reviews of this book, a link to any podcasts that I might make based on the book, links to the websites of my three previous books, and a link to contact me directly via email. Do let me hear from you!

The Bibliography at the back of this book includes all publications cited within the Introduction.

Chapter 1

What Do Anthropologists of Childhood Actually *Do*?

Figure 1.1. Margaret Mead circa 1930s. *Courtesy CSU Archives / Everett Collection Historical. Photo and permission from Alamy Inc.*

1

FILMS INTRODUCING THE MINDSET
AND PRACTICE OF ANTHROPOLOGY

The first two films were made to introduce neophytes to the ways anthropologists think and work.

"Why Study Anthropology?" (2016). Two university students and a professor overview the basics of cultural anthropology, hoping to interest new students in their field of study. Produced by the University of Ottawa Faculty of Social Sciences. 5:17 min. youtube.com/watch?v=vcRqWbhwSq4

"Defining Anthropology and Ethnography" (2018). Introduces basics such as ethnography (participant observation) and the four fields of study within the field of anthropology. Produced by MMOGology (which studies online gaming communities). 7:09 min. youtube .com/watch?v=fMyWotLx6mE

The second set of films introduce Margaret Mead, who was the first anthropologist of childhood.

"Margaret Mead: Exploring the Influence of Culture" (2016). This documentary includes many archival photos. Made for Minnesota State History Day. 10:00 min. youtube.com/watch?v=FnHt8UZ9s5M

"Margaret Mead" (c. 1975). Mead talks about her upbringing, field-work, and perspectives; not an interview. Collected by Footage Farm (# 221564–02). 27:30 min. youtube.com/watch?v=A8uPbRWBUxs

Hot links to all films and videos are at howotherchildrenlearn .info/films.

This book relies fully on the work of anthropologists, so let's begin by exploring what they actually do, including the issues they often discuss among themselves.

The first part of *anthropology*, "anthro-," refers to human beings. The second part, "-ology," designates a branch of knowledge, a science. Anthropologists are practitioners of one of the sciences that studies human beings.

This explanation suggests that anthropologists may study any topic related to humans—someone's skeleton, for example. But that's not the case. Like all the other sciences, anthropology is understood to include some topics and not others. Anthropologists focus on the behavior of humans within their self-constituted groups (families, tribes, teams, clubs, businesses, schools, villages, etc.), together with the background and context that historically gave rise to, and now provides the stage for, group members' characteristic behavior.[1]

Two leading anthropologists once wrote that, "Anthropologists are trained to report shared beliefs systems, value orientations, technical practices, and norms of mundane patterns of interaction" among group members.[2] Note the terms *shared, value, practices, norms*, and *patterns*; these words and concepts often appear in this book. The word *mundane* signals that anthropologists study the ordinary day-to-day lives of a group's members. But the groups they study can be out of the ordinary; one of the films suggested at the beginning of this chapter was made by a group of anthropologists who study online gaming communities.

Let's compare *psychology*, which also studies humans, with anthropology. "Psych-" refers to an individual's mental and emotional processes as well as other internal states. Psychology focuses on humans as individuals. It also looks at relationships between individuals, asking questions such as, "How is Person A affected by such-and-such behavior of Person B?" Compared with anthropologists, most psychologists pay comparatively little attention to the overall background and context within which a person's or group's behavior occurs.

Some anthropologists focus on humans' early years of life. Their field is called the anthropology of childhood. Their interests encompass not only the behavior of youngsters in groups, but also parent–child relationships and the parents' child-rearing practices and patterns. Most broadly, anthropologists of childhood are fascinated by how newborns gradually learn everything they need to know to become productive adults who abide by society's norms. In anthropology-speak, they study the "socialization of children." That's exactly what this book is about.

ANTHROPOLOGISTS STUDY CULTURE. WHAT IS CULTURE?

It's impossible to talk about the work of anthropologists without talking about culture. To study how newborns become *socialized*—that is, become infused with ideas and behavior that fit well with those of other members of their society—is to learn how they acquire the familiar ways and mindsets of their native *culture*.

Many meanings of culture have been proposed since the 1870s. Scholarly treatises have probed its meaning and hundreds of definitions have been put forward.[3] One of the shortest is:

Culture is how we do things around here

In this definition, note the word "we." This indicates that culture involves the meanings and intentions shared by people who self-identify as members of a group such as a family, team, business, or political party. It's true that we refer sometimes to an individual's culture, but that usually refers to the values and ways of living that he or she shares with other members of one or more groups.

Next, note "do." This is "do" in the broadest sense, not merely the skill that's needed to accomplish an activity. It's also about the background and context of the activity, its intended outcome, in what ways group members value it and its outcome, what they gain from doing it (including if the activity fails), how they regard it emotionally, and how they talk about it—or avoid talking about it.

Finally, "around here." "Here" is whatever location the speaker has in mind. If she's discussing recipes and cooking, she might have in mind the food preferences and cooking routines of her family. If she's orienting a new hire to her office, she probably has in mind the work group that the newcomer will join, or the people on that floor of the office building, or the entire company. As they say, "It depends."

Here is a comparison that might help you better understand culture.[4] First, note that when you're in a place with which you are thoroughly familiar, you hold conversations effortlessly with family, friends, and others. You and they share many expectations about your spoken language, and about the rules of grammar and pronunciation governing its use, that enable all of you to share meanings orally. You and they learned the sounds and rules during the first years of life; these are now thoroughly internalized so that no one is conscious of them while talking. You just talk. This is "how we talk about things around here."

The same is true for culture (of which language is a part). You and your local acquaintances share expectations about the meanings of countless gestures, facial expressions, modes of dress and self-decoration, activities of all kinds, symbols (this list could go on and on!), most of which you all came to understand during the first years of life. These common understandings of "how we do things around here" enable you and they to build and sustain relationships, and to get things done, without being conscious of every nuance of meaning. You just act.

Sure, you and others might have different opinions and styles; you might even feel angry with each other. Shared culture does not guarantee warm friendships. It guarantees that when, for example, one frowns or scowls, her behavior won't be misunderstood by members of her culture as signaling warm friendship. Culture includes shared guidelines for expressing anger, disagreeing, even breaking up!

Here's a second short definition of culture:

Culture is our book of *shoulds* and *oughts*

"Value" refers to one's preference for, or dislike of, a certain state of affairs. Values are about the way things *ideally* should, or should not, be regarding events, objects, activities, ideas, intentions, personal characteristics, and so forth. Values are an essential component of any culture because members of the same group tend to share similar values. The similarity of their values explains the similarity of their behavior, which is what we're referring to when we speak of that group's culture. Values don't dictate behavior; they do strongly influence one's behavioral choices.

If you and your young son come to an intersection while walking and he darts across the road to the other side, you recognize a life-threatening tendency. How you react will be influenced by your society's "book of *shoulds* and *oughts*"—your culture's values and norms—regarding the disciplining of children. You could apply corporal punishment instantly or after returning home. You could angrily make him feel shame in the eyes of family and friends, or to feel guilt internally. You could temporarily withdraw something from his enjoyment such as his freedom ("Go to your room!"). You could gravely tell him that the next time he does this, a supernatural being will snatch him. You could calmly try to reason with him about the dangers of the roadway. You could ask someone else to take up the matter with him. You could even do nothing at all. Your choice is driven by your personal values, which are strongly influenced by (but *not* dictated by) your culture's values.[5] What you decide to do, and why, is the kind of topic that fascinates anthropologists of childhood.

While growing up, each child becomes aware of the *shoulds* and *oughts* of the group in which she is living. She observes how people evaluate activities, objects, events, people, ideas, and emotions. In most cases, the child gradually adopts the norms and values shared within her group. She learns to "fit in" and becomes warmly accepted by those around her. (Exceptions occur: A child also may reject all or some of her group's norms and values.) This process of "child socialization" is studied in depth by anthropologists of childhood, as this book will reveal.

One more thing: Culture's "how we do things" and "shoulds and oughts" are gained during the earliest years of one's life, some of it earlier than basic language competence. Culture becomes very deeply ingrained, an essential component of each one's identity and emotional foundation. Each of us is emotionally triggered if we sense that our deep identity is being contradicted or threatened. Even people who have devoted their careers to studying cultures, such as I have, experience an instantaneous negative reaction whenever their cultural values are breached.

Culture is *learned*

This explains how people gain culture. Culture is not acquired genetically. It's not instinctual.[6] An example of an instinctual behavior is that a minutes-old infant reflexively sucks. No time to learn! But 10 years later, whatever meaning and feeling the child gives the word "sucks" has been learned through experience.

People used to assume that all animal behavior was instinctual. Then Jane Goodall discovered in the mid-1960s that chimpanzees learn tool-use from each other. Since then, it's been found that many other animals learn not just skills but also social behavior from their parents and others. Like humans, their groups share practices, norms, and patterns of behavior. They, too, learn culture.[7]

THE WORK OF ANTHROPOLOGISTS OF CHILDHOOD:

1. FINDING FACTS

The work of every scientist includes four indispensable, sequential phases:

1. Within the domain of knowledge studied by their scientific field, their curiosity leads them to form a question that they believe research can answer.[8]
2. They seek facts—data, objects, records, images, and so forth—relevant to answering the question. Each fact must be observable by one or more of humans' five senses.
3. They organize and analyze the facts until they are able to give them meanings that are relevant to answering the question they originally posed.
4. Finally, they share their findings with colleagues so that they can be critiqued and, perhaps, corrected. In this way, human understanding slowly advances.

Just before I wrote this section, a Japanese spacecraft returned to Earth with tiny rocks it had gathered from the surface of a speeding asteroid. Scientists had many questions about asteroids, which they believed were formed at the dawn of the solar system and might preserve the building blocks of organic life. Until now, facts about asteroids were gained through telescopes. Now scientists have better facts: bits of an actual asteroid! Phases 1 and 2 are finished; phase 3 is underway.

Anthropologists of childhood are no different from scientists studying asteroids. They begin with questions that lead them to seek facts about the lives of children and all the ways in which they transform into fully functioning adults. And here's the thing: They *could* simply walk to the nearest location where children and their caregivers live and find facts there. (Occasionally they do.) But that isn't good enough for many anthropologists. They want to go far away.

Why Anthropologists Often Travel Far Away

Previously, I distinguished between instinctual and learned behavior. The former is genetically inherited; the latter is cultural, learned by being passed down to us by our caregivers and others in our vicinity. How can we tell the difference?

Put differently, the key question is this: What features of human experience are universally human? Which traits and behaviors, because they are inherited, characterize *every human* across all geographical locations? That's a Big Question that fascinates social scientists. In order to answer it, they first need to determine that a specific trait or behavior is genuinely universal.

Walking to a nearby location and studying children and caregivers there might yield useful facts for an anthropologist, but it won't answer the Big Question. At any single location, only a few humans can be studied, all of whom will be immersed in the same culture. The question about human universals can be answered only by multiple studies carried out in a variety of cultures around the world. Why do anthropologists scatter far and wide? To discover facts that will enable their scientific field to come up with answers to the Big Question about universals.

The Big Question and Margaret Mead. Margaret Mead (1901–1978) established her reputation by being one of the first anthropologists to contribute— at age 27!—to answering the Big Question. It came about like this:

During the early 1900s, many social scientists agreed that genetic inheritance played a commanding role in human life. A leading psychologist of that period was G. Stanley Hall (1846–1924), the first president of the American Psychological Association. A genetic psychologist, Hall was a leader of the then-fashionable eugenics movement, which sought to reduce the proportion of the population with (what were alleged to be) inferior traits.[9] Together with other prominent thought-leaders, he believed that there was no way for learning to improve any inferior trait that an individual had inherited. Birth was destiny. This view helps to explain why U.S. schools began "tracking" students of differing abilities.[10]

One of Hall's claims to fame was his two-volume book *Adolescence* (1904), which focused mainly on boys. Hall stated that the years of adolescence were a time of overflowing energy, sexual tension, and even rebelliousness that society needed to tame (in ways that he recommended). Hall portrayed adolescent angst as the common experience of all youth everywhere.

Adolescence became a standard reference work and was well known to Mead when she was a graduate student at Columbia University. We can imagine her thinking something like this: "Is adolescent upheaval *really* an inherited universal? Could adolescence actually be learned? Maybe it's a product of *our culture!*"[11]

How could her questions be answered? Hall, a psychologist, was familiar with adolescents in the northeastern United States.[12] Did adolescents there represent the experiences of all adolescents everywhere? If teenaged people residing in any other location on Earth could be shown to not suffer the turmoil and stress that Hall portrayed as universal, his ideas would be revealed as erroneous.

So Mead set off to do fieldwork in the Samoan archipelago of the South Pacific.

The Purpose and Methods of Fieldwork

Fieldwork finds facts. If you're a psychologist, your facts come primarily from surveys, interviews, counseling sessions, and lab experiments with separate individuals. If you're an anthropologist, there's no substitute for facts found by fieldwork among members of a functioning community. Fieldwork denotes the process of an anthropologist's leaving home, decamping to a distant settlement, taking up residence there, then involving herself full-time in local events and relationships for months, often a year or more. Her goal is to learn, in depth, all about local residents' shared values, practices, norms, and patterns of behavior.

The first large-scale fieldwork study by anthropologists of childhood, known as the Six Cultures Study,[13] occurred during the 1960s. Organized by a husband–wife team, a group of more than a dozen anthropologists began by meeting for several weeks to plan and harmonize their research approaches and instruments. Then, in small teams, they dispersed to six field sites: the highlands of western Kenya; Okinawa, Japan; Luzon, Philippines; Uttar Pradesh, India; Oaxaca, Mexico; and a village in the northeastern U.S. Team members lived with local people for months as they carefully observed preteen children and their families; they also gathered a wide range of other data about the societies and their settings. The Six Cultures Study's major contribution to the field of anthropology was to set a high standard for long-term, on-site observation and systematic reporting of the behavior of humans within their naturally occurring groups such as families.[14]

Imagine heading off to do fieldwork. Your flight is comfortable and fast, but how do you get from the airport to your remote fieldwork site? For some, it's a multi-day trek slogging through a rainforest. Your arrival isn't likely to feature warmly welcoming villagers; you might not even be expected! They're distrustful of you. You're not just looking for a bed for the night; you are expecting to live there for months. If you speak the local language, you're probably at the novice level. Will you have your own dwelling or move in with a family? Where will you work? How will you deal with bodily necessities? What if you become injured or ill? Must you eat *everything* they eat? How can you accomplish anything without WiFi?

One anthropologist had this to say about her early fieldwork experiences:

> I learned that you can go days without brushing your teeth or bathing, and wear dirty clothes, and not only do your teeth not rot, hair not fall out, or the earth not stop revolving, but nobody cares! I learned that goat babies sound like human babies (especially when you desperately miss your own children). And speaking of goats, that their turds look like coffee beans, and when turds and beans are mixed together, make for an interesting-tasting morning cup of coffee.[15]

A few anthropologists have written fascinating books for the general public about their fieldwork experiences. Here are five that I have greatly enjoyed:

- *The Forest People* (1961), by Colin Turnbull; 279 pages. [About hunter-gatherers]
- *Never in Anger: Portrait of an Eskimo Family* (1970), by Jean L. Briggs; 307 pages.
- *Into the Heart: One Man's Pursuit of Love and Knowledge Among the Yamomama* (1991), by Kenneth Good; 333 pages. [Includes a cross-cultural love story!]
- *Don't Sleep, There Are Snakes: Life and Language in the Amazonian Jungle* (2008), by Daniel L. Everett; 279 pages.
- *A Death in the Rainforest: How a Language and a Way of Life Came to an End in Papua New Guinea* (2019), by Don Kulick; 272 pages.

Fieldwork leads to relationships. The most common method used to carry out fieldwork is called "participant observation" (also known as ethnography). The anthropologist, living among the local people, simultaneously participates in their daily lives and observes—watches, listens, asks questions, and takes notes about—*what* they do, *how* they do it, and *why* they do it that way.

If you read one or more of the books I just listed, you'll know that "participant observation" is misleading. The anthropologist is *not* a clinically detached "fly on the wall." He or she is a human sharing daily life with fellow humans. The group is small. Relationships develop. Personalities emerge. Unanticipated events bring out the best or worst in people. Mistakes are made. Emotions are triggered . . .[16]

There's also the hurdle of cultural differences. The anthropologist's social expectations differ from those of the locals. What is their conception of privacy? Which behavior demonstrates respect? How is trust established? It's imperative that the anthropologist learns to "fit in" and not remain an outsider. Part of her method is to query individuals about details of group life—including deeply intimate ones. If she's not trustworthy, she's unlikely to be told the whole truth.

In *Never in Anger*, the anthropologist relates that she was well aware of the Eskimos' rigid prohibition against any expression of anger. Yet after months of sharing one family's home (sometimes an igloo, sometimes a tent), she strayed across an invisible line—and found herself ostracized for over three months.

Conversely, the anthropologist whose study provides the basis for this book's chapter on the Quechua became very warmly accepted by her subjects. So many parents asked her to be godmother to their children that she had to start declining.

After a year or more, fieldwork ends; the anthropologist departs. What's next?

THE WORK OF ANTHROPOLOGISTS OF CHILDHOOD:

2. MAKING MEANINGS

After Margaret Mead completed her fieldwork, she returned from Samoa to Columbia University to analyze her notes and draft her Ph.D. dissertation. It soon became a landmark book of the 20th century, *Coming of Age in Samoa*. Although it was neither a diary nor an adventure story, it became an overnight best seller. Its public appeal was due, in part, to its frank discussion of sex. It also addressed another matter of wide interest to parents—the vexing turmoil characteristic of U.S. adolescents. As had been alleged by G. Stanley Hall, that turmoil similarly affected all adolescents living on this planet.

In contrast to the United States, Mead wrote, in Samoa it was hard to identify who precisely the adolescents were. You certainly wouldn't know them by their rebellion, their angst, their peevishness, or their desire to break free of the suf-focating strictures supposedly laid down by their parents. There was no youth culture and no widespread delinquency . . . The reason, she concluded, was that becoming an adult in the United States depended on struggling valiantly against the rules laid down by a puritanical, individualistic, prudish world. "The stress is in our civilization," Mead wrote, "not in the physical changes through which our children pass."[17]

That conclusion contradicted a widely held assumption of Mead's era, that adolescent behavior is determined by genetic inheritance. Now that her research in Samoa showed that one facet of human behavior is *not* universal, scholars felt freer to ask the Big Question about other types of behavior.

Mead's process illustrates a pattern that characterizes anthropology as well as other sciences. She began with a question (about adolescent behavior), carried out fieldwork to amass facts relevant to its answer, then subjected them to an inductive thought process[18] that yielded new insight about the human condition. Mead's findings were shared with others via her dissertation, her book, and several journal articles, all of which opened her findings to debate and critique.[19]

Mead's process illustrates another characteristic pattern, too. Since the early 1900s, anthropologists of childhood often noted that developmental psychologists had published research findings that they (the anthropologists) found intriguing. But the psychologists stated their findings in all-people-everywhere terms—even though their research occurred at *one* location. Fortunately, anthropologists are not the only ones who ask the Big Question about allegedly universal patterns of behavior. Some psychologists do as well, as the following account demonstrates.

The Case of "Attachment Theory"[20]

During the 1960s, a well-regarded British psychologist[21] developed a hypothesis regarding the emotional "attachment" of each infant to his or her mother (or other consistent caregiver). The healthily developing infant, he said, is "securely attached" to its mother, meaning that the infant is confident that the mother will be readily available, sensitive to his signals, and lovingly responsive whenever he seeks protection, comfort, or assistance. Presumably, the infant feels secure because the mother really does consistently behave in these ways.

The psychologist also stated that when an infant lacks a consistently solici-tous mother (or other caregiver), he or she will feel "insecurely attached." This occurs either because the mother's solicitous attention is inconsistent (i.e., on again, off again), or because she frequently ignores the infant. Insecure attachment, said the British psychologist, causes infants to grow up with personality disorders.

An American psychologist[22] then developed a method for assessing the level of an infant's attachment to his mother. This method, known simply as "Strange Situation," separated the infant from the mother for a short time, which upset him, then gauged his reaction when the mother returned. If the crying child was readily consoled by the mother's return, his attachment was judged "secure." But if he reacted with behavior labeled as either anxious-avoidant or anxious-resistant, his attachment was judged "insecure."

You should know that the research with infants and toddlers that led to this new Strange Situation assessment was almost all completed in Baltimore.

The Strange Situation in Germany. Years later in the northern German town of Bielefeld, two German psychologists carried out a study of infants that included use of the Strange Situation method. The Baltimore research had identified as insecurely attached about 35% of infants. In Bielefeld, nearly *two-thirds* of the infants were deemed insecure. Did this mean that a substantial majority of Bielefeld's mothers were doing a really bad job of child-rearing?

Being German, the two psychologists knew that their fellow Germans' ways of child-raising were different from Americans' ways. The Strange Situation method flagged that a difference existed, but the attachment hypothesis did not explain it. The accurate explanation lay in northern German values regarding how parents can best raise a child while preserving a style of family life that's agreeable for adults.

From a north German perspective, American children are spoiled; they get way too much solicitous attention from their mothers and others. Sure, children must have attention. But how often? How much? The relentlessly child-focused family life of Americans was not attractive to German parents, who dared to want quality time just for themselves! So they conditioned their children to accept solitude, expect delayed gratification, and become self-reliant. In Bielefeld, these ways were preferred and viewed as normal. Applying the Strange Situation method branded them as unhealthy, and Bielefeld's mothers as shortchanging their infants.

The fundamental error was the assumption that all good mothers everywhere are readily available to their infants, alert to their signals, and lovingly responsive whenever their infants have needs or desires. That assumption was grounded in the personal experiences of a British psychologist and his American colleague. The two of them were familiar mainly with child-rearing situations infused with Anglo-American middle-class values, in which infant care during the first years involves frequent mother–child encounters featuring pseudo-conversations with a constant display of positive emotions.[23] The experiences of these psychologists hardly could stand as representative of all human child-rearing, past and present, on Earth.

Attachment theory and infant swaddling. One of the anthropologists whose research provides a basis for this book's chapter on the Navajo undertook his fieldwork specifically to discover whether the swaddling of Navajo infants leads to insecure attachment between mother and child. As will be explained in Chapter 4, Navajos swaddle their infants in a rigid but padded "cradleboard" during many hours of the day and night. Compared with typical practices in American middle-class society, a Navajo infant bound tightly to a cradleboard appears to be picked up less often, might be interacted with for shorter periods of time, and clearly is denied the freedom to physically reach out to his mother and others. From the perspective of the attachment hypothesis, this reduction in the interactions between mother and infant obviously could lead to insecure attachment.

After two years of fieldwork and a book in which page after page relates how the cradleboard is used and, more broadly, how a Navajo mother and her child interact during the child's first several years of life, the anthropologist concluded this: "In a word, I could find no evidence of any direct or interactive effects of cradleboard use on mother–child interaction length. The cradleboard had no effect of any magnitude on the characteristics of mother–child interaction."[24]

Again, the basic error was the assumption that all good mothers everywhere are consistently in close, physically responsive contact with their infants. People who are well adjusted in their societies get their starts in a wide variety of ways.

Another basic error was the assumption that all mothers everywhere maintain—or *should* maintain—nearly exclusive, one-on-one relationships with their infants. Actually, most young children around the world are raised by multiple caregivers,[25] with the mother being the most involved caregiver while breastfeeding is ongoing.

This book's main chapters will offer examples of a different approaches to post-weaning caregiving in which the mothers are far less involved than U.S. mothers.

THE WORK OF ANTHROPOLOGISTS OF CHILDHOOD:

3. SHARING CONCLUSIONS

When anthropologists of childhood talk with one another—either directly or, more formally, by means of books and academic journal articles—what are they talking about and debating? What topics often engage their collective mind?

We've already explored two: adolescence and attachment. I selected these because both underscore the danger of assuming that any child or adult behavior is a human universal. Let's close this chapter with some examples of a topic of perennial interest to anthropologists of childhood: In various societies around the world, in what ways do the values and practices of child-socialization differ?

Socializing Children the American Middle-Class Way

If you identify with that loosely defined group known as the American middle class, then it's almost guaranteed that you expect children to be raised by their parents, and only by their parents (maybe with a little help from grandparents). You might never have thought about this, however, because *this is how we do things around here*. Full parental responsibility is taken for granted. Whereas scholars talk about "socializing" children, we Americans talk of "parenting" them.

Our American way of socialization assumes that responsibility for raising one's progeny demands parental commitment 24/7 in terms of being alertly protective and proactively ensuring that one's child will grow up to become an exemplary human being. One clue that this is true is what happens when a friend or neighbor disciplines one's child or suggests an alternative parenting approach. The child's parents usually are offended; this child is their responsibility, and theirs alone!

Yes, delegation is possible: A babysitter during an evening, a nanny if both parents are employed away from home. But parents scrutinize applicants, give explicit instructions, always know that the final responsibility is theirs and, in the case of nannies, often feel guilty about not constantly taking care of their child.

This is normal human parenting, right?

Well, we've already seen one exception. Those parents in Bielefeld, Germany, didn't buy our round-the-clock, child-centered, "active parenting" expectations.

There's No Such Thing as "Normal Human Parenting"

When cross-cultural and historical records are scoured to reveal all the ways in which societies socialize children, every society is found to have at least a few unusual features that make its child-rearing patterns distinct. No single society can be held up as an example of "normal human parenting." Some societies do share similarities—which is why it makes sense for this book to treat "traditional" societies as a loosely defined group. But one society stands out as substantially different from all the others in how it socializes its children—*ours.* Among human societies past and present, our American-style parenting is extraordinary in many ways, including these five:

1. The extent to which youngsters in the United States are raised by older siblings is strictly limited. But across many other societies, child-rearing by older siblings "is the *predominant* socialization experience, more than 70% of every day."[26] For example, among the Dusun of Malaysia, "the two-year-old is usually tended by the next oldest child, *who may be only three or four years old.* Child nurses take their responsibility seriously, feeding, bathing, and singing to their charges."[27]

2. We earnestly keep children out of harm's way. In many other cultures, children learn to avoid danger experientially. No adult shows concern when a toddler wields a knife or crawls toward a fire. A self-injured child is scolded (and cared for), not consoled. Seeing our protectiveness, parents in those cultures wonder why we don't care whether our children learn to avoid danger. How can they ever learn? We don't give them any opportunity to do so.[28]

3. We believe that children's successful maturation requires constant intellectual stimulation. We talk with them, ask questions, read aloud, teach numbers and letters, buy educational toys[29]—and sometimes far more. But societies exist in which very young children are assumed to lack any ability to learn. The goal is to keep them quiet as much as possible so the adults can go about their lives.[30]

4. We play with our children, from roughhousing to board games to skill practice (e.g., ball batting), all the way to adult-organized and coached leagues. In other world regions, adults neither play with children nor organize play for them. Children create their own play, scavenging materials, tweaking rules, inventing new diversions, parodying adult behavior, and learning to negotiate disputes.[31]

5. Much of our adult lives—employment, finances, fights, sex, and entertainment—is kept apart from youngsters, who are deemed too—what?[32]—to witness it. In some societies, children of all ages witness everything. Yes, *everything.* Adults pay them no heed so long as they remain unobtrusive. Observant children learn skills[33] and gain a 100% realistic view of adult life, love, work, and all the rest.[34] In this book, you'll discover a great deal about children's learning via observation, imitation, and participation.

These differences and others like them are interesting, even intriguing. But they lack context. They're like an old carnival freak show—a collection of oddities.

If we want to gain perspective on our child-rearing approaches by learning about others' ways, we need to consider the ways others behave within their natural settings. Each society's child-rearing values and practices are the outcome of adaptations to a combination of historical and contextual factors—economic, political, environmental, spiritual, and others—adaptations that have been fitted together to attain the objectives desired by that society for its progeny.

Over the past 80 years, anthropologists of childhood have been studying children and their caretakers within their natural settings worldwide. For a parent who wants to consider child-rearing alternatives, what the anthropologists have found offers much food for thought—and possibly even for application.

Example of an applicable fieldwork finding. If you are a parent who is immersed in her home culture, you'll probably raise your children according to *how we do things around here* (including passing fads). Fellow parents won't criticize you, but your child-rearing approaches will likely yield a few undesirable outcomes—the same outcomes that many other parents "around here" find undesirable.

Case in point: Many American parents (and teachers, too) lament the lack of a sense of responsibility in children. Is there something about American-style child-rearing that undermines the development of responsibility? Anthropologists of childhood decided to carry out fieldwork to discover whether youngsters in other societies develop a strong sense of responsibility and, if so, how they gained it.

What they found was that, in the societies studied, even young children were actively demonstrating responsibility. They also found that the ways they gained it included thought-provoking, potentially adaptable, ideas for American parents.[35] My first summary chapter, Chapter 7, is devoted to reviewing their findings and others regarding responsibility.

Few parents know of findings like these. Why? Because anthropologists talk using scholarly language, and almost always talk exclusively among themselves.

That's why I wrote this book. First I listen to them, then I talk plainly to you.

NINE IDEAS WORTH REMEMBERING
FROM THIS CHAPTER

1. Psychology studies human individuals' behavior. Anthropology studies the behavior *shared by humans* in their self-constituted groups such as a village.

2. The subfield known as *anthropology of childhood* studies children and their relationships with their parents and other caregivers, and the child-rearing values and practices applied by caregivers to "socialize" a group's children.

3. Anthropologists are interested in *culture*, that is, the values and behavior learned by, and shared by, group members. Culture is "how we do things around here."

4. Until the 1920s, many people—including scientists—assumed that most behavior was determined by genetic inheritance, and thus was common to all humans. Anthropologists set out to question this "universalist" assumption.

5. To question universalism, anthropologists study the behavior of humans in groups all over the world. Any behavior, for example, that of teenagers, that differs markedly from place to place is not universal; it is *cultural*, meaning that it is learned.

6. To study humans in groups, anthropologists carry out fieldwork, which involves participant observation. For a year or more, the anthropologist lives day to day with the group, carefully observing and recording its members' behavior.

7. Participant observation is not clinically detached. To comprehend the shared values and lifeways of a group, the anthropologist needs to actively contribute to community life, build personal relationships, and gradually fit in so that he or she shifts from being seen as a visiting stranger to acceptance as "one of us."

8. Members of the American middle class share assumptions about how best to socialize a child; for example, they hold that families must be child-centered and parents must be proactively responsible 24/7. Fieldwork by anthropologists of childhood shows that parents in other societies hold vastly different views.

9. A society's child-rearing practices result from its adaptations to factors within its natural setting. Understanding that setting and those adaptations must precede any attempt by outsiders to learn about that society's child-rearing practices.

SUGGESTED FURTHER READING

Each of the readings below is profiled at www.howotherchildrenlearn.info /profiles.

Anthropology for Beginners, by Micah J. Fleck (2020); 132 text pages.

"Ethnographic Studies of Childhood: A Historical Overview," by Robert A. LeVine. *American Anthropologist, 109* (2), 2007; 9 text pages.

Gods of the Upper Air: How a Circle of Renegade Anthropologists Reinvented Race, Sex, and Gender in the Twentieth Century, by Charles King (2019); 345 text pages.

The Bibliography at the back of this book includes all publications cited within Chapter 1.

Chapter 2

Raising Oneself in the Forest

Growing Up among the Aka Hunter-Gatherers of Africa

Figure 2.1. An Aka father stays home with his daughter while his wife collects firewood.
From Intimate Fathers: The Nature and Context of Aka Pygmy Paternal Infant Care, by Barry S. Hewlett. Copyright © 1991. Courtesy of the University of Michigan Press.

FILMS ABOUT THE AKA
HUNTER-GATHERER WAY OF LIFE

These films will enable you to more accurately imagine Aka families as you read this chapter.

"A Caterpillar Moon" (1995). Anthropologist Barry Hewlett observes the daily lives of the members of one of the families that he has been studying for decades. Produced by BBC Bristol. 50:00 min. anthro.vancouver.wsu.edu/people/hewlett/; scroll to "Caterpillar Moon," click on "watch it here."

"Pygmies of Africa" (1939). Describes the ways of hunter-gatherers; admires their craft and building skills. Produced by Encyclopedia Britannica. 20:07 min. youtube.com/watch?v=M2NbFY1JdkQ

"Pygmies of Africa" is about a group in Central Africa, but not necessarily the Aka. Note that the filmmaker required his subjects to cover their private parts. Almost certainly, this measure was taken to preserve the tender innocence of pre-World War II audiences in the United States.

Hot links to all films and videos are at
howotherchildrenlearn.info/films

Based on anthropological fieldwork carried out primarily between 1985 and 2015.

When you were a growing child, how would you have reacted to *this* daily life?

You may do whatever you want.[1] No kidding! You don't need any adult's OK. You're surrounded every day by close friends, and you and they may do whatever you choose, wherever you wish, for as long as you like, and come and go as you please. Or just lay around and relax. What if your parents ask you to help with a chore? Sure, help if you like—or say no or ignore them. You'll almost never be punished. Does this idyll end when school begins? There's no school. Suppose you begin feeling tingles around certain members of the opposite sex? Go with it. If you're a boy, walk over to a nearby settlement and check out its girls. They are hoping you'll come. As in your own settlement, many evenings there are filled with singing and dancing, a great time to flirt—or more. But wait: What if you'd rather spend your time learning skills and helping your family? Fine, you may do that.

A few more points to mention: This life occurs in a climate with off-the-charts humidity and in the midst of an endless forest. There's no air conditioning because there's no electricity. No running water or sewers. No flush toilets. In fact, you don't live in a house at all, but in a hut of branches and leaves that's so small you can't stand up in it. Forget privacy. Your only way of traveling is to walk, and occasionally you gather up all that you own and carry it—no pack animals—to a new location, where you build a new hut. That's because, to find food, you must relocate seasonally. Your diet includes rats, termites, grubs, and lots of caterpillars.

A SOCIETY UNLIKE OURS IN
EVERY WAY IMAGINABLE

Compared with our WEIRD society—WEIRD is discussed in the Introduction—a hunter-gatherer society is starkly different in every conceivable way. That's why it's useful for us to get acquainted with the Aka hunter-gatherers.

Useful? Yes. It better enables us to comprehend the full breadth of human potential. For example, we know from research among the Aka that the potential of human fathers to care for and enjoy their infants exceeds what most Americans *think* fathers are capable of. The fact that this was learned by observing the Aka is significant because scholars believe that they and similar hunter-gatherers are living out their lives very much as did *all* human beings 10,000 years ago and long before that.[2] Now, as then, hunter-gatherer societies lack complex social hierarchies, formal social institutions, and ways of gaining and hoarding wealth—not to mention the boundless material trappings of present-day WEIRD societies. So among today's Aka and other hunter-gatherers, we have a near-perfect "state of nature"[3] in which human beings are going about their lives without the myriad complexities and expectations of modern civilization. Hunter-gatherers provide our only opportunity to see ourselves more or less as we were eons ago.

As I've implied, the Aka are not the only hunter-gatherers.[4] Among the main characteristics of groups termed "hunter-gatherers"—or "foragers"—are these:[5] They live in camps of 20 to 35 people in small, easily constructed huts that are left behind when they change locations seasonally in order to be near shifting sources of food. They lack storage capacity and need to find food on an almost daily basis both by hunting a variety of meat-bearing animals and by gathering an even wider variety of plants such as yams and small creatures such as termites. In the forests or savannahs where they live, population density is very low. But in their camps, they live in physically and emotionally close association with each other.

If you're inclined to imagine hunter-gatherers as underdeveloped versions of ourselves, here's an alternative perspective:

> At the individual level, ancient foragers were the most knowledgeable and skillful people in history. Because their survival depended on an intimate knowledge of the animals they hunted and the plants they gathered, they had deep and varied knowledge of their immediate surroundings. They listened to the slightest movement in the grass to learn whether a snake might be lurking there. They carefully observed the foliage of trees in order to discover fruits, beehives, and bird nests. They moved with a minimum of effort and noise, and knew how to walk and run in the most agile and efficient manner. There is some evidence that the size of the average Sapiens brain has actually *decreased* since the age of foraging.[6]

How to Sustain Life in a Tropical Forest

A tropical rain forest is an awesome place.[7] No other ecological niche matches its richness and variety of plants and animals: some 3,000 species. Ecologists classify the tropical rain forest of Central Africa as "marginal" because few plant species are edible and the animals are widely scattered. The Aka disagree. To them, the forest is a plentiful, reliable source of food for those who know how to find it. As for the children, they grow up having an idyllic life in the forest.

> My best memory when I was little was playing in the forest with my friends. I had so many friends and we loved each other. I remember singing and dancing and swinging in the trees. We would build a little house and pretend we were married, finding yams and feeding our babies. Our little husbands would go hunt for rats and bring them back, and we would grill it and eat together. Our parents would call for us, but we were playing so we did not come! This was our good fun.[8]

Regardless of whether the rain forest is marginal or plentiful, it's important to keep two facts in mind about how the Aka sustain themselves. The first is that a high proportion of their daily lives is spent finding food by means of either hunting or gathering. During the dry season, net hunts occur as often as six days a week, up to nine hours a day.[9] Almost all camp members participate. Deep in the forest, they arrange their nets in a semi-circle. One group makes a clamor to flush animals from hiding and drive them toward the net; snared animals—often small antelopes called duikers—are pounced on and killed by those behind the net. Children help by making noise. Babies are brought along, carried by their mothers in slings.

Hunting occurs by other means, too. Monkeys are hunted with crossbows; rats, armadillos, and porcupines with traps; and large game such as hogs with spears or guns. Small game may be hunted by children alone; large game by men alone.

During part of the wet season, the goal of everyone's foraging is to gather nuts, fruits, and yams as well as other roots, fungi, and leaves, notably the large *eru* leaves that are a valued vegetable.[10] Also sought are small creatures such as turtles, snails, termites, grubs, and especially caterpillars when they tumble to the ground in abundance. Large parties sometimes make whole days out of gathering basketloads of caterpillars, which are both eaten and traded. Honey is popular, too; acquiring it is the men's job because it involves climbing tall trees.[11]

The second fact about how the Aka sustain themselves is that, notwithstanding their vision of plenty, the forest cannot provide their complete diet. To sustain life, they must rely to some extent on the village-dwelling farmers, the Ngandu.

The Curious Relationship between the Aka and the Ngandu

Let's begin with the downside: The Aka foragers and the Ngandu villagers do not like each other. Here's how Konga, an older Aka woman, recalls the relationship:

> I never played with villager children because I was afraid of their parents. When I was small, I had no villager friends. The villagers are very difficult. They have a bad character. We have lived together for a long time, but they are not like family. They want you for the work. We are their workers. We work for them, they pay us, and that is all. We work because we do not have many things— money, machetes, cups, pots, clothes—so we work because maybe they will give us these things.[12]

Konga realizes that despite their mutual antipathy, the two groups are drawn together by an economic relationship: labor in return for wages.[13] She forgets to mention the dietary aspect of their symbiosis. The Aka need more vegetables than they can gather, especially those high in carbohydrates such as manioc,[14] which the Ngandu cultivate. The Ngandu need meat but aren't good hunters, so they rely on the Aka.

The Akas labor for the Ngandu during part of the wet season, during which time Aka camps are relocated to be near villages. The Aka carry out a variety of work in the fields as well as transporting produce, making palm oil, and completing daily chores. The Aka are not paid a set rate for a specific job.

From time to time, the Ngandu give the Aka the items that Konga mentions, plus palm wine, tobacco, marijuana, and even cooked food. Also, the farmers turn a blind eye when the Aka take small quantities of manioc leaves or yams from the fields.

Another curious feature of their economic link is that it's not group to group. Instead, most Aka families have a stable partnership with a Ngandu family; the two families typically share the same clan name. When speaking of Akas with whom he shares a clan name, a Ngandu usually talks as though he owns the Akas. He doesn't. But the inequality of their ties is plain to any observer: When there's a job to do, Ngandus tell Akas what to do—often in imperious tones—and the Akas comply. And if a Ngandu and an Aka meet on a narrow trail, it's the Aka who steps aside. Privately, the Aka roundly denigrate their lazy, arrogant taskmasters, likening them to chimpanzees.[15] Unsurprisingly, intermarriage is extremely rare.

Notwithstanding their patron–client economic alliance, the two groups differ sharply in terms of language, physical appearance (Akas are very short, Ngandu are tall), and manner of living (Akas in forest huts, Ngandu in village houses). The Ngandu have much more direct contact with the outside world than the Aka. Of most interest to anthropologists is that their cultures also differ sharply, including many of the values and expectations about raising children.

When the need for farm labor declines, the Aka—breathing sighs of relief, no doubt—relocate again, heading deep into the forest. What does "deep into the forest" mean to you? To the Aka it usually means a trek of from two to four *days*![16]

THE REWARDS AND RHYTHMS OF AKA DAILY LIFE

What is daily life like in the Central African rainforest? Consider this glimpse of the foraging life, recalled by a hunter-gatherer who left the forest and chose to live in Western society:

> Life was very social in the forest. Our small camps had five or six huts, each without a door because no one had any possessions to protect, just a couple of cooking pots. It took Mum and Dad about four hours to make a hut. If you made a strong frame, a hut could last a year. We sometimes cooked inside by making a fire in the middle of three stones and resting a pot on the top. Everyone sat on a log or on the ground. In the forest we didn't wear clothes because they get snagged on branches. When we were hunting, this would be a problem because we had to move fast to follow animals. Both men and women wore only a small

pouch that covered the sex, with a string around the waist and legs. For the men, it made it a lot easier to run.[17]

An American anthropologist was attracted by the warm, communal nature of Aka daily life:

> In their small intimate camps, the number of people varies day to day, as people travel to visit other camps, or relatives and friends visit. The camp is a busy place, with little kids playing and people chatting, cooking, and working.[18]

> It is so interesting here how close everyone sits together. When I want to talk to an adolescent, a whole group of them will pull up a log and lean on each other, giggling and laughing. They even sit thigh to thigh with me. I love this physical closeness; it is comforting somehow.[19]

Camps are described as intimate not only because of the frequent skin-to-skin closeness of their inhabitants, but also because their five or six huts fit compactly into an area the size of a suburban living-dining room.[20] Inside each is a woven twig bed where the family sleeps together, a small fire area, and a few possessions. An Aka's next door neighbor's hut is so close that the two can hand items back and forth without getting up.[21] All daily living occurs in the open: cooking, cleaning, conversations, arguments, caring for children, net- and basket-making, and more. Camp members don't necessarily belong to one extended family, though some of the children will be related. Because of the high rate of child mortality due to infectious and parasitic diseases, most couples raise as many children as they can. Half the population of most camps is under 15 years of age.[22]

A young couple is considered married whenever they start living together.[23] Their shared life begins in the camp of the wife's parents[24] so the husband can perform "bride service." This means that he is available to do whatever work his in-laws need doing, an obligation that continues until the couple's first child is born and begins to walk. From then on, the couple is free to live in the camp of his parents or hers, or wherever else they wish, and to relocate at will.

Marriage among the Aka is a model of egalitarian gender relations.[25] Though most roles are gender-linked, spouses know how to fulfill the other's responsibilities. When circumstances require a spouse to perform the other's role, there's never any teasing from onlookers. Spouses are together much of the time[26] and get to know each other extraordinarily well. They don't hug and kiss like Americans but share all sorts of playful activities and appear to enjoy each other's company. They cooperate to complete tasks, including caring for children. Yes, disagreements do occur, but conflicts are resolved by mediation, crude joking (often about the other's genitals), or one's temporary exit from camp. Physical violence is unknown.[27]

The Aka's egalitarian mindset leads them to avoid any attitude or action that implies prestige or power.[28] So Aka camps have no chief. Instead, each has a *kombeti*, a man with slightly greater influence than others regarding major decisions such as when and where to relocate. Another position of influence is the *nganga*, a man who's learned the traditional arts of healing such as how to cure someone of witchcraft. He often plays a role during hunts by divining where the party should go. The final position of influence is the *tuma*, or great hunter, recognized as the one who has killed the most elephants. Elephant hunts are now rare, so a *tuma* leads hunting rituals and spear hunts for larger, dangerous prey such as hogs, and organizes boys' initiation rituals to join the men's secret society.

Anthropologists are particularly struck by the extent to which the Akas share.[29] Whatever is brought into camp—the bounty of hunting or gathering, even small items obtained in a Ngandu village—is soon distributed among everyone, visitors included, leaving the item's original possessor with as little as 10% of the original quantity. The value and practice of sharing, inculcated in infancy, has come to have specific expectations and procedures too complex to describe here.[30] Note also that the Aka practice "demand sharing," which means that when someone comes asking for something you possess, you are obliged to share it with them.[31] But here's an interesting twist: It is also established practice for one to hide foods, or to eat them in the forest before returning to camp, to avoid giving them all away.

Woven throughout Aka daily life is their culture of music and dance.[32] Babies are lulled to sleep by song and rhythmic patting. Hunts are prepared for by ritual dancing and are accompanied by yodeling in a way that indicates the positions of individuals in the forest. Shared tasks such as washing clothes, preparing manioc, or making journeys to the river to bathe or fetch water can become lighthearted musical renditions. Storytellers are accompanied by a chorus, with the refrain repeated by the audience. The Aka have songs and dances for a variety of purposes such as inaugurating a new camp location, attracting a potential mate, and attending a funeral. For a narrated three-minute video of Aka singing and dancing, search for "The Polyphonic Singing of the Aka Pygmies of Central Africa."

HOW NEWBORNS ARRIVE AND RECEIVE CARE

Here's an eyewitness account of a newborn Aka's arrival in the African rainforest:

In the middle of a circle of children, a young woman in labor gripped a tree and moaned as another woman massaged her back, murmuring encouragement. Squatting down, she gave a final moan, and pushed her newborn child into waiting hands. Quickly assessing the health of the new life, the midwife laid the baby down onto a bed of leaves—the arms of the forest. The baby lustily cried as she was wiped with leaves and water, her umbilical cord cut with a sharp, spiny leaf, then tied closed with a vine. Still gripping the tree, the new mother pushed out the placenta, and the bloody organ was planted, cord up, into the red earth (enabling the mother to have more children). Then the small group made their way back to the camp clearing, where the father first saw his baby daughter.[33]

After this helpless and dependent beginning, it doesn't take long for young Aka children to sense that they may do pretty much whatever they like. For example, they are free to nurse whenever they choose. They are held nonstop, mostly by their mothers, and it's skin-to-skin contact because the Aka rarely wear blouses or shirts. Even when a child is being carried in a sling, mother's milk is immediately available because the carrying occurs on the mother's side (not her back), thus cradling the infant beside the breast. If infants being held or carried by others show signs of wanting to nurse, they are quickly handed to the mother.

Aka parents interact with their infants throughout each day—talking, singing, and playing, showing affection, or even demonstrating to them a crucial survival skill (about which more later). Small Aka children are, quite literally, never alone. They're comforted at once when they fuss or cry. Nursing continues until children give it up, which often does not occur until their third or even fourth year. But if a mother finds that she's pregnant, she usually encourages her child to stop.

Aka mothers have plenty of childcare assistance.[34] When mothers and their babies are in camp, an average of seven other caregivers hold or carry the child during the day, enabling the mother to tend to other matters more than half the time. But when a group is involved in traveling or net hunting, it's the mother who tends to her infant. The practice of bride service, mentioned previously, ensures that a young, first-time mom is in her home camp when she most needs support, which is lavishly available from her mother, sisters, grandmother, and friends.

Later in this book, you'll find that a common practice among traditional societies is for youngsters, after weaning, to be placed very largely in the care of an older sibling, usually a sister. This is true of the Ngandu, but this is not the Aka way. Why? Perhaps because it would infringe on older children's freedom to do pretty much whatever they like.

* * * * *

Let's talk about fathers. Aka fathers are reputed[35] to be more caring toward, more bonded with, their infants and young children than fathers in any other society.[36] Consider this vignette, an example of many similar sights in Aka forest camps:

> Yopo's wife, Bongbongo, gets off the bed, where she was holding their infant, Manda. She hands Manda to Yopo, who is also sitting on the bed, and leaves. As Yopo takes Manda into his lap, he softly hums to Manda and gives him a piece of manioc he is eating. Yopo continues to hum as Manda reaches for and plays with a twig on the bed. Yopo lies down and puts Manda on his chest as he continues to hum. Manda sits on Yopo's chest and smiles and vocalizes to Yopo; Yopo returns the same. Yopo sits up and places Manda on the ground. Manda stands up as he holds onto his father. Yopo lies down again and puts Manda back on his chest. He sings net-hunt songs, then stands Manda on his chest. Manda sits down on Yopo's chest and cuddles up to Yopo's neck; Yopo puts a leaf on Manda's head and Manda squeals with joy. This scene continued for 42 minutes, including 20 minutes after Bongbongo returned.[37]

This vignette accurately represents Aka father–infant bonds by portraying the relationship as *intimate and affectionate*, not rough-and-tumble.[38] Mothers and other caretakers play energetically with infants more than fathers do. Thanks to frequent cuddling, an Aka father learns how to stimulate warm responses from his infant without being vigorous. He also learns the early signs of hunger, illness, fatigue, and need to eliminate, and he is more likely than the mother to clean the infant. If an infant is fussy in the middle of the night, the father is more likely than the mother to take the child outside to walk or dance. Infants and young children often seek out their fathers by reaching toward or crawling to them, or by climbing into their laps; fathers readily pick them up and interact with them warmly. Fathers give every appearance of intrinsically enjoying their infants' company.

Heartwarming, isn't it? But wait, it's not quite so straightforward. Research has revealed a rather complex story about Aka dads and their little ones:[39]

- In general, infants seek to be held by their mothers more often than all other caretakers combined; they seek to be held by their fathers next most often.
- Fathers' involvement is greater during evenings than during daytime; in forest camps, they devote more evening time to infants than to any other activity.
- During daylight, some fathers are more involved with infants than others. One father averaged 13 minutes a day, while another averaged nearly two hours.

- Fathers rarely assist in infant care during net-hunts (because they are the fastest runners) or while engaged in any economic activity in either forest or village.
- Fathers are much more involved with their infants while in their home camps, much less involved while in their wives' home camps where female in-laws are available and eager to assist.[40]

Interestingly, research across several traditional societies has revealed that in populations where wealth is *not* accumulated and men are *not* the primary food-providers, fathers devote more time to their wives and children.[41]

LEARNING TO BE AKA: THE EARLY CHILDHOOD YEARS

If you're an Aka child who recently weaned yourself, the key characteristic of your life is that your parents, though available and unfailingly responsive, are being eclipsed in your day-to-day activities by the other children in your camp.[42]

The children with whom you're spending more and more time are not just your age peers; there are too few youngsters for age distinctions to yield subgroups. A camp's post-weaning, prepubescent children are one group in which boys and girls spend their time very similarly.[43] Throughout each day in camp (i.e., not during hunting or gathering expeditions), these children do whatever they decide to do, mostly in proximity to the adults, but not in alignment with any adult guidelines.

I invite you to consider your mental image of the scene described above. I suggest this because nothing in an American community or school playground, or even a home's backyard, can accurately be the starting point for a mental image of an Aka mixed-age children's group. *Our mental images of young children playing together feature adult supervision*, in the sense of both passive vigilance and rules about what they may not do (don't hit each other, don't go beyond the tree line). We ensure that the area is safe (no sharp sticks, no holes that could trip them), we provide much of what they're playing with (wiffle balls, dolls), and we're ever ready to intervene, if only to say, "Time to come inside."

Forget all that. It is totally off the mark.

Yes, the activities of Aka children very largely occur in the vicinity of the adults, but—I know this is hard to fathom—the children are doing *whatever they decide*, and they're doing it *wherever and for as long as they like*. The adults are tending to adult things, not preoccupied with any mischief their kids might be getting into.

But wait, you say. There are fires and hot coals, there are sharp digging sticks, there are axes and machetes, all within reach. It's downright irresponsible for those parents not to protect their youngsters! Don't they care about their safety?

Aka parents care a lot; infant and child mortality is far higher in Central Africa than in the United States. But generations of experience tell them that what *we* view as a major danger is rarely the cause of serious injury. One anthropologist said that she and her colleagues had never seen young children hurt themselves playing with machetes. Another noted that "it was not unusual to see an eight-month-old with a six-inch knife chopping something."[44] However, one *had* seen a youngster crawling toward a fire being aimed in another direction—not punished, not verbally admonished, just redirected.

So what are Aka youngsters choosing to do?[45] Although they may go wherever they wish, they venture into the forest only about 20% of the time. There, older boys sometimes use lianas—long-stemmed vines—to construct swings. Some of their time is used to explore the camp and the forest's edge, and some is spent relaxing. Sometimes they play games such as *ndanga*, similar to our "keep away" but with this difference: although two teams compete to control the ball, scores are not kept and winners are not celebrated, thus preserving Aka egalitarianism. Whatever they're doing, adults have no direct role in the children's choices or activities.[46]

But adults do have an indispensable indirect role in children's activities. This is because the youngsters devote a substantial amount of time, alone and in groups, to emulating the adults, trying to do successfully what they repeatedly see adults doing. Anthropologists call this "imitation of work in play."[47] Some of it imitates vital living activities such as building little huts and pretending to be husbands and wives. Much of it imitates adults' subsistence efforts, both foraging—such as digging for yams and gathering *eru* leaves—and preparing food for eating. Here's how the hunter-gatherer who left the forest and now lives in Western society recalls his early years:

> When I was about six, I learned how to make a liana net and caught forest rats. Like other kids I also made traps to catch birds. Most of our day was spent gathering food. If we couldn't find fruit we'd go mushroom picking. Our favorite food was porcupine.[48]

American parents sometimes provide their youngsters with small replicas of adult tools including kitchen utensils and even little stoves, manufactured items that have been rendered utterly harmless and signal that they are for play by being brightly colored. Children can be seen using these in apparent imitation of adults' work. Things are different among the Aka. A team of anthropologists reports that

> Parents make small axes, digging sticks, and spears for infants and young children. These are not toys but small-sized artefacts that reflect the size of the child. Mothers place these in their baskets. Then, while resting on a net hunt or other subsistence activity, the mothers give the items to their youngsters, who chip, dig, etc., while the parents watch, laugh, and sometimes physically grasp the youngsters' hands or arms to show them how to use the implement. It is common as well for the mothers to give their young children, including infants, a knife or machete.[49]

Aka youngsters also forage for real food and cook it on real fire. This is why an awed anthropologist tells us that "by three or four years of age, children can cook themselves a meal."[50] Another observed a four-year-old girl using a knife to cut up manioc leaves, pausing to sharpen her knife before continuing to chop; when she was done, she helped to care for her baby sister, carrying the toddler on her back.

Like that four-year-old, boys as well as girls frequently seek out infants simply to interact with them. Their spontaneous contributions to infant care continue into middle childhood. But, as noted earlier, they're never required to take over the care of their younger siblings.

"Children play in order to know *how to live, how their parents do things*." That's an adult Aka's assessment. An anthropologist put it this way: "Play and the social learning that is its outcome is *the work of childhood*."[51]

Consider the context in which all this is occurring.[52] Aka babies grow up among a small group of people, all of whom become thoroughly familiar to them. Their early experience is that everyone adores them and attends quickly to their needs; they are free to nurse at will. In their world, no one behaves as though anyone is better than others, no subgroup dominates the others, and no one even thinks of ranking children according to some performance metric. Wealth is not hoarded by the group or any individual. Everyone widely shares whatever they bring into camp that's useful. Camp members live physically near to each other, to the point of sitting thigh to thigh, and their emotional relations are similarly close. Yes, adults have arguments, but violence is never the outcome.

Children are rarely punished.[53] The high value placed on egalitarianism and freedom to choose means that there's no concept that children ought to obey their parents. Parents might ask their children to assist in one way or another, but if the request is ignored the matter is dropped. Parents sometimes correct a child's behavior that's out of step with Aka values, most notably the obligation to share and the restraint of violence. Common corrective measures are most likely to be either teasing or changing a child's location. Children are very rarely struck; if so, it's more of a light tap.[54]

Growing from infancy to middle childhood within the context described above yields *trust*—trust in the people around you and trust in your own worthiness and competence.[55] Given this self-assessment and living every day among the resources that adults use and models of adult competence, children are motivated to learn. There's nothing to get in their way and they have endless time to experiment and explore. No one is pressuring them. They may learn on their own, they may learn with peers or from older children, or they may approach an adult with a question.

If you're like me, you find this to be an edifying and inspiring account of how children learn. But if you're tempted to share it with others, the anthropologists have a request: Please do not describe Akas as "child-centered."[56] After children are weaned, they are drawn into the camp's mixed-age children's group. There they do their thing while the adults do theirs. If a child is in need (e.g., is injured or ill), adults tend to it. If a child has a learning query, adults respond to it. But adults don't let a child interrupt a conversation. They never ask a child what she wants. They have no active role in children's activities. In sum, adults' lives are not arranged to further their goals for children or children's goals for themselves.

LEARNING TO BE AKA: THE LATER CHILDHOOD YEARS

As Aka children advance toward puberty, much of their time continues to be spent imitating and practicing the endeavors of their role models, the adults with whom they're in close contact every day. One anthropologist tells us that he

> watched two boys of roughly seven and 10 years old climb a tree in the midst of play. The older boy had assembled a miniature replica of the bark basket, or *pendi*, that adults use when honey gathering. The two then tied a long forest cord to the *pendi* and ascended the tree to perform the conventional motions of chopping a hole in a limb to open the imaginary bees' nest, pulling up the *pendi*, filling the leaf-lined container with "honey," then lowering it down to those waiting below.[57]

This vignette is significant in three ways. First, no honey was being gathered, whereas many of children's "imitation of work in play" activities yield edible food. Second, the boys' fathers were not below, anxiously shouting pointers and urging caution; they weren't even present; but it was the fathers' skills that were being practiced. Third, the boys' learning[58]—of the value of honey and of the skills for acquiring it—was occurring via collaboration among children. An element of Aka culture was being learned not via parent-to-child transmission, but by children acting in concert.

Though not fully skilled, a 10-year-old Aka child knows enough to be able to live alone in the forest.[59] Below are a few of the skills children need to learn.[60] Some seem suited for boys, some for girls. But in this society where adult males and females often swap roles, many of these skills are learned to some extent by both boys and girls:

- Kill in net—Kill a large duiker or other animal after it's snared in a net
- Wash nets—Wash nets free of malevolent spirits using a traditional potion
- Make poison—Concoct *ndemele* (poison) for crossbow arrows
- Prepare *kôkô*—Prepare this vegetable dish by shredding large *eru* leaves
- Carry infant in sling—Carry an infant in a sling during a net hunt
- Prepare manioc—Render manioc edible by a long process to remove cyanide
- Obtain palm wine—Use a typical procedure to extract wine from a palm tree
- Make *ekila* medicine—Concoct a traditional medicine to stop infant convulsions
- Craft *mokodi* amulet—Use special vines to weave a cord for luck or protection
- Dance *djengi*—Perform a ritually significant dance after a large animal is killed

Another skill that older children of both sexes learn quite well is how to care for infants and toddlers.[61] Although girls spontaneously care for young siblings more than boys, both appear to become quite attached to the young ones; an adolescent male explained that, "When we are in the forest together, I teach my younger brothers and sisters about the sounds and behaviors of the animals." Older children experience a profound sense of loss and grief when a sibling dies.

As children advance from age six to twelve, they incrementally begin pulling apart into same-sex—but still mixed-age—play groups.[62] Another sign of growing gender awareness is that girls gradually increase—and boys reduce—the amount of time they spend with adult women. When older children choose to accompany their parents on a hunting or gathering expedition, boys tend to follow the father while girls tend to follow the mother. But as previously noted, gender roles are fluid among the Aka, a cultural characteristic to which children will adapt regardless of which parent they spend more time with. A young woman revealed that "my mother taught me how to hunt and kill the animal"; an older boy explained that "father taught me how to care for babies, to soothe and feed them."

While many other traditional cultures convene elaborate initiation rituals for their older children, the Akas de-emphasize theirs in respect for their egalitarian mindset.[63] For boys, the *egengi* initiation occurs whenever two to four boys have passed age seven or eight. They are taken to a special forest path where their bodies are painted red and they spend a few days learning about spirit secrets, the mythical past, honey collecting, and big-game hunting. For girls, the *waya* initiation occurs after menarche. It involves learning about reproductive skills, the mythical past, and female solidarity, and features a spirit dance in which the dancers tease and ridicule men ("Women want young men, not old men!"). At this time girls also are introduced to *ekila*, which refers to menstruation, blood, and certain taboos that, in part, ensure that male hunters are able to find game.[64]

Around the time that children enter what we call the "teenage" years, they build their own huts.[65] A girl's hut usually is next door to her parents' hut and much smaller; there's room inside for, at most, two people to sleep. Boys get together to build a lean-to structure large enough to sleep three to eight people, usually a short distance into the forest. By all accounts, boys' lean-tos tend to be rickety. Whenever the nights become cold, both boys and girls are apt to scurry home to the warmth of their parents' bed. They also often eat with their parents and stay near them during net hunts.

As puberty approaches, most older boys and girls become inseparable with three or four same-sex friends in a small group in which the age range is from 12 to 18 years.[66] These firm friends do things together during the day and sometimes spend a night side by side in their self-made huts. They also unite to hunt and gather, visit other camps, and even explore distant territories. More and more, their constant talk is all about peers of the opposite sex, where to go to meet them, and how best to look alluring to them.

> If you are a young girl, you decide to point your teeth. Pointing the teeth is for beauty. If you do not get your teeth pointed, people will laugh at you and think you look like a chimpanzee, so you get your teeth pointed to distinguish yourself. It is good to do this. If you are a man or woman searching for a spouse, and you see someone who does not have pointed teeth, you say, "You there, you are like a chimpanzee. You have big teeth like a chimpanzee! I do not want you."[67]

Aka young people are completely self-directed in their romantic endeavors.[68] A favorite activity is checking out the opposite sex in other Aka camps. Evening dances provide ideal opportunities to get noticed, to flirt, and to disappear into the forest or the girl's small hut for closer exploration. The fact that a girl has her own small hut signals to visiting boys her readiness for sexual activity. A girl noted that after girls build huts, "the men start coming to ask for them," adding that "it's better if parents like the boy, but we don't need to get their approval." Romantic liaisons aren't necessarily exclusive, even in the short term. A boy explained that "she can have different boys on the same day and take turns."

An attractive potential mate for Aka youth is a "hard worker."[69] Thus, both males and females strive to build suitable reputations. Unfortunately for the males, demonstrations of one's skill and strength can include dangerous activities such as scaling tall trees, leading to high mortality among teen-aged males.

When two young people decide to begin an exclusive long-term relationship, they simply begin living together in the woman's home camp so that the young man can begin his bride service. There is no ceremony, although the man might bring his wife's parents gifts such as meat, honey, an axe, or a net.

Aka children develop their sense of self within the stable, predictable context of camp and kin[70]—the same familiar people, day after day, who share the same values, beliefs, and practices. Aka teenagers know no reality other than feeling that they belong with, and are trusted and accepted by, those among whom they live every day. *They form their identities within, not apart from, their family and camp.* To us, their choices seem tightly constrained. To them, their plainly delineated adult roles are expected, and respected, by everyone they know. Queried about his future plans, one young male replied simply, "I am Aka."

INFORMAL LEARNING BY AKA CHILDREN

Anthropologists have been keen to figure out how Aka children learn. The Aka are ideal research subjects because their ways of living, and the places where they live, are utterly unlike those of WEIRD societies. Nonetheless, the Aka are our fellow human beings. Another attraction is that the Aka have no word for "teaching"; their closest term is *mateya*—advice or guidance that the recipient may ignore.[71]

Three explanatory factors have emerged as significant for our understanding of how Aka children learn.

The first is that there is virtually no separation between the worlds of children and adults.[72] Among the inhabitants of an Aka camp, adults and young children are within each other's vicinity during most of each day and all of each night (when each family sleeps in one small bed). The only routine separation of youngsters and adults occurs during net hunts and other foraging trips, when children too old to be carried in a sling but not yet old enough to keep up the rapid pace are left behind in the camp while almost everyone else is absent for most of the day.[73]

Consequently, youngsters are regularly within easy viewing distance of activities that they need to master. The people carrying out those activities—their role-models—are adults and juveniles with whom they are closely familiar. There is no pressure on the children to learn anything; there's never a comparison of Child A's learning compared with Child B's. Furthermore, all of this is happening in a setting in which children feel known and valued, and where interpersonal trust is high. And there's a visible link between all the skills and wisdom available to be learned and their uses in sustaining and maintaining the child's group. This link between necessary work and informal learning has been termed "the chore curriculum."[74]

The second factor helping us understand how Aka children learn is that there's virtually no distinction between work and play.[75] As one researcher explained, we ought not be talking about their "work" and "play" because Aka children themselves don't make this distinction. It's more accurate to think about a wide range of daily activities in which the children participate, or not, according to each one's ability and interest. *Learning is an incidental byproduct of the ongoing life of the group.*

It's possible that the only occasion in a child's life that is consciously set aside for "learning" is during their initiation rituals (*egengi* for boys, *waya* for girls). Otherwise, a camp's children are doing whatever they wish. What they wish, remarkably often, is to emulate the adults by trying, alone or in mixed-age groups, to do successfully what they repeatedly see the adults doing. These activities are meaningful, enjoyable, often social, and ultimately useful to the group. But in the children's minds, these activities are neither "play," nor "work," nor "learning."

The final factor is that parents, other adults, and older children do not plan ahead to teach or train the younger ones.[76] It's typical of many parents in WEIRD societies (myself included) that we approach child-rearing in a "teaching frame of mind," which might very well be necessary for *our* children's futures. One might expect that the Aka, who live a precarious hand-to-mouth existence, would feel similarly. They do not. So deeply ingrained are the values of egalitarianism and self-determination that Aka adults rarely assume they know what's best for a child. They hesitate to initiate, direct, or intervene in a child's learning. They are constantly near the children, available and willing to assist—if asked. But Aka children don't often ask adults questions; they're busy figuring things out on their own or collaboratively in their multi-age groups.

Revealing insights into Aka children's informal learning are available from two very different sources: scientific research and a brief incident. First, the research.

Researchers were curious about how children use observation and imitation to learn a skill.[77] They set up a situation in which four- to seven-year-olds, one after another, watched an adult obtain a treat. The treat was in a specially built box, concealed behind one of two small doors. The adult sought the treat via six steps: Steps 1 through 3 brought the adult's hand to the incorrect door; step 4 opened it, revealing nothing. Step 5 brought the adult's hand to the correct door; step 6 opened it, revealing the treat. Each child was then asked, "Can you find the treat?"

Of the Ngandu youngsters, 85% imitated all six steps that they had observed the adult carry out while 15% imitated only the two effective steps. Of the Aka youngsters, fully 60% imitated only the two effective steps while ignoring the four useless ones. The researchers interpreted this result as demonstrating that *most Aka children do not view an adult as a source of authority*. The Aka children didn't imitate the adult's useless actions, learning instead the fastest way to get the treat.

Are you curious about how other groups performed? In a WEIRD society, similar-age children studied in a similar way almost all imitated all six actions including the four useless ones. Chimpanzees, however, virtually all went straight to the treat.[78]

The second insight into children's informal learning is provided by the following brief incident. In this case, the neophyte is an American anthropologist and his culturally knowledgeable companion is a nine-year-old Aka girl.

> I was walking down a trail between two girls. The older one had two cookies, acquired via her parents' trading. She handed one to me. When I bit into it, I immediately saw a change in her expression indicating that I'd made a social error. So I broke the cookie in half and handed to the younger girl the piece I hadn't bitten. I received from the older girl a look of reassurance that I had done the right thing.[79]

We will revisit this incident in the following section.

FORMAL LEARNING BY AKA CHILDREN

As the previous section emphasized, Aka children learn a high percentage of what they need to know by informal means. Their language doesn't even have a word for "teach." But this hasn't deterred anthropologists from wanting to determine the extent, if any, to which Aka adults actually *teach* their children.

What mental image pops into your head when you hear the verb "to teach"? As members of a WEIRD society—the E stands for Educated—we're conditioned to imagine classrooms, learning materials, and professionals delivering planned lessons. Clearly, nothing remotely like that is happening in the Aka world.[80]

Hold on. What if we broaden our conception of what teaching involves? How about this: *Teaching occurs when an individual modifies his or her behavior to enhance the knowledge or skill of another.*[81] The modified behavior need not be lengthy or elaborate; it could be fleeting, subtle, even nonverbal. All that matters is that behavior is modified *specifically* to improve another person's capabilities.

Consider the vignette of the anthropologist's cookie. The capability that he needed to improve was how, in daily life, to apply the key Aka value of sharing. The situation was not a class on Aka values, but a momentary interaction on a forest trail. His "teacher," if I may call her that, was only nine years old, but as a native Aka she had a more practical grasp of Aka values than he did. Her method involved no planning, no text materials, no talking. It was a fleeting and subtle show of disapproval (an eyebrow raise?). He "got" it. *His capability improved.*

Driven by this broader conception of teaching, researchers began to discover the very brief, subtle ways in which Aka adults guide younger Akas' learning. Here's how the Aka "teach," listed in order from the least used to the most used:[82]

- Verbal explanation—Explanations, rarely used, never involved "baby talk."[83]
- Opportunity scaffolding—One Aka provides another with a learning opportunity.
- Positive feedback—One Aka displays approval of another Aka's performance.
- Redirect—One Aka redirects another's location or activity to prevent danger.
- Task assignment—An Aka is given a simple task that incidentally helps her learn.
- Move body—One Aka manipulates another's body part to do the right thing.

The following three are the most used ways in which one Aka "teaches" another:

- Negative feedback—An example is the nine-year-old's nonverbal disapproval.
- Demonstration—One Aka shows another how; often includes "move body."

- Natural pedagogy—This term describes a variety of fleeting behaviors such as pointing, using eye contact, calling the other's name, or otherwise using a very brief bodily action to draw the other's attention to some feature of a skill or knowledge to be learned.

Aka infants 12 to 14 months old were found to be on the receiving end of the above approaches an average of 17 times per hour.[84] Their teachers were their mothers far more often than anyone else, plus friends, siblings, and fathers. As children grew, the identity of their teachers gradually shifted away from parents and siblings and increasingly toward older children in their multi-age groups.

There is a general sense among Aka adults that youngsters really do not need sustained direct instruction—"formal" learning—because they will learn all they need to know through imitating their elders—"informal" learning.[85] But Aka adults also want their camp's young ones to learn rapidly and well, a goal they facilitate by using the fleeting, subtle methods listed above. Should these nine methods be classified as "formal" or "informal"? What do you think?

Are you having the same thought that I'm having at this point? It is this: The nine methods listed above are also used by adults in most (all?) other societies, although in WEIRD societies "verbal explanation" plays a far larger role.

Does all this suggest that Aka adults are unwilling or unable to deliver sustained direct instruction? Consider the experience of anthropologist Bonnie Hewlett, who had asked a group of Aka women "how to be an Aka woman." It was decided that Hewlett should begin by mastering the art of weaving a basket.

> A woman sat next to Hewlett, touching her. She started the basket, ripped it apart, then asked Hewlett to try it on her own. As Hewlett tried to weave, some people laughed and commented. After a while, a 12-year-old girl came over, sat next to her in the same way, demonstrated again how to do it, then handed it back for Hewlett to try. Hewlett was not weaving correctly, so the girl took her hand and helped her weave the twine. The mother and the 12-year-old spent three weeks, hours at a time, sitting right next to Hewlett until she completed the small children's basket.[86]

FROM AN ANTHROPOLOGICAL PERSPECTIVE

There are probably no societies on earth right now that are more different from WEIRD societies than those of hunter-gatherers such as the Aka. That

realization, plus the likelihood that they are living very largely as our ancestors did tens of thousands of years ago, combine to make them fascinating
to anthropologists who are trying to grasp the unadorned essence of what it
means to be human.

Physiologically, Akas are virtually identical to us. They reproduce exactly
like we do. Aka fetuses gestate for nine months, just like ours. An Aka newborn slides into the world like ours, where it must be fed mother's milk or
a substitute, like ours. Well, that's pretty much it for the similarities. What
about the differences?

The differences, of course, are far too many and too significant to try to
list. This chapter, I hope, has given you a sense of the chasm that separates
the Aka and American versions of children's learning and adults' childcare
practices.

An idea that keeps occurring to me as I've worked on this chapter is that
Aka childcare practices represent how humans dealt with their young before
parents started to *think* about how they *ought* to raise children. No doubt
there were compelling reasons for all those thousands of years of thinking to
occur. But isn't it intriguing to be able to contemplate this living example of
Original Child Care?

I keep on using the word "childcare," but the meaning we give that expression does not seem appropriate in the case of the Aka. That's why "Raising
Oneself in the Forest" is the title of this chapter. For among the societies
profiled in this book, in none of the other four do adults overtly demonstrate
as little concern for their children's learning of their society's special skills,
values, and wisdom.

Summary of Aka Children's Learning and Socialization

Based on anthropologists' findings, I believe that five key features of how
children are socialized into adulthood are the following. Aka children . . .

- learn as an incidental by-product of doing whatever they wish.
- are allowed, from their first days, almost limitless self-determination.
- constantly experience close-knit companionship in small, stable groups.
- are exposed to the entire scope of adults' daily lives and concerns.
- experience few distinctions between the roles of men and women.

**Aka children learn as an incidental by-product of doing whatever they
wish.** With a single exception—initiation ceremonies for older children lasting a few days—adults never intentionally deliver bodies of information to
children. There's a general sense among Aka adults that children will learn

all they need to know using their own means and on no one's timetable but their own.

When anthropologists made painstaking efforts to detect whether Aka adults were providing any guidance at all for children, they discovered fleeting, nonverbal ways in which adults offered helpful cues. For example, seeing a child struggling to manipulate a small object, an adult might briefly, silently, reposition the child's grip. Or an adult might give a child an opportunity to apply a skill she is learning.

From a very young age, Aka children are not actively cared for. Alone and in multi-age groups, they are on their own day after day (although parents and other adults are responsive to them). After 12–15 years have passed, the children know how to be Aka. Why does this work?

Documented repeatedly in Aka camps are children trying to do as their elders do. Here an eight-month-old girl is chopping something with a knife; there juvenile boys are climbing a tree to harvest "honey"; over there a pubescent girl is building a small hut to entertain friends and lovers. It turns out that when Aka youngsters are left to do whatever they wish, what they wish more than anything else is to figure out how to become participating Aka just like the adults around them.

Children are allowed, from their first days, almost limitless self-determination. Due to the high death rate among youngsters from diseases, adults act protectively as well as warmly toward children. But adult concerns for children's welfare do not lead them to play a directive role. Even the youngest are treated according to a cardinal Aka value: self-determination. Because they have near-constant access to their mother's breast, they nurse whenever they wish; later, they decide when to wean themselves. Then they are absorbed into their camp's multi-age group of freely roaming boys and girls. Parents may ask their child for assistance with something, but if the child ignores the request, the matter is dropped.

It's true that a baby crawling toward danger (e.g., hot coals) is redirected, and a toddler violating a key Aka value (e.g., sharing) is reprimanded. And when almost all adults leave camp to hunt or gather, the very young are brought along whether they like it or not. But after weaning, children are at liberty to do as they wish, alone or with their fellows, with neither adult input nor adult-imposed responsibilities—liberty that continues unabated right through puberty and into young adulthood.

Children constantly experience close-knit companionship in small, stable groups. The progress of children's self-directed learning is facilitated by the stable society into which they were born: a group of 20 to 35 emotionally and physically close people who share everything that comes into their hands, serve as models of egalitarian relationships, and virtually never resort to physical attacks. Adults and older children, including those who support a mother by voluntarily sharing childcare tasks, look out for the interests of the young without trying to control or chaperone them. They don't rank or compare them. They don't task them with responsibilities. They don't protect them from real or imagined dangers. And if they ask the children for assistance, they may be ignored.

Enveloped by this small group of cooperating, warmly accepting people, Aka youth come to trust not only those around them but also their own worthiness and capacity for mastering all that's needed to harmoniously fit in.[87] Under these circumstances, the identity that an Aka child forges is *not* as a unique individual but as a contributing group member.

Children are exposed to the entire scope of adult's daily lives and concerns. An Aka child's family lives in a hut scarcely large enough for the twig bed they all share, so close to the next hut that seated neighbors can hand things back and forth, arranged with other huts in a clearing roughly the size of a suburban living-dining room. Parties of adults and (if they wish) older children go into the forest for much of the day to hunt or gather. When children and adults are constantly in physically close, often intimate contact, there's extremely little that the children—even the younger ones—don't know in real time about real life.

Is an older girl giving birth? Children watch, up close and personal. Are the neighbors having a quarrel? Children know all the issues and the resolution. Did an infant die from a parasitic disease? Children attend the body minutes afterward and join in the mourning. Alien to the spirit of Aka culture are concepts like "PG-13," "developmentally appropriate," and "children under five not admitted."

Children experience few distinctions between the roles of men and women. Until children reach puberty, Aka adults show no preference for boys or girls and treat them identically. They do not assign responsibility for newly weaned children to older sisters (unlike many other traditional societies). Husbands and wives are together during the majority of most days and generally are mutually supportive. Yes, certain tasks are associated with either husbands or wives, but most tasks can, and uncomplainingly will, be performed by the other spouse when necessary.

Within each camp, a few males are recognized as having slightly more influence than anyone else, but they lack authority. And because males tend to be stronger than women, a few hunter-gathering roles (e.g., hunting wild pigs) are reserved for them. On the other hand, Aka males participate wholeheartedly in childcare—and even have a reputation as the world's best fathers.

In sum, Aka society comes as close to being authentically gender egalitarian as any society possibly could be.

SUGGESTED FURTHER READING

Each of the readings below is profiled at howotherchildrenlearn.info/profiles.

"Hunter-gatherer childhoods in the Congo Basin," by Barry S. Hewlett. *Hunter-Gatherers of the Congo Basin: Cultures, Histories, and Biology of the African Pygmies*, Barry S. Hewlett, ed. (2014); 23 text pages.

Listen, Here Is a Story: Ethnographic Life Narratives from Aka and Ngandu Women of the Congo Basin, by Bonnie L. Hewlett (2013); 230 text pages.

Intimate Fathers: The Nature and Context of Aka Pygmy Paternal Infant Care, by Barry S. Hewlett (1991); 175 text pages.

BIBLIOGRAPHY

Bacirongo, Isaac, & Michael W. Nest. (2015). *Still a pygmy: The unique memoir of one man's fight to save his identity from extinction*. Finch Publishing.

Bentz, Bonnie. (2001). Adolescent culture: An exploration of the socio-emotional development of the Aka adolescents of the Central African Republic. *The Oriental Anthropologist, 1* (2), 25–32. [Bonnie Bentz became Bonnie Hewlett.]

Berl, Richard E. W., & Barry S. Hewlett. (2015). Cultural variation in the use of overimitation by the Aka and Ngandu of the Congo Basin. *PLoS ONE, 10* (3), unpaginated.

Boyette, Adam H. (2010). Middle childhood among Aka forest foragers of the Central African Republic: A comparative perspective. *Anthro. Vancouver.WSU.edu*, 1–32.

Boyette, Adam H. (2013). *Social learning during middle childhood among Aka foragers and Ngandu farmers of the Central African Republic*. Ph.D. dissertation, Washington State Univ. (attained via ProQuest).

Boyette, Adam H. (2016a). Children's play and culture learning in an egalitarian foraging society. *Child Development, 87* (3), 759–769.

Boyette, Adam H. (2016b). Children's play and the integration of social and individual learning: A cultural niche construction perspective. *Social*

Chapter 2

Learning and Innovation in Contemporary Hunter-Gatherers, Hideaki
Terashima & Barry Hewlett, eds. Springer Japan, 159–169.

Boyette, Adam H., & Barry S. Hewlett. (2017). Autonomy, equality, and
teaching among Aka foragers and Ngandu farmers of the Congo Basin.
Human Nature, 28, 289–322.

Boyette, Adam H. (2019). Autonomy, cognitive development, and the
socialization of cooperation in foragers: Aka children's views of sharing
and caring. *Hunter-Gatherer Research, 3* (3), 475–500.

Cordes, L., & Barry Hewlett. (May 1990). Health and nutrition among Aka
pygmies. Paper presented at the International Conference on Hunting
and Gathering Societies, Fairbanks, Alaska.

Duffy, Kevin. (1984). *Children of the Forest: Africa's Mbuti Pygmies.*
Waveland Press.

Fouts, Hillary N. (2008). Father involvement with young children among
the Aka and Bofi foragers. *Cross-Cultural Research, 42* (3), 290–312.

Fouts, Hillary N., & Robyn A. Brookshire. (2009). Who feeds children? A
child's-eye-view of caregiver feeding patterns among the Aka foragers
in Congo. *Social Science & Medicine, 69*, 285–292.

Harari, Yuval Noah. (2015). *Sapiens: A Brief History of Mankind.* Harper
Collins.

Hewlett, Barry S., & L. L. Cavalli-Sforza. (1986). Cultural transmission
among Aka Pygmies. *American Anthropologist, 88*, 922–934.

Hewlett, Barry S. (1991). *Intimate Fathers: The Nature and Context of Aka
Pygmy Paternal Infant Care.* University of Michigan Press.

Hewlett, Barry S., Michael E. Lamb, Donald Shannon, Birgit Leyendecker,
& Axel Schölmerich. (1998). Culture and infancy among Central African
foragers and farmers. *Developmental Psychology, 34* (4), 653–661.

Hewlett, Barry S., Michael E. Lamb, Dirgit Leyendecker, & Axel
Schölmerich. (2000). Internal working models, trust, and sharing among
foragers. *Current Anthropology, 41* (2), 287–297.

Hewlett, Barry S., & Shane J. MacFarlan. (2010). Fathers' roles in
hunter-gatherer and other small-scale cultures. *The Role of the Father in
Child Development, 5th Ed.*, Michael Lamb, ed. Wiley, 413–434.

Hewlett, Barry S., Hillary N. Fouts, Adam H. Boyette, & Bonnie L.
Hewlett. (2011). Social learning among Congo Basin hunter-gatherers.
Philosophical Transactions of the Royal Society B, 366, 1168–1178.

Hewlett, Barry S. (2014). Hunter-gatherer childhoods in the Congo Basin.
*Hunter-Gatherers of the Congo Basin: Cultures, Histories, and Biology
of the African Pygmies*, Barry Hewlett, ed. Transaction, 245–275.

Hewlett, Barry S., Richard E. W. Berl, & Casey J. Roulette. (2016).
Teaching and overimitation among Aka hunter-gatherers. *Social*

Learning and Innovation in Contemporary Hunter-Gatherers, Hideaki Terashima & Barry S. Hewlett, eds. Springer Japan, 35–45.

Hewlett, Barry S., & Casey J. Roulette. (2016). Teaching in hunter-gatherer infancy. *Royal Society Open Science, 3*, 150403: not paginated.

Hewlett, Barry S., Jean Hudson, Adam H. Boyette, & Hillary N. Fouts. (2019). Intimate living: Sharing space among Aka and other hunter-gatherers. *Towards a Broader View of Hunter-Gatherer Sharing*, Noa Lavi & David E. Friesem, eds. Cambridge, 39–56.

Hewlett, Bonnie L., & Barry S. Hewlett. (2012). Hunter-gatherer adolescence. *Adolescent Identity: Evolutionary, Cultural, and Developmental Perspectives*, Bonnie L. Hewlett, ed. Routledge, 73–101.

Hewlett, Bonnie L. (2013a). *Listen, here is a story: Ethnographic life narratives from Aka and Ngandu women of the Congo Basin*. Oxford University Press.

Hewlett, Bonnie. (2013b). *"Ekeloko,"* The spirit to create: Innovation and social learning among Aka adolescents of the Central African rainforest. *Dynamics of Learning in Neanderthals and Modern Humans, Volume I: Cultural Perspectives*. Springer Japan, 187–195.

Kitanishi, Koichi. (1998). Food sharing among the Aka hunter-gatherers in northeastern Congo. *African Study Monographs*, Suppl. 25, 3–32.

Lancy, David F., & M. Annette Grove. (2010). The role of adults in children's learning. *The Anthropology of Learning in Childhood*, David Lancy et al., eds. Rowman & Littlefield, 145–179.

Lew-Levy, Sheina., Rachel Reckin, Noa Lavi, Jurgi Cristóbal-Azkarate, & Kate Ellis-Davies. (2017). How do hunter-gatherer children learn subsistence skills? A meta-ethnographic review. *Human Nature, 28* (4), 367–394.

Lew-Levy, Sheina, Noa Lavi, Rachel Reckin, Jurgi Cristóbal-Azkarate, & Kate Ellis-Davies. (2018). How do hunter-gatherer children learn social and gender norms? A meta-ethnographic review. *Cross-Cultural Research, 52* (2), 213–255.

Meehan, Courtney L. (2005). The effects of residential locality on parental and alloparental investment among the Aka foragers of the Central African Republic. *Human Nature, 6* (1), 62–84.

Meehan, Courtney L. (2009). Maternal time allocation in two cooperative childrearing societies. *Human Nature, 20* (4), 375–383.

Meehan, Courtney L., & Sean Hawks. (2013). Cooperative breeding and attachment among the Aka foragers. *Attachment Reconsidered: Cultural Perspectives on a Western Theory*, Naomi Quinn & Jennifer Mageo, eds. Palgrave Macmillan, 85–113.

Meehan, Courtney L., Edward H. Hagen, & Barry S. Hewlett. (2017). Persistence of infant care patterns among Aka foragers. *Hunter-Gatherers in a Changing World*, Victoria Reyes-García & Aili Pyhälä, eds. Springer Switzerland, 213–231.

Takeuchi, Kiyoshi. (2005). The ambivalent symbiosis between the Aka hunter-gatherers and neighboring farmers. *Culture, Conservation, and Development in African Rain Forest*. Core: University of Toyama Repository, 11–28.

Chapter 3

Nothing Special for the Children

Growing Up among the Quechua of Highland Peru

Figure 3.1. Three children of the Quechua ayllu studied by anthropologist Inge Bolin. *From Growing Up in a Culture of Respect: Child Rearing in Highland Peru, by Inge Bolin. Copyright © 2006. Courtesy of the University of Texas Press.*

FILMS ABOUT THE QUECHUA WAY OF LIFE

These films will enable you to more accurately imagine Quechua families as you read this chapter.

"The Original People of Peru: The Quechua" (~1970). Documentary about daily life among the Quechua. Produced by TRACKS Travel. 49:50 min. youtube.com/watch?v=y-4E_VUHKL0

"Peru's Quechua Indians: Culture and Family Traditions" (2019). Traditional practices and rituals. Produced by wocomoHUMANITY. 16:51 min. youtube.com/watch?v=YV6hij9njw8&t=897s

TRACKS Travel makes films about traditional peoples: youtube.com/c/TRACKSTravelChannel.

Hot links to all films and videos are at
howotherchildrenlearn.info/films

Based on anthropological fieldwork carried out primarily between 1988 and 2004.

Picture yourself in Peru, south of Cuzco, on the steep, treeless mountainsides of the Andes, at an altitude that might be higher than you've ever dared to venture—12,000 to 17,000 feet. This region is inhabited by vicuñas (wild alpacas), condors, pumas—and an indigenous people bearing the legacy of the Incas: the Quechua.[1]

Their settlements so little resemble what we think of as a village or hamlet that I will always use the Quechua term: *ayllu.* A typical ayllu consists of a center and four widely dispersed sectors where most inhabitants live. "Widely dispersed" means that, measured from the ayllu's center, each sector is as far as *ten miles distant* (and don't forget the altitude differentials). This four-sector arrangement, carried down from Inca times, ensures that the alpacas, llamas, and sheep of the ayllu's 300-plus families' have sufficient land on which to graze.[2]

The ayllu's center comprises adobe buildings with thatched or corrugated iron roofs: municipal buildings, a school, and a health station staffed by a nurse. The families who live there, and those living in the four far-away sectors, make their homes in small adobe houses—some would say huts—with little or no furniture.

If you were an anthropologist going to do fieldwork in a Quechua ayllu, how would you get there? There's only one option: You'd hike up from the valley.[3]

QUECHUA LIFE: SETTING AND SUSTENANCE

In many societies, children learn about their forebears via stories passed down through generations. The Quechua have an additional way. They take a hike.

If you're a Quechua, you walk *everywhere*, and your miles-long hikes up, down, and across mountainsides[4] take you past archeological remnants from Inca times such as settlements (mini-Machu Picchus), irrigation canals, and stonework carved with intriguing symbols. It's a legacy literally set in stone, open to anyone who happens along, a veritable "please-touch" children's museum.

The Incas spoke the Quechua language and benefited from the cultures of the indigenous peoples who preceded them in the Cuzco region.[5] During their heyday in the 15th and 16th centuries, the Incas built huge stone structures such as Sacsayhuamán, a fortress that you'll want to visit if you're vacationing in Cuzco. Creating it

> required stone blocks to be brought from quarries at least nine miles away. Without wheeled conveyances, this would be difficult enough on the flat, but the blocks had to be moved uphill from their quarries. Even more remarkable is that these blocks, estimated to weigh over 100 tons each, were lifted into place without advanced machinery. The stones of the walls were precisely dressed. They fit together so tightly that even without mortar they've stood for more than 500 years.[6]

And not only that. The Incas knew astronomy, performed brain surgery, and spread their empire far beyond Cuzco—though they lacked both the wheel and a written language. In place of writing, the Inca developed *quipu*, a unique system using colored strings or cords with knots by which they conveyed census, tribute, and storage information, and recorded genealogies, property deeds, and wealth.[7]

The Inca economy was admirably efficient. It included taxation in the form of labor organized to ensure that the overall economy worked well. Ayllu members had a duty to join their neighbors in completing tasks that included major projects such as constructing agricultural terraces and minor efforts such as house repair.

In recent times, the challenge that constantly confronts the Quechua is how to sustain themselves in their marginal environment.[8] Weather in the Andes often is unwelcome but not unfamiliar. As dusk descends, the temperature can drop in a few hours by as much as 35 °F, leveling off below freezing. The Quechua capacity to adapt was sorely tested during 1997–2000 by repeated extremes that probably were related to climate change. Herds decreased by 30%; harvests were wiped out; people went hungry. Some left their ayllus to seek work elsewhere.

Even in "good years," mountainside food production brings adversities that must be routinely overcome. Its necessities determine the rhythms of seasonable and daily Quechua life, sparing only the infirm, the aged, and the very young.

The staples of the food supply are potatoes and other tubers; these are raised in a variety of widely spaced locations, and at different altitudes, to minimize crop failures resulting from frost, hail, floods, and landslides. A few vegetables are grown in sheltered areas; more are acquired by trading animal products and gorgeous woven cloth with lowland farmers. Algae and mushrooms are collected from wherever they can be found. The Quechua also consume small quantities of edible clay.[9] Before anyone can wield a hoe, pluck a plant, or dig a bit of clay, they will have walked on steep trails for miles—and will carry their tools and produce back home the same way.

Consider potatoes. During months when the nighttime temperature is below freezing, hundreds of potatoes are spread out on dry grass where they freeze at night, then dry in the warm sun. Each morning, family members walk on the potatoes in bare feet to squeeze out moisture. After ten days, the resulting *chuño* are hard and grayish-black, but—here's their advantage— can be stored for as much as a decade. Processing doesn't always proceed smoothly. Torrential rains can cause harvested potatoes to rot before they're transformed into *chuño*.[10]

The Quechua don't subsist solely on tubers, vegetables, and algae. They have many domesticated animals that are the main focus of their collective effort.

The Quechua think of themselves as pastoralists,[11] people whose animals provide much of what they require for daily life: wool, blood, skins, tendons, fat, bones (used in tool-making), and of course meat (sometimes dried[12]). Let's not forget dung, which they use wisely: Sheep dung, full of nutrients, is a superb fertilizer; llama dung, full of combustible energy, is dried and used as fuel.[13]

Animals are not thought of only in economic terms.[14] In the Quechua worldview, any animal is worthy of compassion and respect. Domesticated animals evoke feelings of gratitude for their companionship and their provisions. Each has its own name, bestowed soon after its birth during a ceremony thanking the deities. Each animal is recognized on sight; none is ever branded.

Occasionally it is decided to sacrifice an animal as part of a festival. This honors the deities and adds meat to the family's starchy diet. A tender ceremony ensues: The animal is laid on its side with its head in the lap of the owner, who offers thanks to the mountain god. Sad-faced family members take their hats off in respect. A handful of blood is offered to the god of the highest mountain in the vicinity, who is asked to accept the animal's spirit and return it as a newborn.

THE WORLD ACCORDING TO THE QUECHUA

Quechua notions of their surroundings are substantially different from ours. For example, they're mystified by our concept of the "supernatural." Yet far more than we, they are animated daily by forces larger than themselves. The attitudes they gain from communing with these forces shape their human relationships.

A Human Society with Nonhuman Members

In the Quechua worldview, natural places such as mountains, meadows, and lakes are social beings. To each place they attribute the thoughts, emotions, intentions, and capabilities for action of social beings, and even the physiological attributes of social beings such as hunger and gender. Their perspective is that Quechua society includes active members that are not exclusively human.[15]

Note that the Quechua view is *not* that "places have spirits." Instead, places are social beings, located nearby, with whom people have relationships and share kinship.[16] Food offerings are Quechuas' principal way of maintaining a positive relationship with places. After all, places were the original sources of food; life would be impossible without their generosity. So they are repeatedly thanked.

This worldview extends to nonhuman living things as well, including all plants and animals. This is why, a few paragraphs ago, I wrote that *any* animal—even one that is wild—is deserving of compassion and respect. These empathic feelings are part of being Quechua; they are not expressed merely during religious rites.

The Quechua worldview is characterized by feelings of reciprocity. They think of themselves as receiving protection and life-giving sustenance from the places, plants, and animals in their vicinity, to which in their gratitude they return food, compassion, and respect. Thus, they participate in a cycle of giving and receiving that ensures that balance is maintained. Their view of the universe is holistic; all parts of nature are interconnected through this cycle.[17]

Especially important to the Quechua is *Pachamama*, the Earth Mother.[18] Just as human mothers routinely take care of their children, Pachamama is constantly looking after her human children. Women have a special bond with Pachamama; when they sit, it is directly on the earth. Men sit on chairs and benches.[19]

The Quechuas' awareness of their relations with nonhuman beings—relations eliciting feelings of compassion, empathy, humility, and respect—helps to explain how they raise their children, and how their children evolve into adults. As we will see, the word *respect* captures the essential spirit shaping Quechua relationships.

Everyday Relationships Among the Quechua

In Quechua society, all families are striving side-by-side to scratch a living from a reluctant, unpredictable environment; neighbors cooperate to a degree rarely seen in the United States. No family is obviously richer or poorer than the others. No one remains isolated; widows and orphans are absorbed into a relative's family.[20]

The division of labor between males and females is flexible.[21] Normally, men do the heavier work in the fields and with horses. Women take charge of the adobe home and its economics, prepare food, assist with herding, and care for young children. But if only one gender is present, whatever work must be done is done, including infant care. Both spin and weave. Both work side-by-side in the fields during the winter planting season. However, it's the women who actually place seeds in the earth due to their special relationship with Pachamama.

Around 1985, when anthropologist Inge Bolin was working in the Andes, she first encountered Quechuas in a market town below their high ayllu. Bolin writes that she was "struck by their elegant and respectful demeanor," and adds that the priest and several merchants who had first-hand acquaintance with the Quechuas' ayllu "stressed that the herders are more respectful than people elsewhere."[22] Bolin went on to live in that ayllu during parts of 13 years between 1988 and 2004.[23] Her book is entitled, *Growing Up in a Culture of Respect.*

Quechuas' relationships with each other mirror their relationships with the nonhuman members of their society. They maintain the cycle of giving and receiving not only with sustaining places, plants, and animals, but also with family members, fellow ayllu inhabitants and, indeed, with all other humans. Respect is understood as the fulfillment of rights and responsibilities to others, and as the mutual exchange of recognition, empathy, care, and support.[24] (My own preferred definition is, "Respect shows other people that they are valued.")

Bolin writes of respect being shown by older children and even a two-year-old:

> As Luzwilma, Anali, and I crossed a narrow bridge, they noticed that the bridge was not in good shape. They quickly put some of my equipment on top of their carrying bags, and Anali insisted that I hold her hand as I jumped from the bridge to the slippery, muddy ground.[25]

> As we all sat in a circle eating a meal, little Luis noticed that his grandpa wasn't eating his soup with a spoon but instead used his fingers to pick out the potatoes. Luis got up, took a spoon from a pot by the fire, wiped it, and without saying a word stuck it into his grandpa's bowl.[26]

Everyday relationships include the shared activity of chewing leaves from coca plants, which have long grown naturally in South America. The popular belief that chewing coca leaves gives one a "high" is mistaken. Coca leaves and cocaine are as different as rye bread and rye whiskey.[27]

Chewing coca leaves together with a bit of ash is a practice passed down from pre-Inca times. It is now known to reduce hunger and thirst, lessen fatigue, and even diminish altitude sickness, probably by increasing oxygen saturation. Coca chewing seems to improve one's mood, energy, and capacity for the never-ending toil that is necessary in this fickle high-altitude environment.[28]

Coca also plays a role in ayllu members' everyday social routines, which would strike us as unnecessarily ceremonial. Greetings, words of companionship, gratitude, farewells—all are shaped by a stylized etiquette that conveys empathy and respect for human and other beings. Coca chewing is best understood in this context.[29]

Coca chewing—*hallpay*—is simultaneously a ritual act and a pause from daily toil warmly shared with one's companions. Never hurried, hallpay is a meditative interlude for conversation and reflection. Coca is chewed about five times a day by every adult. Here is an anthropologist's account of a hallpay encounter:

> Doña Juana stopped by to visit her sister, Doña María, for Juana had agreed to pasture María's cow. The two sat down to visit for a while and, because Juana was doing her a service, María offered Juana a small handful of coca saying, "*Hallpakuy*" (Please chew). Juana accepted with both hands. The two settled down to visit and chew together. But first, Juana and María shared with the earth and mountains. They searched for their best leaves—dark, shiny green, sweet-tasting, and unblemished. Selecting three leaves, Juana arranged them with

shiny sides up in a small fan, the *k'intu*. Invoking the names of the mountains and lands she was inviting to co-consume the k'intu, she waved it in front of her mouth, blew on it, invoked their powers, and added a petition: "Do not allow more rain." Next, Juana shared with her sister. She made a k'intu, extending it toward María shiny side up. "Let us chew together," she said. María answered with thanks and blew on the k'intu for the other beings. (She had simultaneously offered Juana a k'intu with a similar invitation and thanks; Juana also blew on it.) They both began chewing. Now they added compressed ash from what looked like a charcoal briquette, each taking a small bite and chewing it into her wad. This sweetened the taste and activated the stimulating alkaloids. Juana felt ready to work hard for two or three more hours.[30]

HOW NEWBORNS ARRIVE AND RECEIVE CARE

When he was doing fieldwork among the Quechua, an American anthropologist brought along his wife to a mid-size Andean town. (She played no direct role in his work.) She soon realized that the townsfolk were ill at ease with her because she and her husband were childless, about which *they* were totally at ease.

> It would be interesting for me to become pregnant while we're here so that we'd learn how differently we would be viewed, particularly how differently I would be treated by the women especially. Now, it is impossible for the Quechua to place me comfortably into any known category of being—I behave and expect to be treated as an adult, but in Quechua culture a woman is not an adult until she bears a child.[31]

Among the Quechua, new couples are eager to have children right away even though giving birth in a high ayllu is fraught with danger. The nearest medical facility could be as many as 20 miles away—via trails. Even when a difficult birth can be foreseen, the possibility that the mother will go to a hospital for the delivery is small. Mothers and newborns die during childbirth at a relatively high rate.[32]

During childbirth, mothers usually are assisted by their own mothers.[33] Sometimes the husband assists. In the absence of an adult close relative, children as young as 12 have been known to assist. The newborn's umbilical cord is severed using a sharp piece of tile; it's believed that if the cord is cut using a knife or scissors, the child will wear out his clothes very fast.

Infants are breastfed. If the mother's milk is delayed or inadequate, she is likely to ask a nursing woman, or a woman whose infant recently died, to feed her newborn. A baby is fed when it cries, as crying is interpreted as a sign of hunger. If the mother is working at that moment, she does her best to combine nursing and working. After about two years, the child is weaned.

The first several weeks of life bring threats, especially if climactic conditions have led to loss of herds and crops, resulting in malnutrition. Illnesses leading to fatalities are known to occur in infants' digestive, respiratory, and urinary tracts. Also occasionally fatal is hypoxia (insufficient oxygen).

An infant is in physical contact with its mother or other caregiver (such as its father or older sibling) most of the time. Infants are carried everywhere in cloths worn as a sling in such a way that they are perched high on the mother's back, free to look all around. When the mother arrives at a location where she must work, she places the child on the ground, propped up so that the child can watch her working as well as all her interactions with others.[34] (To anthropologists, these ways of dealing with infants are significant.) Constant carrying continues until the child can walk.

Infants are almost never alone, and then for only very short periods. At night, they sleep together with their mother or on a piece of fur on the floor beside their mother. During the day, family members and others are eager to hold and play with the newcomer. "Women, men, and older children are delighted as infants pull their hair, play with their clothes, and jump on their laps without tiring." Whether inside their parents' one-room home or outside on their mother's back, they not only witness the full sweep of social interactions but also become a focus of frequent face-to-face attention from family members and others nearby.

During each newborn's first week of life, an ancient ritual is performed during which it is given a name, linked with a godparent, and put under the protection of a mountain peak. Although most Quechua are not strong Catholics, they expect a Catholic baptism (performed by a priest who hiked up from the valley), essential because it yields a certificate that puts the child in good standing with the civil authorities.[35]

A young child's main rite of passage is its First Haircut, which occurs between ages one and six years. During the First Haircut additional godparents are named, the child's right to property is confirmed, and gifts of money, clothing, and animals are received. The parents' role is minor to avoid confusing the deities, ensuring that the latter concern themselves only with the child and his or her new ritual kin.

LEARNING TO BE QUECHUA: THE
EARLY CHILDHOOD YEARS

Young Quechuas are not completely different from American youngsters of your and my acquaintance. For example, let's consider the story of

Tomás, Hipólito, and Marcos, ages eight, six, and four, respectively, as related by Bolin:

> Feelings of jealousy tend to mingle with children's urges to get attention. As I admired the spinning and weaving skills of the girls, the three younger boys stood by. Within no time, Tomás climbed to the roof and ran down the wall like an acrobat. Hipólito did the intimate dance of *ukukus*, metaphoric creatures resembling bears or alpacas. Marcos ran to the kitchen to show me the precious carrots his Dad had bartered in the village.[36]

Mischievous Marcos turns up about a year later, doing his best to participate in ways of his culture that he was learning through repeatedly observing adults and older children; unfortunately, he had overlooked one important detail:

> Marcos practiced making a fire with two stones, as he had seen his parents and older siblings do. He sat in the doorway of a small shed. When he finally sparked a flame, it caught the dry grass spread on the floor; soon the roof and some stored objects were burning. Family and neighbors put out the fire with buckets of water. The little boy was scared and ashamed. His father talked to him but there was no punishment.[37]

Bolin tells us that she never saw anyone spank a child. (She was told that it does happen.) She did witness a few "light slaps" when a child played too roughly with his younger siblings. She also found that parents occasionally issued threats, such as that a mythical fox or bull would snatch the child away if the misbehavior didn't cease. Most often, however, parents admonished their naughty child with a serious look or tone. For example, when little Víctor continued bothering his younger sisters, his parents finally admonished him using a serious tone of voice. "Crying, Víctor looked for sympathy from the other family members, but no one comforted him. Only after he apologized did Víctor receive a hug."[38]

Join me in imagining that we can miraculously skip the uphill hike and pay a visit to an ayllu to see what's going on with the younger children there. It's likely that, from our American perspective, the following five features would stand out.

The first is that young Quechua children are constantly with adults.[39] Whether they're riding about on their mothers' backs, struggling to master the skills of walking, toddling around to explore areas near their homes, basking in the loving attention of family members after their evening meal, or bedding down for the night, children are interacting with parents, older siblings, grandparents, and other relatives as well as with their family's neighbors, very nearly 100% of the time.

Given the background and context of the highland Quechuas' lives, it would be impossible to separate adults and children in any sustainable way. But there is no evidence that anyone wants a separation. So from birth onward, children become front-row witnesses to everything that involves the adults. Yes, even *that!*

From an early age, Quechua youngsters' attention is drawn to the pastimes and interests of adults. For example, they come to recognize and then learn the adults' stories, poems, songs, and dances, many of which admiringly depict nature—animals and plants—and love, others of which convey respect for the environment and its nonhuman members. The adults' favorites become the children's favorites.

Second, I believe it would stand out for us that the adults take a laissez-faire stance toward youngsters.[40] *Laissez-faire* is an appropriate descriptor so long as it's understood that adults remain alert to ensure that children don't bumble into serious danger. They do not overprotect. Bolin reports that, "Overly cautious behavior on the part of parents and other caretakers is seldom seen."[41]

Parents allow their children to develop practical skills, such as talking and walking, at their own pace. The little ones are not encouraged; they are not coached; they are not praised for attaining milestones; and their pace is never compared with that of siblings or neighborhood age-mates. For example, if a crawling child attempts to stand on her own, she is neither encouraged nor dissuaded. If she falls, she falls. If she stands, she stands. If she falls and cries, she's comforted. Goading children to attain skills before they're "ready" is not respectful. Remember, this is a culture of respect.

Youngsters are allowed to try to accomplish just about any new task or skill that attracts their interest. With few exceptions, their curiosity is allowed free rein, unconstrained by adults' handwringing about lurking dangers. Consider 18-month-old Luis, who spied a steep staircase without railings and started to climb it on all fours. A family member stood by but neither warned nor intervened.

Third, it would soon dawn on us, I think, that there is extremely little contrast in the way in which parents deal with their male and female youngsters.[42] In some Quechua ayllus, very young children are all called *wawa*, which does not indicate gender. Children of both genders wear very similar clothing consisting of a knitted wool cap, a woven shirt often cut from old adult clothing, and a cloth wrapped around the body and fastened by a woven belt. This manner of dress remains unchanged until the child is five or six years old.

Adults' expectations regarding male and female children's expressions and emotions are indistinguishable. Both are allowed to be sensitive and emotional; both are expected to weep upon appropriate provocation. A cherished trait in both sexes is a respectful demeanor. The "macho" attitude that some people associate with males in certain cultures is absent.

One difference does emerge. As the children get a little older, it is common for them to begin trying to make music together. In these cases, the girls sing and the boys play instruments.

Fourth—and again this might take a while—I think we'd realize that a feature of American childhood is almost completely absent among Quechua children: competitiveness.[43] Some of their play activities are physical contests, but these never result in gloating by the child with the best outcome. The goal seems to be fun, and perhaps subconsciously an opportunity to test one's emerging prowess. Examples include a contest known as either the pushing game or the agility game, in which children playfully press against each other with their shoulders, trying to dislodge the other from a circle. Other games involve daring activities such as energetically climbing on rocks or jumping across creeks. A very common game is hide-and-seek, played just like you and I did all those years ago.

An exception is soccer, played separately by juvenile-age girls and boys. But soccer is not an activity indigenous to the Quechua; it was a European import.

A dramatic example of an activity that certainly *appears* to be competitive is the daring horse races that occur annually during a July festival. Yes, one horse and rider emerge as the fastest—a fact that's noted but not publicly announced. The races have no declared winner. Again we see the Quechuas' reverence for the value of respect. The thrill of the race was made possible by *all* the participants in combination. It wouldn't be respectful to pay tribute to only one of them.

Finally, we would become aware that young children are increasingly drawn into the activities of the adults. As a continual observer of the full sweep of the daily lives of adults and juveniles, and as the continual object of just about everyone's affection, each fledgling Quechua becomes eager to fit in with this loving group. The Quechuas themselves speak of *runa hina kay*, "to be like people."[44]

During our imaginary ayllu visit, you would see youngsters trying to fit in by assisting with day-to-day tasks. At first, they would help to shake out the blankets each morning, run short errands, and hold a bottle so that younger siblings can drink. Months later, they would begin accompanying their elder siblings as they take the animals to the nearby pastures. Next might come helpful tasks requiring more skill, such as lighting the fire, bringing water to boil, and peeling potatoes.

During the 1970s, a group of researchers surveyed an anthropological data base to determine when children in traditional societies begin to take on roles and responsibilities within their families.[45] They found that children usually begin to make significant contributions between ages five and seven. Later fieldwork in a Quechua village in southern Peru provides descriptions of what this looks like:

> Ana, five years old, helped her grandmother with the cattle and regularly joined her mother in grazing the flock. Ana reported that she also assisted with cooking, laundry, cleaning, and feeding hens and guinea pigs. When Ana was six and had started first grade, she explained that she now also cared for her younger sister and helped to harvest potatoes. Her mother noted that the family grew vegetables and sold them in the village market, adding that Ana lately seems to prefer selling to playing.[46]

> Felipe, five years old, joined his mother or his older sister on their visits to the hills around the community to graze the flock or work on the farmland; he helped at home with cooking, washing, feeding the animals, and fetching water and wood. During the following year, Felipe not only expanded these activities but also became closer to his father, helping on the farm, and using a miniature tool, a scythe, that his father made especially for him. He said he enjoyed these activities.[47]

The anthropologist who provided those descriptions adds that besides the development of work skills and feelings of responsibility for carrying them out, these activities imbued the children with "a sense of belonging to the group, which in turn is expressed in a shared identity, and a feeling of overall well-being."[48]

In summary, what you'd see would be children of six, five, or even younger assuming responsibility for the completion of tasks that support smooth group functioning; tasks that could involve danger or discomfort to themselves; tasks that contribute to the well-being of their beloved family group. Writes Bolin:

> When I met three-year-old Anali in her home at 16,400 feet, it was her first meeting with a foreigner. While her parents were busy preparing a meal, Anali took over the role of hostess. She filled two cups with water, kept one for herself, and offered one to me, saying "Let's drink together" in Quechua. She cared for me in an elegant and quite determined way throughout my stay in her home.[49]

That meeting occurred in 1990. By chance I discovered that, some years later, Anali graduated in Cuzco from her studies in systems analysis.[50] As we will see later on, Anali wasn't the only youth from this ayllu to excel academically.

Chapter 3

LEARNING TO BE QUECHUA: THE
LATER CHILDHOOD YEARS

Each child's internal timetable of maturation lets parents know when he or she should begin to wear gender-specific clothing, which occurs roughly around the age of five or six.[51] Despite the switch to more masculine and feminine styles, adults continue to draw few distinctions between older boys and girls.

Much of the daily lives of all six- and seven-year-olds is devoted to assisting parents and older siblings in the various tasks that ensure the family's survival.[52] The Quechua recognized a very long time ago that, given their fickle environment, it is essential for youth to acquire skill and knowledge regarding spinning, weaving, crop cultivation, food storage, births, burials, gala fiestas, traditional medicine, and communal work parties. Learning the what, why, and how of these and other activities is necessary for both boys and girls because, depending on evolving family circumstances including untimely illnesses, injuries, and deaths, they may be called upon with no advance warning to assume full adult responsibilities, age and gender notwithstanding. They learn these responsibilities initially by example and imitation, then by participation.

Starting around the age of seven, a child occasionally will be asked to walk alone to the valley to barter for or buy items in the nearby market town. They've done this before in the company of family members. Depending on a variety of factors, the "nearby" town is 10 to 20 miles away—one way! All downhill in one direction, all uphill in the other, and every step on rough trails while carrying a burden on one's back. Bartering requires an awareness of the relative values of dissimilar items and diplomacy to smooth the process. Potatoes, wool, and finished weavings, for example, might be exchanged for maize (corn), spices, sugar, salt, or tea. Fortunately, bartering usually involves valley farm families with whom the child's family has long had a friendly relationship.

The other activity that requires the attention of every juvenile is their increasing responsibility for the animals. This requires mastering animal husbandry skills such as feeding, shearing, and caring for sick animals in addition to the supervision of mating and even participation in slaughtering. Each young person's most frequent responsibility is to guide the family's herds to and from pastures—by themselves. Again, they will have done this countless times previously in the company of their older siblings.

It's likely that you, like me, have no experience herding, so let's pause to consider what it entails. Pastures are widely dispersed over the mountainsides, each used according to seasonal and other factors. Some pastures lie many miles in the distance, reached only by steep and rocky paths. A pastoralist of any age must be familiar with an array of variables: birthing; specific animals' typical behavior and illnesses; the ownership and physical characteristics of the terrain they're passing through; weather-borne dangers such as lightning, hail, snow-blindness, and torrential rain (which can trigger deadly landslides); and the habits of local predators such as foxes, giant condors, and even human thieves.

A family's wealth is its animals. Each sheep, alpaca, and llama is the equivalent of money in the bank. Each one also is beloved and known by name. If something goes terribly wrong, there is no way for the youthful herder to quickly summon help. He or she alone must analyze, decide, and act.

Think of the eight-year-old children you know. Could any handle this?[53] Would their parents give them even a thin sliver of any equally significant responsibility?

One recurring family activity is available only for boys.[54] When they are about seven years old, they begin accompanying their fathers on journeys to the distant market towns in the lowlands. During these commercial trips, which last from a few days to a month, the goods to be bartered are carried on the family's sure-footed llamas, each of which carry a load of 60 to 70 pounds over a daily distance of about a dozen miles.[55] The men and boys walk. Before nightfall, camp is made at a familiar site such as a cave, rocky overhang, or abandoned house. Food, blankets, and fuel for cooking are part of the llamas' loads; barren mountainsides cannot be depended on to supply anything. Males from several families join each caravan; due to the risks, no family even thinks of undertaking a trading trip alone.

An anthropologist who looked into Quechua trading patterns tells us that

> A family's regular contact with groups of farmers leads to bonds with duties and obligations on each side, such as supplying certain goods even during hard times. Trading occurs as part of a relationship between acquaintances who might have known each other from childhood, when the herder first accompanied his father. Thus, these commercial transactions are not cold and calculating but rather exchanges of goods between friends.[56]

So far, I've portrayed juvenile Quechuas in terms of all work and no play, no doubt because I'm awed by the responsibilities they shoulder at a stage of life that we Americans associate with irresponsibility. This is the same stage of life when hormones first begin to surge. How do these young people respond?

Luckily for them, festivals occur frequently in Quechua life; some are religious, some are national, and some honor their Inca heritage.[57] Festivals provide young people with eagerly anticipated opportunities to notice, and be noticed by, the opposite sex. So when a festival occurs, groups congregate in the four sectors of their widely dispersed ayllu, dancing and singing to *waynus*, the love songs of the Incas, and to more recent melodies. An unmistakable signal that a young person is hoping to make a strong positive impression on the opposite sex during the next festival is when she—or he—is seen devoting hours to the weaving of colorful, intricate designs into their festive clothing.

Teenage romances don't begin only during festivals; far more opportunities present themselves during their long days herding animals in remote mountain pastures. A certain degree of promiscuity is expected, but until recently it was an embarrassment for a baby to be born out of wedlock. Young people tend to marry between the ages of 18 and 30, and it's not a matter of concern if one is significantly older than the other. In choosing a life partner, young people value compassion, ability to work well together, and cheerfulness over attractiveness.

One more type of activity claims a significant amount of each juvenile's time: gaining understanding and practical experience regarding the functioning of their community.[58] Peruvian law sets the age of adulthood at 18, but beginning as early as age 14 boys and girls are encouraged to directly participate in ayllu-focused activities. Doing so signals to all that they are adults in the making.

The first group they join, and the least complicated, is an organization known as *qhaswa*, initiated several decades ago to provide hands-on experience in the functioning of organizations, and to facilitate young people's getting together more often than merely during festivals. They meet weekly to exchange ideas, enjoy recreation including dancing and singing, and gain experience carrying out roles such as president, treasurer, and so forth.

A more direct way for youth to serve their ayllu is by participating in the *cargo* system, a type of non-state organization found in rural Central and South American districts for centuries. *Cargo* is Spanish for "office" or "burden" in the sense of duties to be discharged. The workings of this organization are too complex to relate here, except to say that members, who all are male, shoulder partial responsibility for community safety. *Cargo* positions are unpaid; those in leadership positions are obligated to bear the costs. The Women's Committee has roles parallel to the men's and concerns itself with children, health, food, crafts, and animal breeding.

Similar to the *cargo* organization is *Rondas Campesinas* ("peasant rounds"), a Peruvian public safety organization founded during the 1980s when terrorists were active and cattle rustling was rampant.[59] Young adult members, male and female *ronderos*, take turns patrolling the community 24/7, communicating with whistles and using leather whips as weapons. Animal thefts by bandits from distant regions plummeted after the *ronderos* began their patrols.

INFORMAL LEARNING BY QUECHUA CHILDREN

How do Anali, Luis, Víctor, Luzwilma, mischievous Marcos and their high-altitude mates come to adopt the constellation of values, mindsets, skills, and patterns of behavior that gradually transform them from startled new-borns into confidently contributing members of their Quechua community?

One thing we know for sure is this: Quechua youngsters receive no deliberately planned, formally presented training or instruction from their elders. However, I have come across an adult's first-hand story of how, years earlier, his mother had persuaded him to do as he was told. Not surprisingly for a Quechua mother, she applied her belief in human–animal communication:

> If children refuse to eat, mothers often say that they can hear the dove's song that says *punyay punyay warmachaykita punyay* [hit him, hit him, hit your little child]. According to the mothers, the dove is telling them to hit the child who doesn't obey their mother. As children, we heard this dove song and it seemed to us that it certainly did sound like *punyay punyay warmachaykita punyay*. Normally, after hearing this song children believe that the dove knows of their disobedience, so they eat up their dinner without resistance.[60]

Of course, the dove's song was more for the parents' use than the children's. Among the Quechua, there are no songs or lullabies specially crafted for children. Nor are there stories, poems, or legends just for them. Children's books are unknown. And children are never given manufactured, store-bought toys or other items that are specifically intended for a child's enjoyment or learning. As for locally handcrafted play objects, sometimes an adult will make a spinning top by driving a nail through a piece of wood and attaching a string, but that's about it. Beyond the home there are no day-care facilities and no playgrounds or commercial play centers. And nowhere on the high mountainside are there electronic pastimes of any kind.

With the sole exception of a few warmly welcoming ceremonies such as the First Haircut, there is nothing special for the children.

So by what means are these youngsters learning to fit into their society?

Anthropologist Bolin asks us to set aside any notion that these children are disadvantaged because they live in a "simple" society.[61] On the contrary, they have an exceptionally diverse range of first-hand experiences. They observe and, as they become able, try to contribute to, and eventually participate fully in *all* family and community endeavors. When it comes to people, objects, and ideas to fuel their imaginations and their playtimes—well, let's take stock of what these youngsters *do* have.

It's no exaggeration to say that, if you're growing up in Quechua-land, almost anything within sight can ignite your creative spark and become your plaything.

Inside the home, small children are encouraged to occupy themselves with utensils, dishware, pots, candles, blankets, and bottles—anything they can't seriously damage and won't damage them. In a nearby shed they can find tools the family uses for cultivation and herding. They often play with food. Potatoes are always lying around, and there might be other vegetables and fruits (bartered in the valley) as well. In their shapes they soon are imagining things such as an animal, a relative's face, or a feature of the landscape. It isn't long before they discover that they can creatively alter a food item's shape. Bolin relates that she once gave three-year-old Víctor a cookie. After selectively nibbling bits of it, he imagined a donkey. He made his donkey jump across the adobe floor, up the wall, along the earthen stove, and into the middle of the room where it roused the cats and guinea pigs. Then Víctor ate the whole thing.

Outside the home, the high-altitude landscape seems barren to our eyes, but not if you're a youngster becoming acquainted with her environment for the first time. In the distance there are features of the landscape such as a boulder that can be imagined as a condor or mountain lion. Within reach are countless objects that are curious and overflowing with potential for creative endeavors: dirt, sticks, stones, grass, leaves, branches, water, mud, flowers, and tufts of wool. One morning, Bolin watched as five of the children

> filled their hands and skirts with found objects, settled on the ground, and began building tiny houses. Each soon had a corral and connecting path. Luzwilma outlined a sacred corral used for ceremonies. Both corrals were filled with stones imagined to be herd animals; outside the corrals were donkeys, horses, and dogs. In the house appeared, via a handful of mud, an elevated area for a bed. Tomás placed bits of earth, representing a load of dung, on his largest llama. Anali placed tufts of alpaca hair on another, which it will carry to market. The children now designate a stone to be the herder, who is walked to the pasture nearby with his animals. A jagged stone condor is balanced on a large stone representing a mountain peak. The condor might snatch a young animal, observes Tomás. So he takes a blade of grass to serve as a slingshot and places it on the herder, who needs it to protect his herd.[62]

This peaceful tableau led to a commercial transaction.[63] Luzwilma saw that Anali had stones that she wanted to use. So she took two yellow leaves and one green one, signifying paper money of different values, and offered to buy a couple of Anali's "animals." The exchange completed, Anali put the bills into her *unkuña*, a woven cloth handbag. Luzwilma then realized that she forgot to prepare lunch, and fashioned it out of grass and tiny flowers as well as pebble "potatoes."

The children's inventive animation of their mini-homestead came to an end when Tomás's mother called him to fetch fresh water from the spring. That reminded Anali and Luzwilma of their own roles in preparing their family's next meal, and they ran off as well. But it would be a mistake to conclude that the children sharply distinguish between enjoyable play on the one hand, and burdensome chores on the other.

The children's collaborative and creative endeavor gave them a sense of pride in accomplishment. Such emotions similarly characterize how Quechuas feel about their work. Like play, work is a companionable and mutually supportive endeavor of relatives and close friends.[64] What any group's efforts produce is an essential ingredient in ensuring that the entire community will survive and, in good years, thrive. Hard work is admired. One's standing in the community is largely a function of one's demonstrated ability to complete work expertly. For example, the best weavers achieve superior status and enjoy much prestige.[65]

Bolin once came upon some young men during a break from their communal work, and asked permission to photograph them. They agreed—but jumped up, grabbed their foot plows, and resumed working so that the photo would record their productive labors instead of their leisure.[66]

FORMAL LEARNING BY QUECHUA CHILDREN

The small school in the ayllu's central area is staffed, one at a time, by teachers sent by the Peruvian government. If you were the teacher, there'd be a lot *not* to like: responsibility for all the lower grades, isolation from family and friends in an ayllu with no shops or restaurants, an exhausting hike at the start and end of each week, and icy nights in sparse quarters with neither electricity nor heat.

Yet many teachers prefer to teach in the high-altitude ayllus. They say that Quechua children, in contrast with those in the valley's urban areas, are more respectful, attentive, and eager to learn. They admire that the ayllu children "know what's right and wrong" and are innocent, caring, and willing to share. Others described their pupils as "much better behaved, more curious, and more creative in their approach to different tasks" than other children.[67]

In the ayllu frequented by Bolin, a small adobe school was built in 1938 by community members. At first, it was attended only by boys. Never did all the children attend. The daily roundtrip walk for some was as much as four hours, which in stormy weather could be brutal. Others were needed at home due

to ill or deceased parents. And the school was too small; some children had
to sit on the floor or stand. (The government built a new, four-room school
during 2000.)[68]

Here's the good news: The ayllu's children did remarkably well in
inter-school competitions, often winning singing, dancing, and running
contests. Those who continued their education in the valley town were consistently at the top of their classes academically. Referring to the ayllu's children, the middle school principal described them as "curious, self-confident,
and always respectful."[69]

And here's a mystery: Recall three-year-old Anali, who cared for Inge
Bolin in an elegant way, then graduated some years later as a systems analyst.
Anali is not the only student from one of the mountain ayllus who excelled in
math; many other children do so, too. Educators and anthropologists would
like to know why.

The children consider math to be their favorite subject, experiencing it
as both interesting and fun. Many who continue their studies become math-
ematicians, statisticians, engineers, systems analysts, computer scientists, or
teachers of those subjects.[70] No one expects this from children who grew up
on mountainsides.

But wait. Could they excel at math *because* they grew up on mountainsides? This is what some have speculated. Consider three thoughtful guesses:

First, at an age when their American peers are in kindergarten, ayllu children are accompanying their older siblings as they take the family's animals
to pasture.[71] A herd consists of about 35 animals of three types. Each animal
has a name. Each belongs to a family member—parent, grandparent, uncle,
aunt, sibling, or cousin; a few belong to the children themselves. The herder
must know how many white, brown, black, and checkered animals she has.
Another family might be taking its animals to a nearby pasture; herds could
begin to mingle. Individual animals must be recognized on sight, for the
herder must be able to tell at once if an animal is missing and which one it
is. Thus, a high standard of counting-related *detail-orientation* is learned and
practiced.

Second, ayllu youngsters are encircled by seemingly desolate mountainsides, providing them with sight lines that extend long distances.[72] By accompanying their elders on foot through this expansive environment, they learn to
find their way to locations, some many miles distant—and to find their way
home again. Along the way are streams to leap over, boulders to climb on,
caves to crawl into, and Inca ruins to clamber on as well as plots of arable
ground for their potatoes and steep meadows for their herds. Also, both boys
and girls must learn to masterfully deploy the traditional sling to hurl stones
in order to drive away a predator or startle a straying animal to return to the

herd. In these ways, ayllu children become deeply acquainted with *spatial relationships*.

Finally, ayllu girls eventually become skilled at weaving, but boys practice it, too, focusing on learning how to braid slings and ropes.[73] Both weaving and braiding are intricate skills that develop one's visual acuity, manual dexterity, and grasp of spatial configurations. Intricate patterns are mastered and embellished, as discussed in this account:

> The decorative motifs can be grouped into four principal categories: geometric, zoomorphic [animal-like], phytomorphic [plant-like], and anthropomorphic [human-like]. Geometric patterns comprise rhombuses, crosses, arches, triangles, hexagons, pentagons, stripes, checkerboard patterns, and angles. Combinations are limited only by the imagination of the weaver. Skilled women can reproduce letters and phrases without knowing how to read and write. They can imitate any pattern in front of them.[74]

Weaving is grounded in math and, of course, *plane geometry*. Another benefit is that learners gain the ability to *focus and concentrate* for extended periods.

FROM AN ANTHROPOLOGICAL PERSPECTIVE

Food insecurity is the daily reality that drives the Quechua way of life. Most of us would describe their environment as "barren," but they have evolved ways of surviving there and, occasionally, of thriving. Those ways constitute their culture.

Quechuas have very little control over their environment. But their forebears did figure out how to control the values, mindsets, and patterns of behavior that have come to characterize their culture, the key attribute of which is that the allyu's need to survive and thrive takes priority over any individual's desires. But that explanation isn't quite right because it suggests a clash of wills—individual vs. ayllu. It's more accurate to portray Quechua culture as one in which *the desires of each individual are intuitively aligned with the needs of their shared community*: What I desire is the same as what our ayllu needs.

Such an alignment of personal desires can be relied on if, and only if, the ayllu's infants are raised in a manner that results in each one's intuitions being molded into an ayllu-focused frame of mind. This molding is what Chapter 3 has described.

Summary of Quechua Children's Learning and Socialization

Based on anthropologists' findings, I believe that five key features of how Quechua children are socialized into adulthood are the following. Quechua children . . .

- learn by contributing to family endeavors from an early age.
- are immersed in a culture in which productive work is highly valued.
- are accepted by adults regardless of their developmental paths.
- are exposed to the unrestricted scope of adults' lives and concerns.
- witness adults living lives infused with empathy, gratitude, and respect.

Quechua children learn by contributing to family endeavors from an early age. The highland Quechua live a precarious existence and their mortality rate is relatively high. Family and community need every capable member to contribute to the group's survival according to each one's ability, age notwithstanding. Thus, at very young ages, children are drawn into the essential activities of the group, their initial bumbling efforts gladly tolerated, their learning advanced mainly by observation and imitation. A three-year-old lights the fire and boils the water for the family meal. A five-year-old herds the animals all day in one of the nearer pastures. A seven-year-old barters for vegetables in the distant valley. Each is performing a service that visibly contributes to his or her family's sustenance.

Perhaps it's significant that Quechua adults provide nothing special for the children—no toys, no special poems or songs, no diversions of any kind. Children are warmly welcomed into the adults' world while also being free while still quite young to develop their own make-believe activities, as in the case of their building the model community. But expectations for them to share their family's workload begin early, far earlier than most Americans would ever think appropriate.

Children are immersed in a culture where productive work is highly valued. The dividing line between play and work is indistinct. Recall again the five youngsters constructing a model community—that's an example of play that enables children to progressively grasp the practical knowledge, procedures, and skills they'll soon be applying for their family's benefit. As well, play is the setting in which children activate their growing awareness of the community's work ethic, shaped by the keystone values of respect, reciprocity, empathy, and admiration for effort.[75]

Note as well that children's play is never organized or suggested by adults, and that their play depends on initiative, imagination, cooperation, and creativity.

In the high-altitude ayllus, work is accomplished with pride. Outstanding skills garner admiration and prestige. When Bolin asked a centenarian what he viewed as most important in his life, he replied, "That I do good work every day."[76]

Children are accepted by adults regardless of their developmental paths. *Laissez-faire* aptly expresses the adults' stance regarding their little ones' cognitive, social, physiological, and emotional development. Yes, adults keep one eye open for threats, but they're slow to act preemptively: think of 18-month-old Luis, seen climbing the stairs without sides or railings, but not pulled away from them. Adults respect each child's own internal timetable.

Children are not hurried. What we call "developmental milestones" are unknown to their parents, who don't push, encourage, incentivize, or applaud their child's striving for the next level. It's not a competition. (Competition is absent from children's experience until they begin attending school.) In addition, each child's burgeoning curiosity is unconstrained, though adults are alert for danger. When a child begins trying to pitch in on daily chores, her efforts are accepted and her missteps are overlooked.

Children are exposed to the unrestricted scope of adults' lives and concerns. You'll recall, a few pages back, my parenthetical comment, "To anthropologists, these ways of dealing with infants are significant." I was describing how mothers and other caretakers carry infants on their backs, and put them down on the ground, in ways that enable the infant *to see everything going on nearby.* (Many American parents use carriers that oblige the infant to look at the parent's upper chest, and put them down on their backs, facing straight up.) These ways of handling infants are the first instance of a general pattern of exposing children to everything occurring in their family and community.

Like fledgling anthropologists, youngsters are participant observers of every aspect of adults' lives and concerns—initially observers, then imitators, and finally participants. They are not distracted by any item or activity intended by adults to educate, entertain, or distract children; there are none. Witnessing the full reality of Quechua life 365/24/7, children make sense of its values, regularities and, yes, it's contradictions. Slowly they learn to pitch in, fit in, and participate.

Children witness adults living lives infused with empathy, gratitude, and respect. Quechuas view themselves as actively participating in a community of both human and nonhuman members. The latter are the places, plants, and animals in their vicinity, to whom the Quechuas ascribe the characteristics of humans including feelings and intentions. From these nonhuman members they sense protective energy and life-giving sustenance, for which they express gratitude daily by offering coca, food, compassion, and respect in a cycle of giving and receiving.

These empathic feelings are not expressed merely during religious rites but appear to infuse the Quechua mindset. This mindset shapes their moment-by-moment relationships with each other, becoming the behavioral example that they consistently exhibit to their watching, yearning-to-participate children.

Why the Herders' Children Do So Well Academically

It's intriguing to speculate why illiterate herders' children distinguish themselves in math classes. What interests me more is why they generally distinguish themselves in school.

A few years ago, I became interested in why East Asian students always gain high scores on international comparative tests[77] while American students always gain middling scores. "Always" means *since the 1960s*. What's the explanation?

Others have wondered, too. Since 1970, dozens of researchers have been inquiring into how East Asian youngsters are raised at home and taught in school, yielding a mountain of published findings. After reading some of their findings, I realized that the principal reason for East Asian students' superiority was how they are raised at home. I wrote a book about it: *The Drive to Learn*.

There's a big difference between how East Asian and Quechua children are raised: Most East Asian parents' top priority for their children is attaining academic excellence and high marks. Most Quechua parents are illiterate or nearly so, though they do recognize the value of education for their children.[78]

But there's also a striking similarity between how East Asian and Quechua children are raised: Both East Asian and Quechua cultures are "communitarian" in their value structure,[79] and both emphasize respect. In fact, the Quechua word *uyakuy* references a way to show respect that includes "listening for one's own benefit," and implying "minding" in the sense of paying attention to someone else.[80] A deeply ingrained habit of respect serves children well in classrooms because it conditions them to carefully attend to teachers and to the process of learning (class meetings, textbooks, assignments, etc.). And most teachers react favorably to those students who (unlike many others) consistently show respect for them and for learning.

SUGGESTED FURTHER READING

Each of the readings below is profiled at howotherchildrenlearn.info/profiles.

Growing Up in a Culture of Respect: Child Rearing in Highland Peru, by Inge Bolin (2006); 160 text pages.

"Respect and autonomy in children's observation and participation in adults' activities," by Fernando A. García. *Advances in Child Development and Behavior, 49*, 2015; 14 text pages.

"Places are kin: Food, cohabitation, and sociality in the southern Peruvian Andes," by Guillermo Salas Carreño. *Anthropological Quarterly, 89* (3), 2016; 22 text pages.

BIBLIOGRAPHY

Allen, Catherine J. (1981). To be Quechua: The symbolism of coca chewing in highland Peru. *American Ethnologist, 8*, 157–171.

Allen, Catherine J. (1982). Body and soul in Quechua thought. *Journal of Latin American Lore, 8* (2), 179–196.

Ames, Patricia. (2013). Learning to be responsible: Young children transitions outside school. *Learning, Culture, and Social Interaction, 2*, 143–154.

Bolin, Inge. (2006). *Growing up in a culture of respect: Child rearing in Highland Peru.* University of Texas Press.

Dougherty, Martin J. (2018). The Inca civilization. *Aztec, Inca, & Maya Empires: An Illustrated History of the Ancient Peoples of Mesoamerica & South America.* Amber Books, 125–170.

Flores-Ochoa, Jorge A. (1968). *Pastoralists of the Andes: The alpaca herders of Paratía.* Institute for the Study of Human Issues.

García-Rivera, Fernando. (2007). *Runa Hina Kay: Imágenes de la Educación Familiar y Comunitaria Orientada al Respeto en una Comunidad Quechua.* Doctoral dissertation, Departamento de Investigaciones Educativas, Centro de Investigación y de Estudios Avanzados, Mexico City.

García, Fernando A. (2015). Respect and autonomy in children's observation and participation in adults' activities. *Advances in Child Development and Behavior, 49*, 137–151.

Lane, Kevin. (2022). *The Inca.* Reaktion Books (Distributed by The University of Chicago Press).

Meyerson, Julia. (1990). *'Tambo: Life in an Andean village*. University of Texas Press.

Núñez del Prado, Juan Víctor. (1985). The supernatural world of the Quechua of southern Peru as seen from the community of Qotobamba. *Native South Americans: Ethnology of the Least Known Continent*, Patricia J. Lyon, ed. Waveland Press, 238–251.

Rogoff, Barbara. (2014). Learning by observing and pitching in to family and community endeavors: An orientation. *Human Development, 57*, 69–81.

Salas Carreño, Guillermo. (2016). Places are kin: Food, cohabitation, and sociality in the southern Peruvian Andes. *Anthropological Quarterly, 89* (3), 813–840.

Winterhalder, Bruce, Robert Larsen, & R. Brooke Thomas. (1974). Dung as an essential resource in a highland Peruvian community. *Human Ecology, 2*, 89–104.

Chapter 4

Parenting by Persuading

Growing Up among the Navajos of the U.S. Southwest

Figure 4.1. A Navajo mother and her infant in a cradleboard, circa 1940. *No known copyright. Made available by the Princeton University Library.*

FILMS ABOUT THE NAVAJO WAY OF LIFE

Although several of these films offer an idealized portrayal, watching some or all of them will enable you to more accurately imagine Navajo families as you read this chapter.

"Navajo Indians" (1939). Focuses on tribal social life and courtship rituals; includes building a hogan. Produced by Encyclopedia Britannica. 10:35 min. aifg.arizona.edu/film/navajo-indians

"The Navajo Indian" (1945). Focuses on how the Navajo live and sustain life, especially sheepherding. Produced by the U.S. Office of Indian Affairs. 8:54 min. aifg.arizona.edu/film/navajo-indian

"Navajo Canyon Country" (1954). Overviews the practical aspects of Navajo life. Produced by filmmaker Florence Avalon Daggett. 12:19 min. aifg.arizona.edu/film/navajo-canyon-country

"Navajo Indian Life" (1956). Reviews the formidable challenges facing the Navajos. Produced by the National Council of American Indians. 11:33 min. aifg.arizona.edu/film/navajo-indian-life-0

Many similar films are retained at the American Indian Film Gallery at the University of Arizona.

Hot links to all films and videos are at
howotherchildrenlearn.info/films

Based on anthropological fieldwork carried out primarily between 1940 and 1990.

Anthropologists who spent years living among the Navajo[1] have described them as genial, humorous, and imaginative as well as hard-headed and practical. Many also report that Navajos have a tendency to be anxious, fearful, and suspicious due to a preoccupation with life's uncertainty and a variety of threats to their personal safety. One concluded that, for the Navajo, "life is very, very dangerous."[2] Is there an explanation for Navajo apprehensiveness? Consider first the historical record.

A HISTORY OF LIVING WITH
UNCERTAINTY AND THREATS

The Navajos' ancestors entered the Arizona–New Mexico region from northwest Canada, where they had relied on hunting and gathering.[3] Soon after arriving, they began exchanging raids with their neighbors, the Pueblos; why raiding began isn't clear. When Spanish explorers introduced horses, sheep, and goats to the region during the 1500s, the benefits of raiding increased. If your group often raids the neighbors, you can expect the neighbors to retaliate; life becomes more perilous.

After the U.S. government gained control over the Southwest in 1848, raiding continued as a way of life for several groups. As the largest native group in the region, the Navajo's raids were conspicuous, to the point that government people spoke of "the Navajo problem." So Colonel Kit Carson was sent in 1863 under orders to raze structures, destroy fields, poison wells, and kill animals. Facing starvation, most Navajos gave themselves up at Fort Defiance. But the United States wanted to detain them near Fort Sumner, 300 miles to the east.[4] Thus began the devastating Long Walk for thousands of Navajos. Many perished during this forced march.

Eight thousand Navajos were held captive for four years. They suffered gravely due to the government's giving them inadequate provisions and the shame they felt at depending on handouts. This period became known as The Fearing Time.

Allowed to depart in 1868, the Navajo faced insurmountable obstacles as they returned to areas that Carson had deliberately ruined—and these were years of drought as well. Almost every Navajo was miserable. Only after multiple delays did the government issue seed, tools, and livestock—more shaming handouts.

A boy named Left Handed was born during the Fort Sumner captivity. During the 1930s, an anthropologist recorded his recollections from childhood and youth. Here is what Left Handed related about the early 1870s:

> A year after we returned from Fort Sumner there were no sheep, and we had nothing to live on. My mother had gone to Black Mountain, but it was the same. At that time her husband had a slave, a Paiute woman. He took his slave to a man who owned many sheep and traded her. He got seven head and brought them back to where he lived.[5]

Eventually, conditions improved somewhat; the population began to grow. But new disillusionments arrived with the railroad, for which the Navajos were compelled to give up huge tracts of preferred range land. The railroad also brought disease, alcohol, and more Anglo[6] settlers and agents of the government and the railroad, many of whom viewed Indians with contempt.

During the first decades of the 20th century, a period of relative stability was welcomed by the Navajos, and their flocks of sheep and goats burgeoned.[7] Then another threat arose. During the 1930s, the agency now known as the Bureau of Indian Affairs noticed that far too many animals were being pastured on the reservation, resulting in malnourished livestock and severe soil erosion. So the government instituted a "stock reduction program" requiring each family to give up, on average, half of its flock in return for cash compensation.

On a practical level, the stock reduction program probably was in the Navajo's long-term interests. Government agents certainly tried to present its rationale to gatherings of Navajo. But the tribe bitterly opposed it. Sheep were the mainstay of their economy and the focus of their family lives. Not only did their sheep have market value; they also had emotional and prestige value. The Navajo bitterly resented that their sheep by the thousands were allowed to die in holding pens; some were driven into box canyons and slaughtered. They saw the government as barbaric and disdainful of their way of life. As you can see, the Navajos' past gave them reasons to be distrustful and wary regarding what their future held in store.

THE NAVAJOS' WORLD: NATURAL AND SACRED

There are other reasons why some Navajos might envision their world with distrust. Let's begin with language.[8] The structure of Navajo is such that "I" am not the initiator of an action; I am its passive recipient. We say, "I am hungry"; hunger occurs inside us and, to a considerable extent, is under our control. Navajos say, "Hunger is killing me," implying that hunger is an outside force that is largely or entirely beyond their control. If pressed for an explanation, a Navajo is likely to say, "The spirit of hunger sits here beside me."

Next, consider their natural world.[9] Their reservation is classified as arid semi-desert. Streams and springs are few. When the rain does come or the snow melts, erosion of the sandy soil can be severe. Looking out across their high plateau, you or I would never think, "Wow, what a great location for a ranch!"

You're probably familiar with one location on the Navajo reservation, at least via photos: Monument Valley. Search the web for Monument Valley; study the photos to determine the ground cover. That's where many Navajos traditionally made their living.

Now consider their concept of what we call the "supernatural." Our concept is a poor guide for grasping theirs. Most of us conceive of a natural world and a separate supernatural one; we live largely in the natural world, paying attention occasionally to the supernatural one, typically via religious rites. But the Navajo language has no word for "religion." Its speakers live in one seamless world, home to two types of people. There are the Earth Surface People, living and dead; these are ordinary human beings. And there are the Holy People, mysterious, potent beings who belong to the world's sacred realm (as opposed to its secular realm), and who travel about on sunbeams, rainbows, and lightning bolts.[10]

First, the good news about the Holy People: One of them, Changing Woman, is the Navajos' favorite. She had much to do with their creation. She consistently sustains them and furthers their health and prosperity. Her name cites her power to repeatedly reach old age, then return to youth, reflecting the seasons.

Regarding all the other Holy People, our meaning of "holy" is seriously misleading. They are not paragons of virtue. Our concept of "god" is off the mark. Neither all-knowing nor all-powerful, the other Holy People are mysterious, fickle, and not necessarily well disposed toward the Navajos—especially if the latter commit taboos or fail to do required things. Fortunately, the Holy People can be propitiated and supplicated, even coerced. A typical concern of the Navajos is finding ways to keep all the Holy People except Changing Woman in a benign frame of mind.

The Navajo theory of ill health historically held that diseases, mental disturbances, and injuries are likely the result of either an attack by the Holy People for a taboo violation, or by some other mystical force. Efforts to restore health involve ceremonies known as "sings," which intend to appease the harmful influences and restore the condition of *hózhó*: balance, beauty, and harmony. Sings are led by a Singer, involve the patient's kinfolk and many others, last from one to nine nights, and require vast preparation (including food for all).

The Navajos' personal ethics are shaped by their concept of one seamless world inhabited by both Earth Surface People (the secular) and Holy People (the sacred).[11] Growing children are not taught about any divine being who has established principles of virtuous living and ultimately will reward or punish each person's adherence to them. This explains why traditional Navajos rarely align their behavior with abstract principles of behavioral "shoulds" and "should nots."

The key phrase is *abstract principles*. The Navajo have received none from On High; nevertheless, they have a perfectly serviceable sense of ethics. At its foundation are *practical considerations*: "If I don't give sheep to my cousin who's starving, my kinfolk might refuse to help me when I'm down." Even when the Holy People are involved, the mindset is not, "Do this because a Holy Person says so," but rather, "Do this because otherwise I might soon get sick or have an accident."

Here's the thing: If you're a Navaho, you are mainly absorbed in the goings-on of your extended family. Not all family members are physically close every day, but their activities and anxieties are among your consequential concerns every day. You all are wresting a living from an erratic semi-desert; to do that well, each one needs all the others' cooperation. You treat them all with respect, but not because it's the moral thing to do. Rather, it's the *practical* thing to do.

LIVELIHOOD AND DAILY LIFE IN
AN ARID SEMI-DESERT

Here's how one Navajo woman recalls the years after their flocks were reduced:

> We didn't have very many sheep then. After the Government reduction there was a dry spell and we lost a lot, and then there was the big snow. We did not lose any ourselves, but we had to give away a lot because our relatives needed them. That year the coyotes were bad. They would go right into the corrals and take full-grown goats.[12]

After herding was curtailed, it was replaced by other means of subsistence.[13] Keep in mind that a family hauls its own water, gets electricity (if any) from its own generator, and pays no rents or mortgages. Members consume most of the produce from a family's fields and gardens, but less than half of its sheep and goats. The remaining meat, plus wool, is sold to yield much of a family's income. If a member is employed, their wages bring in cash; so do Social Security and welfare[14] receipts, if any. The rugs and jewelry they sell to tourists bring in a tiny fraction of most families' income.

As already noted, Navajo values strongly encourage mutual support within extended families and local residence networks.[15] The woman quoted above said that they gave away sheep "because our relatives needed them." Also routinely shared are tools, labor, produce, transportation, even cash. An elderly Navajo observed that, "You can't get rich if you look after your relatives right."[16]

Poor soil, struggling vegetation, and cycles of droughts and floods necessitate that small groups live far from their neighbors so that each group is relatively near its fields and other scattered resources. Each small settlement is called a "camp." Some Navajos feel crowded if the nearest camp is under four miles away.

Pickup trucks are a common feature of reservation life. A pickup is viewed as highly desirable because families rely on widely dispersed resources. Pickups are used to visit distant fields, fetch water and wood, make shopping or selling trips to town, and benefit from distant opportunities such as a rich piñon nut harvest. For families that can afford one, a truck and its upkeep is its main expense, much greater than the means of travel that the pickup largely replaced: the horse.

To coax a living in this demanding environment, more strong backs and nimble hands are always welcome. Children are needed! As young as age five, they begin to herd sheep, till gardens, gather and cut firewood, and care for younger siblings. So useful are they that a family with many children will "give" one to a related family that has none. The average number of children per family is five.

Here's a passage from "My Life Story" by Betsy, a third grader:

> At home I help my mother wash dishes also clean the house and help cook. Then I wash clothes with her. Also I get the horses in when daddy wants to use them. I water them at the Well too. During the summer I just take care of the sheep with my aunt because I have my sheep and goats in her herd. It is always hard to herd sheep when they are lambing.[17]

Did Navajo girls contribute solely to completing domestic chores and caring for animals? Not if this adult Navajo woman's testimony is any evidence:

> I'm married to a white guy. He couldn't believe what I can do. One time, he watched me work on the tire. He said he was going to bring it to Crownpoint, and I said, "No, I don't think so." He went outside to another shed. When everything was all ready, he says, "I'm surprised." I said, "That's what I've been doing, mostly, since when I was big enough to do things."[18]

The general pattern is that men do the heavy fieldwork; haul wood and water; build dwellings, corrals, and fences; and look after horses, wagons, and pickups.[19] Women oversee children; keep dwellings and utensils clean; and cook, butcher, weave, and gather crops. Men sometimes help women and vice versa. As noted, children begin helping at a very young age, fetching wood and water and, within the camp's confines, herding sheep. Left Handed recalled that . . .

> about this time I began to herd around the hogan in the morning and evening when the sheep came home. But I was so small. I went out with the sheep like a dog. I just walked along with them and staying right in the middle of the herd. I was afraid to go around them, but while I was in the middle of the sheep I wasn't afraid of anything.[20]

Herding is the main organizing principle in most Navajos' daily lives, even though livestock constitutes roughly only half of a typical family's sustenance. Each camp's activities are driven primarily by its animals' daily and seasonal needs, in part because of Navajos' deep emotional identification with their sheep.

The principal Navajo dwelling is the *hogan*.[21] The traditional variety looks like a hollowed-out mound of soil (although it is built with forked poles for support) with a smoke-hole at the top and a low door. Its inside diameter is up to 25 feet. Newer, larger varieties use more wood in addition to soil, and appear to be a six-sided log cabin. Hogans are adaptive to the climate. Early anthropologists reported them as more comfortable than the thin-walled cabins of Anglo homesteaders.

On a typical day, few family members are present in the camp. Some will be visiting relatives or running errands; others will be living near their fields in a small hogan. Children sometimes are away for weeks at a sheep camp with an aunt or other children. Ceremonial occasions are when most family members all come together in one camp.

During ceremonies and other events, Navajos visit with those they haven't seen in a while. Singing often occurs, as do foot and horse races as well as "American" card games. At night, myths and folk tales are told around the fire.

Within a family, each Navajo addresses the others using only kinship terms, such as "maternal nephew." With outsiders, however, kinship terms don't work. So Navajos acquire a variety of nicknames. For example, if a child is sent away to school or joins the armed forces, he is likely to get a new name. Some we know of are Angel Whiskers and Fish Sombrero.[22]

HOW NEWBORNS ARRIVE AND RECEIVE CARE

Navajos consider pregnancy a well-state.[23] Pregnant women continue their chores but strenuous work is avoided. Taboos are observed. For example, a knot tied by the mother- or father-to-be must not remain tied, or the fetus will become tangled in the umbilical cord. Baby clothes are not made until the infant is two weeks old; this is less a taboo than an acknowledgment of high infant mortality.

Awareness that a birth is imminent sends women collecting sheepskins and old rags on which the event will occur—leading to a high infection rate.[24] Births are aided by female relatives and, often, the husband. An anthropologist branded as a "fable" the notion that traditional women give birth with little pain. But he added that "There's little doubt that they make less fuss about their pain."[25]

Here are excerpts from that anthropologist's account of a typical birth:

The husband brings sand and spreads it on the floor. Upon it women spread the old rags and the sheepskin, woolly side up. The mother-to-be kneels on this padding and takes down her hair. Over her head a woven red sash is suspended from the ceiling and sprinkled with corn pollen. During pains, the mother holds onto this as high as she can reach and supports herself. When labor pains become harder and more rapid, pollen is taken from the mother's buckskin pouch and rubbed on her belly. As the final pains approach, a woman kneels in front to receive the baby, and another assistant—often the husband—stands behind with his arms around the mother's abdomen, applying pressure to push the baby downward. The woman who receives the baby cuts the cord with a kitchen knife or old pair of scissors, then ties it with any available piece of string. Unless the baby is already breathing well, it is shaken, massaged on the chest, patted on the back, or held upside down. Then it's tightly wrapped in a sheepskin or woolen blanket and placed near the fire. The placenta, the sheepskin and old rags, and anything on which there's blood are burned or buried to keep them out of witches' hands.[26]

After the newborn is bathed, its head is anointed with corn pollen. One of the attending women then "shapes" the infant manually,[27] beginning with its nose and continuing to the head and limbs. The goal of this molding is to ensure that the infant grows to be strong and attractive.

After the mother recovers from her ordeal (two or three days), her immediate response to her infant's cries is to place him to her breast. Nursing in response to crying occurs within seconds because mothers and infants are constantly in close physical proximity—wherever mother goes, whatever she is doing, day and night. If suckling does not produce satisfaction, the mother will take other measures such as cleaning the child or cuddling and singing to him.

As the first months pass, no adult shows concern about whether the newborn is getting enough sleep or eating an appropriate diet. The child sleeps, or not, as she pleases. When she cries, she's nursed or fed other food; when she quiets, she's satiated. She is never coerced to take any food. Navajos say, "The baby knows what's best for her." Does this portend a neglectful permissiveness? As we will soon see, it's evidence of a bedrock cultural value in traditional Navajo thinking.

Let's not forget those necessities of infancy: diapers. Wild rose bush pulp is placed around the genital area; it is very soft and nonirritating, has a pleasant smell, and is highly absorbent of liquid and odors. It's held in place by the cloth in which the infant is wrapped, and usually by its cradleboard as well.

Navajos show little interest in the products of an infant's nether region. They don't fret over whether a bowel movement has occurred; they don't examine its appearance; and they don't decry its odor. Except when an infant clearly is ill, what occurs naturally is assumed to be right for that child. Baby knows best.[28]

You've probably seen photos of an infant swaddled on a cradleboard. It looks like a cloth-wrapped parcel tightly laced with cords to a squarish board; only the infant's head is visible. The infant appears immobilized. It's true; it *is*.[29]

A day or two after birth, the infant is lovingly placed in the cradleboard that the father has painstakingly crafted. During the first several months, infants spend about two hours a day *out* of the cradleboard; by nine months, they average six hours out. Cradleboard use usually is discontinued after a year.

The Navajo word for "cradleboard" means "baby diaper," but diapering is only one of its functions. Some say it originated to facilitate transport—in pre-pickup truck days, it was hung from the saddle—but that, too, is only one of its functions. A cradleboard is a baby-tending aid. Many infants sleep satisfactorily nowhere else. It shields the infant from romping siblings and cousins and spares the mother the need to regularly monitor her newborn. Propped upright, it aids digestion and promotes interactions with family members by bringing the infant to the same eye level as adults seated on the ground.

The effects of cradleboard use on infants has been studied. Here's why: Recall that Chapter 1 discussed Attachment Theory, which hypothesized that a healthily developing infant feels "securely attached" to his mother, confident that she will respond quickly and warmly. An infant lacking a consistently attentive mother will feel "insecurely attached," sparking a personality disorder. What about swaddling? If an infant is restrained for hours at a time, does insecure attachment result? Thus, the Navajo swaddling device came under scholarly scrutiny.

A major study[30] concluded that cradleboards do *not* inhibit the development of positive mother–infant relationships. Yes, it's true that whenever infants are on cradleboards, their verbal and tactile interactions with their mothers are reduced. But also reduced are mothers' frustrations with their infants, who are not free to get into mischief. The study also found that an infant on a board is "significantly more likely to be within arm's reach" of his mother.[31] And when an infant frets, she's released from the board and, usually, cuddled intensely by the mother.

LEARNING TO BE NAVAJO: THE
EARLY CHILDHOOD YEARS

If you're a newborn Navajo, the social world of which you gradually become aware is populated by individuals to whom you are closely related.[32] Many of those who show up are siblings and cousins who want to play with you; those who are a bit older than you will be deputized to help your mom by looking after you. Camps often include members of an extended family. Mothers can count on an average of 6.5 people over the age of three who are regularly available to relieve her either of child-care duties or of her camp duties so she can spend time with her youngest.

So routinely are camp children together that sibling–cousin distinctions usually vanish. (Children visit at will, no play dates needed.) For a growing child, the mother–aunt distinction also wanes; a woman and her sisters share childcare. A child calls an aunt "little mother" and can come to feel very close to her.

Even so, mother is central in a child's life.[33] His clan membership is traced through her; he was "born of" his mother's clan. He was "born for" his father's clan, but his mother's clan matters more. The mother–child bond is exceptionally close, enduring while both are living. Newly married Navajos usually live in the camp of the bride's mother. One reason why fathers tend to be absent is that they're visiting their own mothers' camps.

Let's mentally visit the Navajo reservation as it existed during the period when much anthropological fieldwork was being completed. Imagine taking historic Route 66 to Gallup, New Mexico, then driving 30 miles to Navajo Tribal Park near Window Rock, Arizona. Before entering the reservation, we'll pause before the monument to the Code Talkers, WWII Marines who used the Navajo language to confound Japanese code-breakers, saving countless American lives.

What would we observe going on with the youngsters in the reservation's various camps?

We would quickly notice that fathers, siblings, aunts, uncles, and grandparents all vie for opportunities to hold, talk to, sing to, and generally fuss over infants.[34] We'd see that every advance the newborn makes toward social participation and self-locomotion is encouraged, coached, and applauded. Because someone is always talking to the child, language learning gets constant support. She's praised when a babble sounds like a word and later when she begins to grasp her tribe's vast array of kinship terms. Walking is encouraged much like talking. Adults and older siblings take turns leading the child around and murmuring approval of her efforts to stand and step forward. However, this encouragement does not come with pressure on her to attain a specific milestone by a predetermined age. Her timetable is best.

If we were lucky, we'd encounter a First Laugh celebration, the Navajo way of welcoming a new member into a family. The child's first laugh is believed to indicate that she has attained basic awareness. To the person who made her laugh goes the honor of giving, entirely at his expense, a feast for all the parents' extended family, clan members, and friends; his generosity ensures that the child will become similarly generous.

We'd soon notice as well that the less agreeable aspects of early childhood are tolerated. There is no pressure on a toddler to regulate elimination. Little tantrums and aggressions are allowed to pass. If children scream at not getting what they want, efforts are made to distract them, or the adults just give in. At weaning time, however, this idyll ends.

If our imaginary visit lasts long enough, we'd notice that adults mold youngsters' behavior via persuasion and attention to practical outcomes.[35] I have emphasized the Navajo belief that whatever a child does is best for that child. This helps explain why adults rarely consider corporal punishment; instead, they either distract errant children or persuade them to adopt new behavior.

To entice pre-verbal youngsters away from mischief, Navajos use distraction and its group-focused equivalent, herding. For children who can talk, persuasion begins with teasing. If a child doesn't take the hint, this tactic inflates to ridicule, then to warning that others will shame her and, if that fails, to direct shaming.[36]

Another way of persuading youngsters to stay in line is via an initiation ritual for children featuring alarmingly masked figures called *Yeibichai*.[37] Children who've been insubordinate are publicly singled out for the *Yeibichais'* special attention. Once a child becomes conscious of these dreaded beings, adults can threaten their reappearance if he doesn't behave. Left Handed recalled his father saying that

> the *Yeibichai* are going around to different hogans today. They have a sack into which they put the children who have disobeyed. So you must do what you're told. Get water and wood so they won't bother you. They take bad children home, dig a hole, build a fire, bury the children and cook them. So behave and obey; herd the sheep all the time.[38]

As noted earlier, Navajos usually don't align their behavioral standards on abstract principles of "should" and "shouldn't." Parents' scolding focuses on the practical, real-life consequences of one's actions. As a youngster, Left Handed had a puppy he loved to play with. But one day

> all at once, I saw a coyote running towards me. The coyote caught the puppy and carried him off. Then I cried more than ever. My mother said, "I told you not to go far from the hogan. If you'd minded me you'd have your little dog with you now."[39]

Note that Left Handed was *not* condemned as "bad" because he disobeyed mama. Instead, mama pointed out the practical benefit of being guided by her voice of experience. She had foreseen that if he took his puppy far from the safe area, he would invite a coyote attack.

During our imaginary visit to the camps, we'd realize that children are not constantly being shielded from danger.[40] Growing youngsters are not assumed to remain thoughtless and helpless indefinitely. The assumption is that they will explore their world and figure out how to take care of themselves within it. A toddler will be warned about touching a hot or sharp item, or after she's hurt by one she will hear the experiential lesson verbally reinforced. But after she's been alerted to a danger, *she* becomes responsible for her own well-being.

So we are unlikely to witness a mother's moving knives out of her baby's reach. Nor will we see an adult snatching a knife or scissors out of a young child's hands or blocking her from nearing the fire. If a youngster gets injured, she learns from experience to be careful. Children learn on their own how to handle knives, fire, and other potentially harmful things to benefit themselves and their families.[41]

Finally, during our visit we would notice that recently weaned children encounter many new expectations.[42] Weaning isn't rushed; even some two-year-olds have access to the breast. But when that ends, the child's life changes.

The newly weaned child sleeps with the other children and learns to wash and dress himself. Dressing is not a daily event and washing involves only face, hands, and an occasional yucca suds shampoo. The child now is asked to help around the hogan, such as to fetch small sticks for the fire or snow to be melted for water. Neglect of his chores will bring reminders, then a scolding.

Expectations about bladder and bowel control begin. Often it's an older sister or the mother who takes the child with her into the bushes and encourages imitation of her actions, including concealment of the waste. After a suitable period for learning, the child who doesn't comply is unmercifully teased.

The weaned child no longer receives his mother's rapt attention. In the camp much of the time are many other caretakers: siblings and cousins who are barely older than him, plus his aunts and grandmother. These kinfolk have more stringent expectations about his behavior than his mother. *T'adoo*, the equivalent of "Stop that!," is often heard wherever adults and youngsters are present.

I'll end this section by quoting an anthropologist who knew the Navajos well:

> Although usually unwashed and uncombed, the average Navajo child of six is found to be winsome by most Anglo observers. Lively, curious, relatively free and easy with his familiars, he is apt to be silent, shy, and diffident with strangers because he has been taught to believe that one is safer with relatives than anywhere else.[43]

Chapter 4

LEARNING TO BE NAVAJO: THE
LATER CHILDHOOD YEARS

Among the ways of life that children begin learning around age six, two stand out: accepting increased responsibility, and mastering gender-linked mindsets and skills.

Accepting Increased Responsibility

The Navajos reckon an individual's maturity in terms of how far beyond himself his sense of responsibility extends.[44] The child begins by learning to care for himself, which some can do at age five. Maturity grows in tandem with one's responsible activities beyond self: first to things; then to animals; then to family. The top level of maturity is leadership, which for the Navajo means that one doesn't merely care about, but also *cares for*, others beyond his extended family, such as one's clan or tribe.

A responsible Navajo is one whose activities contribute in practical ways to the well-being of others. The just-weaned child is expected to assist communal well-being by fetching sticks; if she doesn't, others' fires won't burn well. To encourage her to accept this entry-level responsibility, sanctions follow if she fails to fetch sticks—a stern reminder, a light switching on the back of her legs. As she gets older, fresh expectations emerge: emptying ashes, husking corn, and so forth.

We Americans tend to shield youngsters from having to expend effort or endure inconvenience. Not so in the case of those societies that inhabit environments where sustenance must be wrestled from the land, such as an arid semi-desert. Children's assistance is *genuinely needed.* Contributions are expected from them at the youngest possible age.

Children as young as three start "helping" with the sheep. Actually, they're hindering, but it's crucial that they get into the swing of things. Within a few years, they start accompanying a herder to the pasture. At first, they prefer to chase or ride the animals, bringing a scolding. Or they go to sleep or play with other young herders, allowing animals to become coyote bait. This brings public shaming that might include, "Are you lazy or shiftless, or do you have a girl out there, my son?"

Left Handed recollects the following from around the time he was 12:

> In the winter when it was lambing time, either my mother or I would go out to the corral when a sheep lambed. We'd bring the lamb into the hogan and take care that it was dry and warm, then return it to its mother. If my mother stayed up until midnight I'd sleep, and around midnight she'd wake me and go to bed,

and I'd stay up the rest of the night. Every few minutes I'd go out into the corral and look for lambs.[45]

Responsibility for the family's animals is strengthened by the custom of setting aside each year one or two sheep that the child herself is given to own, together with any lambs that are born to those animals.[46] The young herder thus begins to look after the welfare of her own animals as well as those of other family members.

Mastering Gender-Related Mindsets and Skills

Beginning around the age of eight, boys and girls increasingly are separated so that each group can become familiar with the mindsets and skills of their sex.[47] Under the tutelage of her mother, grandmother, and aunts, a girl is drawn into cooking, weaving, and child-tending while continuing her involvement in herding. Under the tutelage of his father, grandfather, and uncles, a boy is drawn into agriculture, house building, leather work, animal husbandry, and especially horseback riding.[48]

By the time Gray Girl was 10, she always had a rug on her loom, and even had made a saddle-blanket for her father according to old methods that most women didn't know. She'd already learned to use her mother's sewing machine. By the time she was 14, her family depended on her to stitch the women's velvet blouses and ruffled skirts, and to serve as principal cook during sheep-dipping:

> She had assembled her pots and pans around the glowing coals. In one boiled goat stew to which corn had been added. Pots with hot water stood ready for coffee. She had mixed a pan of thoroughly kneaded dough from which she had already shaped tortillas. Watching each tortilla in the pan, she turned it with a skillful flip; when it showed a nicely browned center on each side, another was ready to take its place. A pile of tortillas was ready as the family began returning.[49]

Here's a vignette from the life of a 10-year-old boy, Little Policeman:

> When his father was branding, he expected Little Policeman to ride as hard as the men and valued his help. It didn't matter to the boy that at the end of the day he was dead tired. The days he found trying were those when he *couldn't* work with his father. Today he would drive the main herd to water, pumped by a windmill two miles south. He would drive the flock slowly, but if a wind came up to pump water, he would hurry them. Small for his age, he could hardly get the saddle on the horse. Six-year-old Alaba was going along. Little Policeman would ride; she'd follow the sheep on foot.[50]

One key assumption Navajos make about child-development is completely different from the one we make. For Navajos, "adolescence" is not a thing.

By adolescence, I refer to a span of several years when young people, male and female, are no longer children but still aren't quite adults. In some WEIRD[51] societies such as ours in the United States, "adolescence" is associated with overflowing energy, sexual tension, and tumultuous behavior. The key fact about adolescents in such societies is that sexual maturity has been attained *but social maturity has not been granted.* Adolescents in WEIRD societies must remain dependent on their parents because they're thought to require monitoring, guidance, and protection.

As noted in Chapter 1, about anthropologists of childhood, an early controversy in their field concerned adolescence: Is it a human universal and thus inherited by all, or is it learned in some societies but not in others? The Navajo experience suggests that it's *learned.* Navajo youth who are sexually mature are assumed by all to exercise socially mature judgment—and to live with the consequences. Let's turn now to how Navajo girls are helped to embrace their coming of age.

Recall that women in Navajo society are at least the equals of men, and in some ways are more central.[52] Womanhood is something a girl can look forward to.

Each girl's first menses prompts a four-day celebration, a religious and social event central to Navajo culture: *Kinaaldá.* The contrast with the response to an American girl's first menses is stark. Noted one young Navajo, "White people try to hide it. We celebrate it. It is womanhood."[53] Another remembered that

> I was around 14 when I had my first period. I woke up and felt wetness, and saw spots of blood. I put a blanket around myself and went to my paternal aunt. She said, "What's wrong with you? You became a woman right there!"[54]

Around the time the first menses occurs, a female relative, often the maternal grandmother, shares with the girl her experience with regard to heterosexual relationships. Of course, this child has spent countless hours with sheep, not to mention being raised in a one-room hogan, so mechanics isn't the focus of this chat. Neither is morality. Advice tends to be practical, such as, "Don't give yourself to a man or you'll have a baby and then a good man won't marry you."[55]

The *Kinaaldá* ceremony culminates during the final 36 hours when the batter for a large corn cake is prepared by the old women in the area together with the young woman being fêted, then baked overnight in the ground. According to one account, the cake was to be six feet in diameter and a foot thick.[56]

The *Kinaaldá* celebration announces that a girl is ready for marriage and may participate in the next Squaw Dance, during which marriageable girls invite young men to dance. The latter turn out in droves. Mothers sometimes urge daughters to invite a "catch" to dance: "Go ask *that* boy; his mother has two thousand sheep!"[57] A young man who dances with a girl must give her something of value. Here's Left Handed's recollection:

> A girl got hold of me and started dragging me out of the crowd. She was strong, so I just went with her. I was ashamed to dance at first, but soon my shame had gone and from then on I went right ahead. I had a long string of copper buttons and began giving her three at a time. Every time she wanted me to pay, I gave her three buttons.[58]

Left Handed doesn't reveal what went down after the music stopped.

INFORMAL LEARNING BY NAVAJO CHILDREN

Earlier I noted that, from birth, infants and children are assumed "to know what's best" for themselves, calling this a bedrock cultural value.[59] Stated formally, this value is: *No person has the right to speak for or direct the actions of another*.

Youngsters become accustomed to this guiding principle while being nudged to act appropriately via parenting by persuading. They rarely experience parenting via demanding, commanding, punishing violently, or threatening to withdraw love.

This "ethic of noninterference" means that even young children have occasions to choose for themselves. Imagine that a mom and dad will take the pickup truck to the store and want their four-year-old to come along, but she wants to stay near the hogan. She will stay unless some compelling reason makes that impossible.

But this does *not* mean that youngsters are left to figure out everything on their own. Beginning around age six, children are guided by their elders' informal methods into learning the skills of daily work and the norms and emblems of Navajo culture.

Learning How to Work—and How to Respect

We've seen that boys and girls are separated to learn their respective responsibilities and skills. What is not clear is how much of what they learn is due to observation and imitation, and how much is due to their elders' deliberate instruction.[60]

Relatives often demonstrate and instruct. But practical training may be provided by *any* adult in the child's vicinity. Left Handed was expected to grind corn for his family's meals. One day while he was grinding, "a man came in."

> He said, "Get up." He began to grind the corn. While he was grinding, he said, "Look, and watch how I'm holding this rock. Watch how I'm working it." I did, and I learned how to hold the grinding-stone and how to work it. My mother never did show me.[61]

The anthropologist who tells of the responsibilities willingly discharged by Gray Girl writes that, "elders felt the responsibility of showing and explaining to their children every detail of their work as soon as the young were able to use it." Yet she also observes that for Gray Girl, "merely seeing an adult do something like spinning yarn inspired her to try to do it as well; she was allowed to try anything."[62] Other children also are portrayed as eagerly observing and imitating elders' skills:

> When my mother puts up a loom to start a rug, I used to watch and try to learn how she puts in all those yarn. When she gets up to rest or to cook, I would get in there and try to do what she did, but I make mistakes, and she would get after me.[63]

One anthropologist believes that, while Navajo children were learning to accept responsibility for things, animals, and people beyond themselves, they also were learning respect.[64] Respect for the Navajos means *knowing the importance of*. If one experiences a thing, animal, or person as important to one's own well-being, one will want to skillfully take responsibility for *its* well-being.

Respect, he continues, resonates with the bedrock ethic of noninterference. Navajos demonstrate that they know the importance of fellow humans by reserved behavior that avoids imposing on their space, senses, or self-determination. Accordingly, Navajos talk slowly and in soft tones, and touch others gently. In conclusion, he writes, "This is where, I think, Navajo children learn respect: from their parents' quiet and controlled ('polite') behavior toward them."[65]

Learning the Norms and Emblems of Navajo Culture

The effort of adult and juvenile Navajos to shepherd youngsters into familiarity with the norms and emblems of their culture is deliberate, ongoing, and insistent.

Grandmothers play a significant role in cultural instruction.[66] Besides sharing their technical skills, they often are key transferers of traditions such as First Laugh, of behaviors associated with ceremonies (of which *Kinaaldá* is one of many), of traditional teachings about how to live wisely and productively, and of relationship patterns among clans and kinfolk on both the mother's and father's sides.

Fathers are also important in instilling fundamental Navajo norms and values despite their frequent absences to pursue wage labor and visit their mothers.

> My mother taught me how to boil coffee, fry bread, teach me how to milk the goat. Father is the one who taught me to do the right thing. I get punished when I do bad things and do not do what my father tells me to do.[67]

What types of activities are embraced by the term "do the right thing"? Some of them are related to a complex panoply of taboos that impact every Navajo's life. As well, we have this recollection from Left Handed about his father:

> He told me I shouldn't sleep too much. Early in the morning he'd say, "Wake up, get up and dress yourself. Your sheep are calling you to let them out; they're hungry."[68]

Earlier, I noted that myths and folk tales are told around campfires at night. Their purpose is largely to instruct and inculcate the camp's children regarding desirable attitudes and behavior. Listening children are not left to reach their own conclusions about their elders' anecdotes and tales. After each rendition, the speaker or another senior person will point out explicitly the implications for daily behavior. Recalled one adult, "They used to get us together to tell us what to do, and what not to do."[69]

Campfires are frequent (especially during winter) and lengthy, and every child in the camp, excepting infants, is expected to attend *and* be attentive. "If I went to sleep," said a boy, "my grandfather would pull my hair and shake my head."[70]

FORMAL LEARNING BY NAVAJO CHILDREN

During the late 1800s, the government established the now-notorious boarding schools for Indian children.[71] The goal was to strip the children of all native ways, including cutting their long hair, insisting on Anglo clothing, assigning new names, and prohibiting native languages, all strictly enforced. Many students attempted to escape. During summers, some children were sent to live with Anglo families. (These schools are being investigated; the first report was recently published.[72])

The government's approach changed during the 1970s, and schooling became less distasteful for the Navajos. Parents realized that learning English benefitted the children and their elders. The high dropout rate continued, but most children stayed long enough to become their family's trusted interpreter.

The government's attempts to provide formal schooling for Navajo children offers us examples of three types of education-related cross-cultural clashes.

The first type of clash was between parents and teachers.[73] The Navajos' bedrock principle of noninterference upset the Anglo teachers, who viewed the parents as "permissive," "uncaring," and "lacking control." Because the teachers never set foot in the camps, they had no opportunity to see noninterference being balanced by an ethic of sharing, cooperation, and responsibility-building.

Teachers claimed they needed parental involvement; to them, this meant that the parents would come to the school for meetings. But the parents soon realized that teacher meetings were virtually always about behavioral infractions, rarely academic challenges. At group meetings such as PTA events, communication tended to be unidirectional. By the way, most schools were *hours distant* from the parents' camps.

Could teachers and parents find common ground in striving for the children's school success? Not likely. For teachers, school success meant transforming children into cultural Anglos who could compete with native Anglos for jobs and even live in Anglo society. For the parents, success meant that their youth could remain cultural Navajos, gain employment, and continue to live with their tribe.

The second type of culture clash was between the children and the teachers.[74] One source of friction was grounded in the principle of noninterference: no one has greater worth than another. But in school, children found themselves in a realm of publicly proclaimed hierarchical rankings. The notion that you would vie with your friends for high ranking on a 0–100 scale contradicted Navajo norms. So while the teachers saw the grading system as encouraging and rewarding hard work, the students experienced it as a *disincentive* to work hard.

Another source of teacher–student friction concerned contrasting ways of approaching the learning of a new topic or skill. The Navajo norm is that the learner works to improve competence *in private*—though perhaps with private expert coaching—until mastering a high level of skill. Only then is the learner comfortable demonstrating it in public. *Competence precedes performance.*

That pattern is 180° contrary to the "progressive" style of teaching,[75] which holds that immediate public engagement with a new topic is the superior path to learning, and mistakes be damned. *Performance precedes competence.* This approach was seen clearly in foreign language learning; Anglo teachers expected students to practice speaking new words and phrases moments after they were introduced, guaranteeing public failure. A failed public performance is deeply shameful in Navajo culture.

But wait; there's an upside: The government curriculum included biology, and biology includes human reproduction. An Anglo sixth-grade teacher wrote that:

> I think that the girls who have had the *Kinaaldá* and the boys who saw the ceremony are a lot more mature. They don't giggle and get all silly when we talk about reproduction. They seem to have a grown-up sense about it all, to sort of take it for granted.[76]

The final cultural clash is especially poignant, for it's between the children and their parents.[77] Initially, most parents reacted to the possibility of schooling with ambivalence. A child in school was labor lost. Girls might be led astray. And those who had previously attended the government schools viewed progressive methods as relying on fun and games and avoiding rigorous learning. On the other hand, English proficiency was useful for purposes of interpretation *and* because parents had discovered that English greatly facilitated agricultural record-keeping.

A Navajo chief expressed why parents sent their children to school:

> Our children need to go to school and college and get everything they want. Then come back here, to their homes, here between the four sacred mountains. They need to bring their education back here to their home. Then we can be a whole people.[78]

But most parents could only lament the reality of their returned students:

> They teach them in the schools that they don't need to mind their mothers and fathers. They are supposed to go the white man's way and we don't know that way. So we can't even wake them up in the morning. They even cuss their parents out.[79]

An anthropologist summed it up this way:

> The adjustment is often painful on both sides. The student has become accustomed to Anglo food, clothing, standards of cleanliness. His impulse to participate reverently in native ceremonials conflicts with what he's heard in school about "ignorant superstitions." He sometimes feels called upon to be apologetic to his Anglo friends about the behavior of his parents: "These Navajos are kinda funny."[80]

FROM AN ANTHROPOLOGICAL PERSPECTIVE

Navajos' daily lives are dogged by uncertainty and threats to an extent that I, and perhaps you as well, have never experienced. They've dealt with challenges not only historically but also as features of their belief system, their language, and of course their lifelong location within an arid semi-desert.

One reason Navajos have been able to cope, and occasionally even to thrive, is their culture, which values sharing during hard times and cooperation at all times. As we are learning in this book, theirs is hardly the only society guided by group-oriented, or "communitarian," values. What makes Navajo culture unusual is that it pairs group-orientation with an ethic of noninterference, a radical form of individualism: *What each person wants is what he gets.* Even a four-year-old.

Group-orientation and individualism: an odd couple. How come it works?

One factor is that I-get-what-I-want applies to everyone; it's not only for the elite. Another is that noninterference isn't only about your not interfering with my self-determination, it's equally about my not interfering with yours. Before anything important can be done, you and I need to come into alignment.[81]

Summary of Navajo Children's Learning and Socialization

Based on anthropologists' findings, I believe that five key features of how Navajo children are socialized into adulthood are the following. Navajo children . . .

- learn by means of imitation, persuasion, and instruction.
- are frequently instructed regarding their society's norms and values.
- are socialized by many relatives and friends, including older children.
- are expected to shoulder gradually increasing responsibility.
- are exposed to the unrestricted scope of adults' lives and concerns.

Navajo children learn by means of imitation, persuasion, and instruction. Navajo children are more actively socialized by parents and extended family members than children in the other four societies described in this book. Like children everywhere, including in WEIRD societies, they absorb a great deal by observation and participation. But they also are the recipients of parenting by persuasion, and of deliberate, direct efforts (such as during lengthy evening campfires) to instill in them Navajo norms and values.

A central behavioral element in Navajo culture is the ethic of noninterference, which applies to individuals of all ages. Adherence to this ethic would seem to render parents powerless to guide their children through the early years of life. But instead of trying to overtly guide or control them, parents resort to persuasive tactics. The toddler headed for mischief is distracted. The three-year-old who prefers his diaper over the bushes is teased. The contrarian five-year-old is reminded of the *Yeibichai's* imminent arrival. The herder who allowed sheep to stray while playing with her pals is shamed. And the boy who took his dog far from the hogan is told again of the likely practical consequences; lesson learned too late, doggonit.

In these ways, the parent or caretaker is *redirecting the child's own preferences and intentions*—without resorting to physical violence, threats to withdraw love, appeals to moral strictures handed down from On High, or claims of his or her own hierarchical superiority (". . . because I am your *mother.*").

A description that resonates with these tactics is "manipulative." It's too bad this word has become a pejorative because it is accurate in implying that much Navajo parenting occurs by persuading the child to want to do the right thing.

What is not clear is the extent to which caretakers actually resort to more direct interventions. We know only that *T'adoo* ("Stop that!") is frequently heard wherever adults and young children are present.

Children are frequently instructed regarding their society's norms and values. The principle of noninterference applies to children's behavior, but not to their emerging ideals, norms, identities, attitudes, and emblems. When it comes to their fitting in with their elders' values and beliefs, adults leave nothing to chance.

Although a child's father is frequently away, for many children he is the leading dispenser of explicit advice about becoming the right sort of person. Another key player is the child's grandmother, who often takes the lead in sharing traditions, skills, and help in navigating the Navajos' complicated panoply of clan relations.

Finally, the norms and values of Navajo culture are made plain to children at informal learning events—campfires—that are frequent, lengthy, insistent ("Wake up!"), and mandatory (no ethic of noninterference *here*). They also are didactic: Each myth or tale is followed by its implications for children's behavior.

Do we have any continuous, insistent way of indoctrinating our kids with the reigning norms and values of contemporary American society? Social media?

Children are socialized by many relatives and friends, including older children. Until an infant is weaned, it's the mother who tends to his needs. She is aided by the cradleboard's calming effect. Relatives visit to ooh and aah over the baby, but rarely share in its care.

But after the child is weaned, all those relatives—even those only two or three years older than the youngster—contribute to its minding and learning. We've seen that Navajo children often forge close relationships with their aunts. Grandma plays a major role. Fathers and uncles help though not always present in the camp. And there are all the other older children of different ages and both sexes. As in most other traditional societies, a large portion of each youngster's day is spent in the company of this multi-age group, roaming about the camp. Adult relatives and other children play significant roles in bringing up recently weaned youngsters, thus lifting much of the responsibility for child-minding from mothers' shoulders.

Children are expected to shoulder gradually increasing responsibility. Children barely can walk when they're given responsibility for tasks that make miniscule contributions to family well-being. Bigger tasks come earlier than we might see fit: Children are drawn into herding at such an early age that they get in the way.

One way that a child is encouraged to actively assume responsibility for more than just herself is by being given a sheep each year, beginning at a young age. Her sheep is immediately integrated into the flock, the same flock that anchors her family's livelihood. So while she's herding the sheep all day long, enduring rotten weather and scaring off coyotes, her interests and her family's are merged.

For the Navajos, a young person's maturity is gauged by the span of items for which he or she demonstrates active responsibility. The lowest level is taking responsibility for inanimate things. Taking responsibility for animals, the next level, is actively promoted, as reviewed in the previous paragraph. Adult-level responsibility involves taking care of one's extended family. Leadership positions go to those who demonstrate responsibility for their clan or even the whole tribe.

Around the time that Navajo children reach sexual maturity, they also begin being accepted as socially mature, available for marriage, and fully responsible for the outcomes of their judgment and actions. The contrasts between that and our modern, middle-class way are huge and will be revisited in Chapter 8 of this book.

Children are exposed to the unrestricted scope of adults' lives and concerns. Another major difference between traditional Navajo society and our modern middle-class one is the extent of what children know about the daily lives and concerns of their parents and other close adults.

From the time a Navajo newborn is propped up in his cradleboard to face every activity in his vicinity, through his watching the camp's womenfolk struggle to deliver his new baby sister, through his hearing his parents' night-time discussion of how to pay for the pickup's new clutch, to his attendance at his cousin's four-day *Kinaaldá* ceremony—and much more—Navajo children come to know in real time virtually everything there is to know about real life.

SUGGESTED FURTHER READING

Each of the readings below is profiled at howotherchildrenlearn.info/profiles.

Children of the People, by Dorothea Leighton & Clyde Kluckhohn (1947); Part I, 112 text pages.

Navajo Infancy: An Ethological Study of Child Development, by James S. Chisholm (1983); 249 text pages.

"Cultural differences in child development: Navajo adolescents in middle schools," by Donna Deyhle & Margaret LeCompte. *Theory into Practice, 33* (3), 1994; 10 text pages.

BIBLIOGRAPHY

Abraham, Kitty G., Victor A. Christopherson, & Robert O. Kuehl. (1984). Navajo and Anglo childrearing behaviors: A cross-cultural comparison. *Journal of Comparative Family Studies, 15* (3), 373–388.

Chisholm, James S. (1983). *Navajo infancy: An ethological study of child development.* AldineTransaction.

Chisholm, James S. (2014). Learning "respect for everything": Navajo images of development. *Images of Childhood*, C. Philip Hwang, et al., eds. Taylor & Francis, 167–183.

Deyhle, Donna. (1991). Empowerment and cultural conflict: Navajo parents and the schooling of their children. *Qualitative Studies in Education, 4* (4), 277–297.

Deyhle, Donna, & Margaret LeCompte. (1994). Cultural differences in child development: Navajo adolescents in middle schools. *Theory into Practice, 33* (3), 156–166.

Deyhle, Donna, & Frank Margonis. (1995). Navajo mothers and daughters: Schools, jobs, and the family. *Anthropology & Education Quarterly, 26* (2), 135–167.

Downs, James F. (1964). *Animal husbandry in Navajo society and culture.* University of California Press.

Downs, James F. (1972). *The Navajo.* Holt, Rinehart, & Winston.

Dyk, Walter. (1938). *Left Handed, Son of Old Man Hat: A Navajo autobiography.* University of Nebraska Press (2018).

Kluckhohn, Clyde, & Dorothea Leighton. (1946/1974). *The Navajo, Revised Edition.* Harvard University Press.

Lamphere, Louise. (1977). *To run after them: Cultural and social bases of cooperation in a Navajo community.* University of Arizona Press.

Lee, Dorothy. (1961). *Freedom and culture.* Prentice-Hall.

Leighton, Dorothea, & Clyde Kluckhohn. (1947). *Children of the people.* Cambridge University Press.

McCloskey, Joanne. (2007). *Living through the generations: Continuity and change in Navajo women's lives.* University of Texas Press.

Phillips, Suzanne, & Sandra L. Lobar. (1990). Literature summary of some Navajo child health beliefs and rearing practices within a transcultural nursing framework. *Journal of Transcultural Nursing, 1* (2), 13–20.

Satz, K. J. (1982). Integrating Navajo tradition into maternal–child nursing. *Image, 14* (3), 89–92.

Willeto, Angela A. A. (1999). Navajo culture and family influences on academic success: Traditionalism is not a significant predictor of achievement among young Navajos. *Journal of American Indian Education, 38*, 1–24.

Witherspoon, Gary. (1975). *Navajo kinship and marriage.* University of Chicago Press.

Witherspoon, Gary. (1977). *Language and art in the Navajo universe.* University of Michigan Press.

Chapter 5

According to Nomads' Values

Growing Up among the Village Arabs of the Levant

Figure 5.1. The males of a Bedouin family, including boys, gather near their tent and camels circa 2003. *Photo by Frans Lemmens. Photo and permission from Alamy Inc.*

FILMS ABOUT THE BEDOUIN WAY OF LIFE

These films will enable you to more accurately imagine Bedouin families as you read this chapter.

"Bedouins and Early Life of Muhammad" (2017). Deep background regarding the Bedouins' values and lifestyle. Origin indeterminate. 9:22 min. youtube.com/watch?v=2qLMeBWTszk

"Desert Arabs" (1948). A fascinating silent film depicting features of the daily lives of the Bedouins. Produced by Encyclopedia Britannica. 11:00 min. youtube.com/watch?v=VYtYTTd5afA

"The Bedouins about 100 Years Ago" (c. 1920). Silent film about desert tent life, focusing on women and children. Produced by Pathé-Baby. 2:12 min. youtube.com/watch?v=2ig6TtQDf_Y

"Life in a Bedouin Encampment" (1922). Silent film about couscous that also reveals Bedouin family life. Produced by Pathé-Baby. 2:05 min. youtube.com/watch?v=vJrcxppL6oQ&t=20s

Other films were readily available, but almost all were advancing a political perspective.

Hot links to all films and videos are at
howotherchildrenlearn.info/films

Based on anthropological fieldwork carried out primarily between 1960 and 2000.

It's possible that you've heard of the Bedouin Arabs but know little more than that they are desert nomads. So let's begin getting acquainted with them via firsthand accounts from two men who are recalling events of their boyhoods.

The first is by an Arab who became a scholar of Bedouin life despite not being a Bedouin. But as a boy growing up in the Levant (the region at the eastern end of the Mediterranean[1]), he often encountered the Bedouin, as here in roughly 1915:

> A desert tract lay between our village and Homs, where my father had sent me with my brother to a boarding school. I will never forget the many times that bedouin raiders set upon the caravan in which we were traveling and seized whatever it pleased their hearts to take. On one occasion, the people of the caravan began to shout, "The Arabs! The Arabs!" Bedouins surrounded the

caravan, and some of them began to close in and shout, "Strip, boy! Strip, boy!" My brother was so terrified that he began to cry. The heart of the bedouin leader was moved to pity for him. He walked his charger around the donkey we were riding, preventing his comrades from plundering us, and we were spared. The others were robbed, and some were stripped of their clothing, then given enough bedouin garments by the raiders to cover themselves.[2]

The second is by a Bedouin born in 1935 whose childhood was as a nomad in the Saudi Arabian desert; he went on to a career in the world of global oil:

> For the first eight years of my life I was a Bedouin nomad. We moved across the Arabian Peninsula in groups of fifty to a hundred or so. We would barter our sheep, goats, or camels, along with their milk or wool, for grain and other dry goods and staples. We had no vegetables or fruit beyond dates. Days started with the predawn call to prayer. Prayer rugs were lined up on the ground facing Mecca. Then the male elder ground coffee beans and called us to a breakfast of coffee with dates. Beginning when I was four, my stepbrother and I were sent each day to tend to the family's lambs. We kept the flock of about 150 close to our camp. We found plenty of time to get into mischief. We would catch small lizards and roast them on sticks. Later I learned how to catch birds and roast them as well.[3]

COUNTLESS GENERATIONS OF DESERT NOMADISM

The Bedouin are believed to have originated around 6,000 BCE. They are spoken of, or alluded to, ten times in the Koran and ten times in the Old Testament.[4] For example, Isaiah 13:20 says that "Arabs will never set up their tents [in Babylon]"; some versions replace "Arabs" with "nomads," others with "Bedouins."[5] Since antiquity, *a'rāb* and *badawī* ("bedouin") have often been used interchangeably.

The Bedouins had a well-earned reputation for raiding,[6] but another way of sustaining themselves was through pastoralism, the raising of domesticated animals. Why this way of life began is not clear.[7] What is clear is that pastoralists cannot live exclusively off the land. Their animals must provide their owners with not only food but also items to trade for supplies that aren't available in the area.

Pastoralists eat no plant products except those acquired by gathering or trading; the future oil minister had no vegetables or fruit except dates. Anchoring the Bedouin diet is mutton and goat meat, followed by that of the camel, plus the animals' milk; these also are traded.[8] Camel hair has its uses but isn't sought by merchants. Camel hides, on the other hand, are a major trading item; village craftsmen make them into shoes. Wool and goat hair also are reliably tradable; villagers weave the goat hair into tent panels and sell them back to the Bedouins. The Bedouin also collect and sell truffles, which are resold in Arab cities.

Traditionally the measure of economic value was stated in terms of camels. The Bedouin scholar quoted previously recalled watching a companion of Lawrence of Arabia offering to buy a Bedouin's binoculars for three camels.

For countless generations, all family members were cooperatively involved in animal husbandry. Men and boys herded the sheep and goats, sheared the wool, and ensured that adequate fresh pasture was available by searching for it or making agreements with landowners. Women and girls cared for young and sick animals, milked the camels, sheep, and goats, and turned the surplus, if any, into clarified butter[9] to sell; some women took temporary wage-paying jobs, such as cotton picking, in nearby settled areas. Some families also raised horses, including fine Arabian ones. During busy periods, young children were left with elderly kin.

The driver of the nomads' lives was that, to maintain their animals, they had to change locations often. Doing this required two essentials: camels and tents.

The camel has been called a "land-ship," a vessel that makes desert travel possible.[10] Known for tolerating lack of water, camels also can be content to eat thorny shrubs. Camels carry literally every item the Bedouin use. They also transport women and children in a *howdah*, a saddle with a cloth sunshade. Yes, sometimes a howdah and its passengers fall off.

Camels aren't merely beasts of burden. Besides being a trading item, camel hides are used by the Bedouin to make sandals and water containers. From camel fur they weave rugs and bags for storing grain and flour. Camel dung is a fuel for Bedouin fires; it's also a fertilizer. Camel urine, containing ammonial salts, is used by women to wash their hair, thus protecting it from infestation by vermin.[11]

Bedouins have mastered everything to do with tents.[12] Their black tents are woven mainly from goat hair, which is water resistant and keeps heat inside during the winter. In the summer the back wall is raised to allow air to circulate. The women sometimes weave tent panels from goat hair, though they often buy them instead. Tents belong to the women, who are responsible for pitching, maintaining, and striking all of the family's tents.

Viewed from the front, Bedouin tents are at least 13 feet wide. On one side is the men's section, the focal point of which is a fire in a pit or a brazier, where the male household head continually makes coffee to serve to the family's ever-present visitors. Women are often in this section of the tent but withdraw when a stranger enters. Men, guests, and (if guests are not strangers) women arrange themselves on rugs and cushions around this fire; young children roam among them. The household head is the host, who ensures that guests are provided with open-hearted generosity.[13] An Arab poem expresses his perspective:

> The servant of the guest I am while at my tent he'll stay.
> In no other situation at all do I have this role to play.[14]

The other side of the tent is the women's section, walled off from the men's side with cloth panels. Here household supplies are stored and women prepare food and care for children; only men of the immediate family may enter. Some tents have a third room where women and children care for young and infirm animals. These rooms are side by side under one or more center poles; more poles (five, six, even more) allow greater width and signal higher status of the family.

THE 20TH CENTURY BRINGS TWO TRANSFORMATIONS

Since the mid-20th century, the Bedouin have experienced two transformations in their way of life. One was that they gave up their camels in favor of half-ton trucks.[15] This switch reverberated throughout their daily lives. Campsites ceased to be scattered in remote areas and appeared by the side of roads, and they were shifted far less frequently. The need to pasture herds near the tents diminished; young boys had fewer opportunities to serve as shepherds of lambs. Fresh food and items such as butter, previously made by the women, could be bought. There was little camel hair to weave. Women acquired unaccustomed free time.

As destabilizing as was the swap of camels for trucks, the other 20th century change had even greater consequences. Most Bedouins gave up nomadism and began to live sedentary lives in permanent settlements. Known as "sedentarization," this process didn't necessarily occur because of choices made by the Bedouins.

Governments in the Levant region made it their policy to encourage the Bedouin to cease their nomadic ways and take up farming and settled sheep-raising.[16] For example, governments began to privatize landowning and to outlaw raiding. Some governments granted land for farming to the Bedouins and even helped them build stone houses. Another enticement was that the burgeoning oil industry on the Arabian Peninsula had hundreds of low-level jobs to fill. Traditional Bedouins viewed manual labor (except in agriculture) as *'aib*, contemptible.[17] But if one male did take a low-level job with Aramco or Kuwait Oil, many of his male kin soon followed. There were also negative motivators for the Bedouins to agree to sedentarization. In some areas they were harassed by police and officials as well as local people, including having their tents pulled down and even burned.

Why did governments encourage the Bedouin to give up their nomadic ways? The rational reason is that their leaders recognized that, unless a population is permanently settled, it is all but impossible to administer government services. The subjective reason is that many governmental leaders regarded Bedouins as ignorant and uncivilized. This might be why some not only pressed the Bedouin to settle and submit to centralized authority, but also denied them citizenship. For Bedouins in some areas, the outcome was that, when a group of families did find a place to settle, their existence was ignored by the state, thus depriving them of services such as schools, roads, sanitation, water, electricity, and health care.[18]

One of the nations where this process has been documented is Israel, where some Bedouins established villages that became "unrecognized." A scholar who visited one of these villages to learn how its families were coping recalls that

> The bus dropped me off at the intersection in front of a bridge that leads to the village. To get to the bridge, I first needed to cross three lanes of traffic going in one direction, and then three lanes of traffic going in the other direction. Only a week before, two girls had been seriously injured while crossing the same road. At the entrance to the village, I found that the dirt road to Fatma's house was an elongated pool of mud.[19]

Whether in an encampment of tents in the high desert or a desert-edge village of small houses, the social patterns of Bedouin life have remained substantially the same. Try to imagine yourself in the sandals of someone who, from infancy, has lived every single day in one dwelling with members of your extended family: paternal grandparents, father, mother, unmarried siblings, and married brothers with their wives and children. Able-bodied members, including youngsters, all cooperatively contribute to sustaining their shared lives by raising animals. You and your family sleep, eat, entertain, and (if living as pastoralists) migrate as a unit. In nearby dwellings are members of your clan, most of whom are related to you by blood or marriage. Social interaction is constant. No one is alone—*ever*.[20]

To many Americans, this seems like too much of a good thing. Yet this is how Levantine nomads have lived for as many as *eight millennia*. When they settled in villages, their dwellings changed but their pattern of family relations did not.

THE EXTENDED FAMILY AS ONE'S
CENTER OF GRAVITY

Nomadic Bedouins knew that they exercised no control at all over the sands and the weather. Complete reliance on their families was indispensable. Surviving, even thriving, was possible only if all able-bodied members contributed to the gaining of sustenance, which required harmonious coordination with each other and constant collaboration with extended family members nearby. Each individual grasped a chilling fact: Separated from my family, I'm dead.

These attitudes and values have remained active among the village Arabs of the Levant, descendants of the Bedouin nomads. Thus, the key to appreciating the role of each family member lies in the phrase above, "if all able-bodied members contributed." In the desert, *able-bodied* meant "able to do any task of use to our family"; *contributed* implied "with unceasing dedication."

Another key phrase above is "harmonious coordination." Maintaining harmony and coordination of family survival activities wasn't left to individuals' goodwill. Each family had a leader, the father.[21] Known as *rabb al-bayt*, "master of the household," the Bedouin father's decisions were binding; all expected to do as he directed. During the millennia of nomadic wandering, it was the father who, joined by his adult or nearly adult sons, provided for his family by raiding as well as by making decisions about the family's herds and other economic activities. Yes, this *could* lead to despotism, but generally it did not. Many a father sought the views of his wife and older sons. Then *he* decided.

Don't envision mothers as simply taking orders. They were responsible for the tents, for preparing meals, and for provisioning the family with fuels, water, woven textiles, and food that could be gathered. They ensured the herds were watered, fed, and pastured. In their husbands' absence, they were masters of their households. Most important for us, mothers oversaw the children and made all day-to-day decisions regarding them.

Encircled by seemingly endless desert, knowing that only coordinated effort made survival likely, composed of close relatives, and steered by unquestioned leadership, the Bedouin family was *one complete whole*. It viewed itself this way; all others did as well. This is the practical, mental, and emotional pattern shared by Levantine Arabs across countless generations; sedentarization and stone houses did not dislodge it. In keeping with the ways of their recent Bedouin ancestors, a village Arab family is *a single unit*, not a group of self-reliant but voluntarily cooperating relatives. This is the central fact of the village Arabs, the fact that enables all others to fall into place.

If you had been born into an Arab village family, you would have learned how the world works from people who see that you inhabit your own body, but do not regard you as a being separate from themselves. From birth until death, your social status, feeling of worth, sense of security, expectations, and more would be determined by your family, your life's center of gravity. *This tightly knit group would infuse your life with meaning and relevance.* In return, your family would expect from you conformity, allegiance, and participation in providing all other family members with similar comprehensive support.

What is it like to be a caring parent or growing child in such a family?[22]

HOW NEWBORNS ARRIVE AND RECEIVE CARE

Pregnant women generally continue their work routines right up to the day of birth. (Said one agricultural laborer, "We keep working until the last. We are *fellaheen* here, what should we do?"[23]) When a pregnant woman senses that the birth is imminent, just about every woman in the neighborhood shows up to encourage and assist her.[24] Her husband and sons? They leave the premises!

Pregnant women must not attend the birthing. But a woman with no children who wants to have a child should attend, though often she's kept at the back of the crowd so she won't become too anxious. If a midwife is present—not always—she takes charge. Known as a *dāya*, the midwife is a woman who no longer menstruates.

After the birth, the new mom is expected to rest and recuperate for forty days.[25] During this time she is considered "unclean" and therefore must not cook, wash herself, or even say her prayers. Together with her newborn infant, she is segregated from the household as much as possible while female relatives tend to her needs. They feed her rich foods so she'll produce enough milk for her baby.

A recuperating mother receives a constant stream of visitors, but there are a few restrictions: A menstruating woman, being "unclean," should not visit, and it's best if men who visit stay outside, sending in their gifts of money on a tray. Otherwise, the women of the village—many will be relatives—keep the mother company. Marguerite van Geldermalsen, a New Zealander who married a Bedouin and raised their children in one of the caves at Petra, Jordan, writes of her visitors:

> All of the women, lots of the men, and most of the children of Petra came to visit us. Men mostly came in the afternoons. They usually just popped in to shake my hand and give me more money before going back outside to stand around the fire. But the women arrived in the mornings dressed in their best clothes;

mostly they stayed the day. The beauty of the children who came with them was camouflaged for protection against the evil eye by unkempt hair and ragged clothes. Everyone brought something. By the fifth day we had a hundred and twenty eggs despite frying huge panfuls of them.[26]

A word about that "evil eye," which is believed to be real by people in several Middle Eastern and Asian societies.[27] If a youngster becomes ill, it's often assumed that the evil eye is the culprit.[28] Blue beads are thought to ward off the evil eye and protect one's youngsters. Another preventative measure is for parents to deliberately allow their children to remain dirty and disheveled day after day; snotty noses are common in some villages.[29] And Arabs know that one never, ever, compliments a child directly, as this might rouse an inattentive evil eye hovering nearby.

After the 40-day recuperation period, an infant is constantly in the mother's or someone else's arms or lap, and it always sleeps beside the mother. Swaddling, a Middle Eastern custom, is thought to keep the infant's body firm and legs straight and make him easier to care for. Swaddling continues for up to a year, though most babies spend many daylight hours unbound. Van Geldermalsen observes that other mothers

> wrapped their babies in swaddling clothes, some of them so fastidiously in such straight, tight bundles that they reminded me of the old wooden clothes-peg dolls we made as children; only their heads rolled loose.[30]

On the seventh day after the birth, the child is named by its mother with input from her female relatives.[31] A typical feature of the ceremony is the killing of a ram or sheep. The infant is passed over the blood seven times, which is said to be another way of protecting it from the evil eye. The married women of the village attend, bringing small gifts and enjoying the resulting feast.

Never scheduled, breast-feeding follows two principles: One is that whenever the infant becomes restless, it is given the breast.[32] The other is that it's also suckled when the breast becomes "compassionate," that is, full. Unlike attitudes about breasts in the United States, in the Levant they're a symbol of compassion. Mothers may nurse their children any time, any place, in the middle of any activity—including while riding a bus or train. Breast feeding does not conflict with strict sexual mores.

Toilet-training isn't rushed.[33] Cradles generally have matching holes in the mattress and bottom board, which are positioned directly over a chamber pot on the floor. The child is gently bound in place so that its bottom is directly over the pot. When the child isn't in the cradle, the mother—who's the one carrying him by day and sleeping with him at night—learns to detect the subtle signs of imminent evacuation and rushes the child to a chamber pot or outside location. No precautions are taken when a child is being held; women seem unperturbed if their arms or laps are soiled. Toddlers go around bare-bottomed and are mopped up after like an unhousetrained puppy.

Women give birth often.[34] It's widely accepted that children bring joy and that a childless woman is incomplete. But after several children, some parents express reservations. Men worry about the financial burden. Women's eagerness for yet another little one wanes. One anthropologist who returned after 14 years to the village where she did her fieldwork writes that, in every household she visited, the mother took her aside and asked what she'd done to limit her children to three.

LEARNING TO BE ARAB: THE EARLY CHILDHOOD YEARS

Anthropologist Andrea Rugh has written about her months living with a family of seven members in a Syrian village. The family soon accepted her presence fully, calling her Um Dawud (Mother of David, her oldest son). Here is one of the experiences that Rugh recounts in her book:[35]

During the hours I spent daily sitting with family members, I often worked on complicated embroidery. Miriam, the five-year-old daughter, showed an interest in my work. When I offered to let her do a stitch or two, she seemed pleased. But the stitches were so tiny that she had difficulty. So when I returned after Christmas, I brought along a simple piece of cross-stitch work for Miriam. Soon after I'd settled into the family room with Um George, Miriam's mother, Miriam slipped in and nestled in her customary place by my side. I pulled out my embroidery along with the cross-stitch I had for her and slipped hers into her lap. I showed her how to pull the threads and helped her take the first stitches. Um George seemed concerned. "Oh, Um Dawud, it's very nice of you to bring Miriam the embroidery, but really, she is too young to learn that." I replied, "I'll teach her, Um George. Won't it be nice that she'll be able to do it all by herself?" That evening I visited the family again, but the cross-stitch was nowhere in sight. "We need to continue the lesson, Um George," I said. She took the missing cross-stitch from a high cupboard saying, "She gets it all mixed up." I corrected Miriam's problems, and she got to work again while her twelve-year-old cousin, Muna, settled in beside us. When Miriam went to the bathroom, Muna seized the cross-stitch and started to work on it herself. When Miriam returned, she said nothing to Muna, instead passively watching her work. Each day it became increasingly difficult to find Miriam's cross-stitch when I wanted to begin. Um George obviously was irritated by this project. In addition, I had noticed one day that, when I handed the cross-stitch to Miriam, she received it with a sigh of resignation. Disappointed, I accepted that this project had ended. Miriam showed no emotion.

What we have here is a "culture clash." What clashed?

Rugh's American values led to thoughts like these: Miriam has an interest in learning a skill I've mastered.[36] I can help her. When she finishes the cross-stitch I'll say, "Look, everyone, even though she's only five, Miriam can do embroidery by herself." She'll gain self-esteem; others will be impressed. Uh-oh, why is Muna highjacking Miriam's project? Why does Miriam not seem to care? Why has Miriam started sighing whenever we begin? Why is her mom upset?

Village Arabs' view of this situation is molded by another set of values. A family is a single entity, the welfare of which is paramount. Any individual member's interests are irrelevant. A child shouldn't try to learn a skill before she's physically able because attempting this wastes the time and energy of competent elders as they try to support her learning. And her mediocre results will be useless.

In addition, a village Arab child has no expectation that anything belongs to her alone. Items that interest the children are shared by all of them; each is passed around. It was routine for Muna to pick up the cross-stitch when Miriam went away, routine for Miriam to find a sibling using it when she returned.

Rugh came to understand that, at first, Miriam's enthusiasm had been about helping a fascinating foreigner.[37] The cross-stitch project transformed Miriam's help into a D.I.Y. project that prevented her from pleasurably sharing activities with her siblings. In fact, Miriam's siblings were pointedly not invited to join in completing the cross-stitch. As a task solely for Miriam, cross-stitch became an unwelcome expression of individualistic values, and thus a burden for Miriam; hence her sigh of resignation. She continued doing it merely to please Rugh.

The Role of Children in a Village Arab Family

Village Arabs fuss over their newborns like we do, so you might expect them to provide infants with toys and experiences that promote fun and early learning—like we do.[38] But you'd be mistaken because the way Arabs think of childhood is *not* like we do.

Instead, they regard early childhood as an annoyance that's worth their effort because it will yield an able-bodied family contributor—and sooner is better. At first, "able-bodied" doesn't imply much. Still, even a toddler can fetch and carry. A young lad can shepherd a herd; a girl can nurse injured animals. Such mini-contributions, beginning as early as possible, usher the youngsters into the life-spanning habit of promoting their family's well-being.

In this culture, play isn't emphasized. Because of their desert heritage, adults emphasize the discharging of family responsibilities. A child's role models are his or her elders, especially elder siblings and cousins, and they are not often seen spontaneously playing. Nevertheless, the younger children do discover ways to play—ways that do not involve manufactured toys or games.

Baby birds or insects can be collected as pets. Girls might make dolls out of sticks and rags or hold make-believe weddings. Group games rely on improvised materials, though hide-and-seek needs only players. Courtyards can be marked off for hopscotch. Winter rain brings glorious mud. Play, when it occurs, usually involves siblings and cousins; few non-family children live nearby.

But here's the thing: Parents ignore children's play. It does not further the family's well-being. Mothers never hesitate to interrupt play by calling their child to do tasks that benefit the family; eldest daughters are most likely to be the ones summoned home. Disputes among playmates? That's *their* concern. If a child bawls to mama about so-and-so's hitting him, mama will reply, "Hit him back!"—or punish her child for *not* retaliating. It's not mama's problem.

The role of children is to learn how to participate, as much and as soon as possible, in advancing their family's interests and well-being. Think of them as pint-sized apprentices in terms of both mastering useful tasks and fitting in to the family's we-are-one ethos.

Imagine being a young child in an Arab village.[39] Your many relatives would not call you by your given name, but by your relationship to them. If a village visitor asked your name, you'd reply, "I am the son (daughter) of so-and-so." If the visitor was impressed by your fine qualities, she'd say something like, "You are the child of people who are like princes," praising not you (which might rouse the evil eye), but your family—of whom you are a representative sample.

You wouldn't have your own bedroom, nor your own bed. You wouldn't have exclusive access to a closet or dresser. No one would ask you what you'd like for breakfast or which clothes you want to wear. Choices would be made *for* you by parents who are older and wiser than you, who love and accept you just as you are. You'd never question that they know, in the context of your family's long-term welfare, what is best for you now.

"Dethronement" and the Role of Older Siblings

The term "dethronement" captures the practical and emotional effects of weaning a child in an Arab village.[40] Weaning is usually abrupt; many mothers claim the process needs merely a day or two, facilitated by rubbing quinine on the nipples or leaving the child in the care of a grandmother for several days.

The resulting anguish is not because the child is hungry; for some time, he or she has been fed semi-solid foods such as rice cooked in milk or bread softened in the mother's mouth. The reason is that, to a considerable extent, the mother has vanished along with her breast. For as long as two years, the mother had been at the disposal of her child nonstop, sleeping beside him at night and taking him everywhere during the day. She had been quickly responsive to his first stirrings of hunger, need to eliminate, or other discontent.

My child, today that's finished.

The contrast is stark. The mother abruptly starts delaying her response to the child, in spite of relentless crying, for what must seem to the child like forever. ("Dethronement" is an apt word, don't you think?) This new pattern, termed "inconsistent nurturance," has been hypothesized as appropriate in cultures that value familial interdependence. The reasoning is as follows: Because the mother usually *does* respond after considerable delay, the child's assistance-seeking behavior is reinforced. And because the child is not told or helped to figure things out on his own, dependent behavior also is reinforced.[41]

I said above that breast-feeding continued "for as long as two years" because girls are nursed for barely a year, while most boys are nursed for two, even more. Arabs say that shortened nursing helps a girl more quickly gain control of herself, lest she bring shame on her family (more about this later). An Arab saying advises mothers that, "Pampering a girl disgraces thee; pampering a boy makes thee rich." Nevertheless, as soon as a mother becomes conscious of a subsequent pregnancy, she usually weans a nursing child.[42]

So who takes over the main caretaking role when a mother ends her unceasing involvement?[43] There are other adult family members around who *could* step in. No. The responsibility goes to one or more older siblings, usually girls of at least age four but, ideally, age six or seven (four-year-olds can't easily carry infants). Sibling care leads to a variety of developments.

If the child hasn't already learned to walk steadily, this skill will be developed under the guidance of one or more siblings. Even when the toddling stage gets underway while the child still is suckling, it's not an adult concern. Nor do adults concern themselves when the child falls down. The same with learning to talk; the sibling caretaker is far more involved than adults.

When the child wants to go outside, his caretaker comes along. The youngster is led by hand or perched on his sibling's shoulders to watch the activities of older children, who probably will be cousins. In this way plus frequent visiting, a child begins building lifelong bonds with relatives who are similar to him in age.

LEARNING TO BE ARAB: THE
LATER CHILDHOOD YEARS

In an apparently effortless manner, growing Arab village children are integrated into their family's ongoing labors. They don't view their involvement as "work" in the same way we might.[44] They want to fit in with their family, and these activities are what family members are doing.[45]

Here's an account of an eight- or nine-year-old boy's work:

> His father wants something from the city; the boy gets it. Yesterday his father said, "Take to my sister her festival meat." When his mother is absent, he takes his four siblings down to the garden, which he waters. He rode the ass to the villagers' fields, two hours distant. I asked, "With whom did you go?" He said, "Alone." "Who pulled the grass?" "I pulled it myself; Yamne helped me load it on the ass." He brought the grass for the cows because his father was ill. He also brought dung for the oven.[46]

The activities of a girl of nine are similarly depicted:

> She assists in the kitchen, following her mother's directives. She carries her brother, puts him to sleep in the cradle. She airs the bedclothes and sweeps. If her mother is absent she looks after her little brother. She announces, "I want to go and gather dung." Her mother adds, "Gather stones for the baking-oven. Get petroleum and matches from the shopkeeper." She gathers small wood and dry dung and readies them for burning. If her little brother is sleeping, she fetches water and gives it and food to the chickens. In the evening she closes the chicken-house. She gathers the eggs.[47]

Andrea Rugh records that . . .

> The older children started coming home from school around 1:30. The girls threw down their school-books, changed out of their uniforms, and immediately set to work without being told. The boys went off to turn on the hoses to fill the water carts to take to the chickens. After lunch, the adults relaxed over tea while the girls cleaned up.[48]

Learning Responsibility through Participation in Work

Previously I said that Arabs regard early childhood as an annoyance that's worth their effort.[49] It's worth it because they view children as miniature adults who can be eased into responsible roles by joining their elders in the family's routine activities.

Arab children become full participants in *activities commensurate with each child's current level of ability and understanding.* They're not just building skills for adulthood. There's no point in having a child assist in an activity that they're unable to readily master; everyone's time is wasted. Recall Miriam's cross-stitch. Her mother objected because five-year-olds cannot master cross-stitch. Miriam's labor might yield a finished product, but it would be inferior. Useless kid-stuff.

Village Arab parents expect differing contributions from each child based on their age, gender, strengths, and natural tendencies.[50] Lisa was a good student, so she was relieved of some housework to free time for studying. Muna was good at serving guests, so she was expected to do less homework. Hanna, a mediocre student, was manually adept, so he did home maintenance. The parents assigned jobs based on capacity to perform for the common good, not because every child ought to learn certain skills. "The children seemed to have acknowledged these differences," noted Rugh, "and did not themselves expect to develop all skills to the same degree." Their parents talked openly about each child's strengths and weaknesses, their appraisals never being taken to indicate different levels of love or approval. The children's varying abilities were common knowledge.

Absent among these children was concern about "fairness." The parents had no motive to ensure that all were sharing equally in the work. The needs of this family, now, governed the deployment of their young specialists. None of the children claimed ownership of a new, interesting item; instead, they passed it around among themselves. No "accounting mentality" ever emerged.

Two more outcomes of village family culture are worth noting. First, children don't defend their "rights," that is, what is due to *me*. Instead, they gain awareness of their obligations to others, which shift as they grow. Second, in this culture, seniority counts. As lives advance, people become worthy of increasing respect, authority, and responsibility. We're not talking only of the big distinction among children, adults, and seniors. If I am nine years old, you are seven, and something goes amiss while we're together, our parents will hold *me* responsible.

Adopting the Traditions of Gender Relations

You and I know that many followers of the Islamic faith believe that it's essential that women be veiled, and in some cases secluded. Often overlooked, however, is that these gender expectations did not originate as articles of faith; they were added three or four generations following the death of the Prophet Mohammad.[51]

Village Arabs' gender expectations derive principally from the Bedouin, who maintained an intense solidarity with their family and clan, leading to sustained consciousness of their descent lines. The Bedouin have tracked their genealogies since pre-Islamic times.[52] This practice continues: One anthropologist encountered preschoolers who could recite five generations of their genealogies on both sides.[53]

This brings us to the Arabs' patrilineal system and its determination to ensure that each child's paternity is known. Maternity is empirically verifiable; paternity, not so much. One way of being sure that each new child's paternity is known is by controlling who your womenfolks' sexual partners are—and aren't.

The accounting of each child's paternity became part of the "honor" concept, which refers to the reputation of one's group for morality, courage, religiosity, and hospitality. A male's honor, *sharaf*, concerns all these desirable qualities. A female's honor, *'ard*, zeroed in on morality and became defined as her chastity before marriage and sexual fidelity afterwards. Her honor, once lost, could never be regained. And given the potency of family identification, if a female's honor is lost, then her family's honor is lost—an unmitigated disaster.

These assumptions are absorbed by every growing youngster because every family member shares them. It's the nature of things, the way we do things around here. Supporting this implicit assumption are explicit events that shape a child's understanding. One of the most memorable occurs when children attend weddings and, on the following morning, join the adults in watching the ritual display of a blood-stained sheet that demonstrates the bride's virginity. Helping the youngsters "get" both the mechanics and the meaning of this display are the adults' conversations that accompany this event.[54]

This brings us to the restrictions on the dress, behavior, and activities of juvenile girls that are a common feature of village Arab child-rearing. The objective isn't just to avoid premarital sex, it's to avoid the tiniest temptation toward premarital sex. Even gossip about a girl's suspected loose behavior can permanently wreck her family's honor.

There's a second element in this intense focus on descent. In a carefully tracked patrilineal system, males obviously are key.[55] Without a direct male ancestor, a descent group cannot continue. Thus, familial pressure, openly applied, is placed on newly married couples to produce at least one son who, as an adult, will carry forward the family's name and take over the family's leadership and sustenance. It's not that newborn girls aren't loved; they will have important roles to fulfill, too. Yet in response to male and female births, there are distinct patterns of behavior by family and neighbors.

Three examples: First, whoever tells a father the news of his wife's delivery receives a reward from him; the reward is greater if it's a boy. Second, the
parents' names change on the day their first child is born. Assume the infant
is a girl, Leila. Her father's name becomes "Abu Leila," father of Leila; her
mother's, "Um Leila," mother of Leila. If and when these parents later have
their first boy, their names change permanently: If the boy is named Husayn,
they become "Abu Husayn" and "Um Husayn."[56] Finally, an anthropologist
recalls that one day while walking to visit the parents of a newborn, she
passed a villager, who inquired about her destination. The villager's response
was, "Why are you going? It was a girl."[57]

Beginning around the age of 10, the maturing girl is increasingly kept
under the surveillance of her parents and (if any) older brothers.[58] Depending
on local custom, she might be allowed to run errands. Perhaps she may go
alone down the street to the fountain to fill the water jar—*if* she is certain to
conduct herself with conspicuous modesty, shawl over hair, sleeves to wrists,
behavior restrained. But outside of the village she must never go unaccompa-
nied. Meanwhile, her brothers are kept in the foreground of social activities,
circumcised in a ceremony so lavish it rivals that of marriage,[59] and increasingly allowed freedom of movement.

* * * * *

Though it's beyond the scope of this book, I'd like to share an observation
of several anthropologists, both male and female: It is not accurate to portray
Arab village wives as subservient to their husbands.[60]

What *is* accurate is to say that the wives' sphere is "private" and "domestic," while the husbands' is "public" and "income-producing." The roles
of spouses are complementary *and are accepted by all as complementary*,
a way of organizing family life traced back to the Bedouin. Andrea Rugh
stated that she

> had trouble reconciling the rhetoric about the oppressiveness of women's lives
> with what I saw in our household. Um Abdalla was the center of household
> arrangements, the core around which the rest of the household rotated, the
> one who decided on major household purchases and projects. It's true that she
> worked almost every waking hour to maintain her standards, but to a large
> extent they were *her* standards.[61]

INFORMAL LEARNING BY ARAB VILLAGE CHILDREN

Very young Arab children are said to be without *'aql*, or reason. A central
goal of child-rearing is to instill and develop reason, an important aspect of
which is to learn a system of etiquette called *adab*.[62] *Adab* comprises not only

obeying one's parents but also demonstrating respect for adult elders in ways such as talking in a respectful manner, offering one's seat to an older person, and declining food until everyone who is older or of higher social standing has been served. Girls, in particular, must assume a subservient attitude in the presence of elders. Some *adab* habits are carried into adulthood, such as guests' never eating all the food offered by a host, signaling that the host was generous beyond the guests' needs.

There are two categories of *adab* behavior. One is expected when outsiders are watching; the other is acceptable solely within the privacy of the family circle. For example, a child may sit on a bed while his father is sitting on the floor, or sometimes might even get away with hitting his mother after she scolds him.

The mother is the first person to help a youngster develop *'aql* and conform to the behavioral expectations of *adab*.[63] Her arsenal includes requesting, demanding, scolding, teasing, shaming, and even "beating" (we'd say "spanking"), depending on local community norms. An often-used alternative is to tell the child about a huge ogre, *al-Ghūl*, that attacks misbehaving youngsters as they sleep; its name is the origin of our word "ghoul." A mother's ultimate recourse is to threaten the intervention of a higher power: father. This threat often restores peace and quiet. Threatening the intervention of a much older brother can be just as effective.

Many village fathers are affectionate toward their children—in some families, especially toward their daughters—but fathers also are quite capable of assuming an authoritarian stance and disciplining them harshly. When children are small, fathers typically play no direct daily role in instilling *adab*, but as children gain in years, fathers become more involved, especially with their sons.

As children's capabilities increase, they are expected to complete tasks that maintain the family's well-being.[64] Some children shirk these responsibilities. Upon seeing such a child eating his dinner, a parent might apply shame by saying, "You only know how to increase the size of your butt." Tellingly, a very effective way to shame a misbehaving child is to remark that he "has no people to discipline him," implying that he is behaving like a child with no family (for Arabs, a terrible fate).

It would be a mistake, however, to assume that the instilling of *adab* is wholly up to the parents.[65] Recall that many village households include three generations; some even include four. So in many cases, actively present almost every day are not only paternal grandparents but also adult aunts and uncles, all of whom are expected to participate in a child's rearing, and usually do. Ideally, these adults support the parents' efforts. But if the parents are perceived as too lax, they can step in with needed rigor, or if the parents are perceived as too harsh, they can affectionately support the child.

Grandparents, parents, uncles, and aunts are present in abundance—and we still haven't mentioned those who are among the most effective *adab* agents of all, the child's own siblings and cousins who are older by three or four years.[66] All these children are regularly together, giving the older ones daily opportunities to informally act as instructors, role models, and mentors. Among these groups, peer pressure is exerted mainly via mocking, ridiculing, and scoffing at the younger ones who are lagging in their acquisition of the next level of *adab* conformity.

During nomadic times, it was common for the adult men of the camp to get together for discussion sessions known as *majālis*. Sometimes the men would permit juvenile-age boys to attend. Sitting at the back and never uttering a word, the visitors nevertheless gained indispensable understanding of the personalities of members of their clan, and of the clan's system of justice, accounts of raids and heroism, news of the settled Bedouin, practical information about pasturage and water, odes of the poets, the occasional love story, and more.[67] This tradition has continued in some village communities in the form of men's clubs, meetings of which older boys are able to observe quietly. Although older girls' movement about the village is restricted, they have countless similar opportunities to listen to conversations among adult women, thanks to frequent visiting back and forth among their relatives.

FORMAL LEARNING BY ARAB VILLAGE CHILDREN

The nomadic Bedouin had nothing similar to schools.[68] Rarely did they encounter a literate person. They judged a stranger by assessing his or her genealogy plus adherence to *adab* and devotion to Bedouin culture, especially to its main art form, poetry. Such factors were the best guarantees of an individual's worth.

When governments began encouraging the Bedouin to end their nomadic ways, opportunities for schooling began to appear. Schools were established on the desert's edge; some governments even sent mobile classrooms to desert camps to teach the shaykhs' sons. Many shaykhs agreed because the service was free and evidence was accumulating that having a literate male in the family would be useful.

After the Bedouin began transforming to a sedentary existence, families other than the shaykhs' encountered opportunities for schooling.[69] But each family's decision was *not* a no-brainer. In the case of each child, the choice was guided by the well-being of the family. If a son was expected to indefinitely assist with the family's fields or herds, parents asked what benefits book learning might bring, and whether it could lead the lad to feel too good for farm work. Questions about a daughter included how literacy might affect her marriageability and what threats to family honor could occur by her attendance. Not many girls attended school; only a fraction advanced beyond primary level. For busy eldest daughters, schooling was a near impossibility.

Many a *fellaheen*[70] father, who had never darkened a classroom door, conjured up a transformed family future if a son could become educated.[71] His vision, often shared by the son, did not include manual labor but otherwise was hazy at best. After a few years of attending the inadequate local school, the hapless son almost always remained prepared solely for manual labor; now, though, he resented his fate.

The inadequacy of schools was due in part to their being starved of resources. One anthropologist wrote that a visit to the school in her village

> tells much of the story of education here. The small, barren, uncompleted cement-block structure is surrounded by a sea of mud. Inside it is ill-lit, damp, poorly heated. Partitioned into three small rooms, it houses children at narrow, closely set-together desks and benches. But for an oil stove and blackboard, the rooms are bare.[72]

Another aspect of being starved of resources was that the poorly paid teachers were insufficiently prepared; also, many were socially isolated because they weren't in their native villages.[73] Another reason for the inadequacy of some schools was intermittent attendance. During the wet winter months, attendance was high, but as soon as work in the fields began, it dropped sharply. Autumn saw a slow drift of children back into their classrooms.

Many villages had two types of schools: the type we've been considering and the Koranic school, the *kuttab*.[74] In terms of material and human resources, *kuttabs* tended to adhere to the description above. Most parents, even the poorest, tried to send their sons and sometimes their daughters to the *kuttab* for a few years.

Whether in *kuttabs* or schools that taught literacy and numeracy, the method of instruction usually was rote memorization. In fact, to complete the *kuttab* course of study meant that the child had memorized the entire Koran by heart, which occasioned a gala celebration by his or (rarely) her extended family.

What was the stance of parents regarding formal schooling? It's clear that many considered it a "nice-to-have," mainly for their sons, so long as attendance didn't prejudice the family's work. But that's not the full story. With respect to the Syrian family with which she lived, Andrea Rugh relates that, during evenings in the sitting room where everyone was gathered, each child was "figuring math problems or reciting lessons that had to be memorized, with Abu Abdalla answering questions or listening to a recitation."[75] And before Rugh came to Syria, she had carried out participant observation in a village in Egypt. She tells us that

> the Egyptian household focuses its activity on the study tasks of the children; parents frequently feel they must "study" with their children. During holidays, although school children assume some household chores, these are viewed as peripheral because the parents believe the children need to "rest up" for the next arduous school year.[76]

FROM AN ANTHROPOLOGICAL PERSPECTIVE

Arabs who live in small villages across the Levant are the direct heirs of the desert Bedouin, nomads whose ways of living began to be forged as long as 8,000 years ago. Bedouin traditions are indelibly ingrained among those villages' inhabitants, especially those who have avoided modern Western influences. Chief among those traditions is the all-embracing cocoon of the extended family.

In the five main chapters of this book, societies are explored in which the well-being of the group is valued much more highly than the needs or desires of any individual. In the cases of the Aka, Quechua, and Navajo societies, the well-being of one's settlement—for example, the *ayllu* of the Quechua—seems at least as important, perhaps more important, than that of one's extended family. But in the case of the village Arabs, the well-being of one's extended family takes precedence. They inherited their focus on the family from the desert Bedouin, who lived in small, widely scattered, tightly knit groups composed largely or entirely of relatives.

A child born in a Bedouin camp was absorbed into his family group, never to be dealt with as a person with interests distinct from those of his group. He was addressed by each relative not by name but by the nature of their relationship, which he reciprocated. A youngster owned nothing, had exclusive access to nothing, and was rarely if ever asked for their personal views. Decisions large and small were made by senior adults, who were mindful of the family's needs, honor, and well-being. In this setting, a child effortlessly gained a *we-are-one* mindset and set of values.

Summary of Village Arab Children's Learning and Socialization

Based on anthropologists' findings, I believe that five key features of how village Arab children are socialized into adulthood are the following. Village Arab children . . .

- learn through being immersed in their families' activities.
- and their childish concerns are very largely ignored by adults.
- are cared for and raised, following weaning, by an older sibling.
- are expected to fulfill responsibilities suitable to each one's strengths.
- are dealt with from the day of their birth according to each one's sex.

Village Arab children learn through being immersed in their families' activities. The village Arab household is the scene of frequent activity involving three, or even four, generations of close relatives, who typically live nearby. The activity tends to center on the mother of the household. Until each newborn is weaned, the mother cares for him virtually non-stop. After weaning, the child constantly is witness to the ideas, activities, and relationships of his extended family members. Surrounded every day, hour after hour, by these models of Arab values, behavior, and competence, the child has limitless opportunities to learn his family's ways by observation and imitation, and then increasingly by participation.

Parents and other adult family members pay very little attention to the growing child, whom the mother has consigned to the daily care of a slightly older sibling. The exception is that parents and others, including siblings and cousins, do concern themselves with the child's mastering of *adab* behavior, for it is largely on this basis that he, and the entire extended family, will be judged by others. So far not clarified by research is the extent to which the others go out of their way to help the child develop any of the skills of practical competence.

To a village Arab, it never occurs that a child should, or even could, acclimate to being alone from time to time, "entertaining oneself" as we say. Life means togetherness; togetherness means grandparents, parents, siblings, cousins, uncles, and aunts all the time. Village Arab children, the heirs of the nomadic desert Bedouin, learn to be Arab in the crucible of their extended family.

Children and their childish concerns are very largely ignored by adults. Like us, village Arabs are apt to coo and fuss over newborns, but they show scant interest in them during toddlerhood and beyond, including what we tenderly call the "milestones" of child development like walking and talking.

Dealing with children and their childish interests is a necessary annoyance, tolerable because the young one is on a path to becoming a useful, adult-like contributor to the extended family's well-being.

Adults' care for and love of their fledgling apprentices occurs in spite of the trappings of childhood.[77] Adults almost never show any interest in playing with children, providing them with play opportunities, or intervening in squabbles that arise during play. It's all kid stuff, useless to the family, not worthy of an adult's notice. Adults want youngsters to start behaving like adults ASAP, which they promote by not patronizing them.[78] Instead of lowering themselves to enter the world of children, adults maintain grown-up standards of behavior and expect children to figure out how to expeditiously join them at that higher level.

Children are cared for and raised, following weaning, by an older sibling. Village Arab weaning is characterized by sudden denial of access to the breast and abrupt curtailment of access to the mother's highly responsive nurturing. Sure, she's still nearby, as are several other adult relatives. But none of those adults is interested in the prospect of being a growing child's caretaker, disciplinarian, and cultural guide.

The nurturing and mentoring role goes to a slightly older sibling or cousin, preferably a female aged six or seven. From then on, it's largely under *her* guidance—monitored at a distance by the mother—that the youngster learns basic life skills, *adab* behavior, and how to fit in with the family. Frequently, a strong lifelong bond is forged between the youngster and their caretaker.

Children are expected to fulfill responsibilities suitable to each one's strengths. No child is allowed to think of their self as separate or unique, but parents do view each child as potentially possessing distinctive abilities. The nature of each child's distinctiveness is gauged in practical terms relative to the family's needs.

Along comes a new youngster. Which tasks are they best qualified to be assigned for the common good? Considered are age, strengths, and interests, and what's appropriate for boys and girls differs. What's appropriate for a child of eight isn't for a child of five. Miriam at five lacked the dexterity to do cross-stitch well, so why should she even try? Just as we all can see that Miriam cannot do cross-stitch yet, we also can see that Hanna is manually adept and that Lisa is a scholar. Children's varying strengths are on public display, so we all may discuss them openly without any implication that our frank assessments signal more or less love. In the assignment of roles and tasks, each is treated as a specialist.

Children are dealt with from the day of their birth according to each one's sex. This is the Arab characteristic some love to hate: the subjugation of women begins with strikingly muted responses to the birth of a girl. But history offers another perspective. Common among the Semitic peoples was an interest in kinship and descent.[79] Do you have an Old Testament handy? Scan the first four chapters of First Chronicles, where countless genealogies are delineated, father to son. Genealogical precision is a deep Semitic tradition requiring accounting of paternity, which in turn has led to the honor concept and the expectation that the home is where women's indispensable contributions to their families should be made.

Andrea Rugh once observed an Arab woman being asked, "Do you feel you realize your full potential as an individual?"[80] She replied, "I am a daughter, wife, mother, sister, aunt, grandmother. What else do you want me to tell you?" In those roles and relationships, one *can* live a fulfilling life that others admire.

SUGGESTED FURTHER READING

Each of the readings below is profiled at howotherchildrenlearn.info/profiles.

Within the Circle: Parents and Children in an Arab Village, by Andrea B. Rugh (1997); 245 text pages.

Married to a Bedouin, by Marguerite van Geldermalsen (2006); 276 text pages.

The Bedouins and the Desert: Aspects of Nomadic Life in the Arab East, by Jibrail S. Jabbur (1995); 537 text pages.

BIBLIOGRAPHY

Abu-Rabia, Aref. (1993). Educational anthropology in Bedouin society. *Practicing Anthropology, 15* (2), 21–23.

Al-Naimi, Ali. (2016). *Out of the Desert: My journey from Nomadic Bedouin to the heart of global oil*. Penguin U.K.

Ammar, Hamed (1966). *Growing up in an Egyptian village*. Routledge & Kegan Paul.

Beck, Dorothy Fahs. (1970). The changing Moslem family of the Middle East. *Readings in Arab Middle Eastern Societies and Cultures*, Abdulla Lutfiyya & Charles Churchill, eds. Mouton, 567–577.

Blunt, Lady Anne. (1879). *Bedouin Tribes of the Euphrates, Vol. I.* John Murray. This volume contains no information about who republished it.

Blunt, Lady Anne. (1879). *Bedouin Tribes of the Euphrates, Vol. II.* John Murray. Republished by Franklin Classics, an imprint of Creative Media Partners.

Brink, Judy H. (1994). The effect of infant rearing practices on the personalities of children in Egypt. *Pre- and Perinatal Psychology Journal, 8* (4), 237–248.

Brink, Judy H. (1995). Changing child-rearing patterns in an Egyptian village. *Children in the Muslim Middle East*, Elizabeth Warnock Fernea, ed. University of Texas Press, 84–92.

Chatty, Dawn. (1978). Changing sex roles in Bedouin society in Syria and Lebanon. *Women in the Muslim World*, L. Beck & N. Keddri, eds. Harvard University Press, 399–415.

Chatty, Dawn. (2010). Bedouin in Lebanon: The transformation of a way of life or an attitude? *International Journal of Migration, Health, and Social Care, 6* (3), 21–30.

Fernea, Elizabeth. (1991). Muslim Middle East. *Children in Historical and Comparative Perspective*, Joseph Hawes & N. Ray Hiner, eds. Greenwood, 447–70.

Fernea, Elizabeth Warnock. (1995). Childhood in the Muslim Middle East. *Children in the Muslim Middle East*, Elizabeth Warnock Fernea, ed. University of Texas Press.

Fuller, Anne H. (1970). The world of kin. *Readings in Arab Middle Eastern Societies and Cultures*, Abdulla Lutfiyya & Charles Churchill, eds. Mouton, 526–534.

Ghannam, Farha. (1995). Kuwaiti lullabies. *Children in the Muslim Middle East*, Elizabeth Warnock Fernea, ed. University of Texas Press, 77–83.

Granqvist, Hilma N. (1947). *Birth and childhood among the Arabs.* Söderström. Reprinted by AMS Press.

Haj-Yahia, Muhammad M. (1995). Toward culturally sensitive intervention with Arab families in Israel. *Contemporary Family Therapy, 17* (4), 429–447.

Hamamsy, Laila Shukry el. (1970). The changing role of the Egyptian woman. *Readings in Arab Middle Eastern Societies and Cultures*, Abdulla Lutfiyya & Charles Churchill, eds. Mouton, 592–601.

Jabbur, Jibrail S. (1995). *The Bedouins and the Desert: Aspects of Nomadic Life in the Arab East.* State University of New York.

Katakura, Motoko. (1977). *Bedouin village: A study of a Saudi Arabian people in transition.* University of Tokyo Press.

Lichtenstadter, Ilse. (1970). The Arab-Egyptian family. *Readings in Arab Middle Eastern Societies and Cultures*, Abdulla Lutfiyya & Charles Churchill, eds. Mouton, 603–618.

Lutfiyya, Abdulla M. (1970). The family. *Readings in Arab Middle Eastern Societies and Cultures*, Abdulla Lutfiyya & Charles Churchill, eds. Mouton, 505–525.

Marey-Sarwan, Ibtisam, Hiltrud Otto, Dorit Roer-Strier, and Heidi Keller. (2016a). Parenting among the Arab Bedouins in the Naqab Desert in Israel. *Contemporary Parenting: A Global Perspective*, Guerda Nicolas et al., eds. Routledge, 105–123.

Marey-Sarwan, Ibtisam, Heidi Keller, & Hiltrud Otto. (2016b). Stay close to me: Stranger anxiety and maternal beliefs about children's socio-emotional development among Bedouins in the unrecognized villages in the Naqab. *Journal of Cross-Cultural Psychology, 47* (3), 319–332.

Marey-Sarwan, Ibtisam, & Dorit Roer-Strier. (June 2017). Parents' perceptions of risk for children: A case study of Bedouin parents from unrecognized villages in Israel. *Social Service Review*, 171–202.

Nydell, Margaret K. (2018). *Understanding Arabs: A contemporary guide to Arab society, 6th Ed.* Intercultural Press.

Patai, Raphael. (1970). Familism and socialization. *Readings in Arab Middle Eastern Societies and Cultures*, Abdulla Lutfiyya & Charles Churchill, eds. Mouton, 578–582.

Peraza, Alfonso Fanjul. (2015). Desert stories & Bedouin legends. Self-published.

Prothro, Edwin Terry. (1961). *Child rearing in the Lebanon.* Harvard University Press.

Prothro, Edwin Terry. (1970). Patterns in child-rearing practices. *Readings in Arab Middle Eastern Societies and Cultures*, Abdulla Lutfiyya & Charles Churchill, eds. Mouton, 583–591.

Rugh, Andrea B. (1984). *Family in contemporary Egypt.* Syracuse University Press.

Rugh, Andrea B. (1997). *Within the circle: Parents and children in an Arab village.* Columbia University Press.

Suwaed, Muhammad, & Faten Swaid (2015). Relations between mothers and adolescent daughters in the Israeli Bedouin society characterized by education of traditional values. *International Education Studies, 8* (5), 75–87.

van Geldermalsen, Marguerite. (2006). *Married to a Bedouin.* Virago.

Williams, Judith. (1968). *The youth of Haouch el Harimi, a Lebanese village.* Harvard Center for Middle Eastern Studies.

Zahr, Lina Kurdahi, & Marianne Hattar-Pollara. (1998). Nursing care of Arab children: Consideration of cultural factors. *Journal of Pediatric Nursing, 13* (6), 349–355.

Chapter 6

The Total Immersion Family

Growing Up among the
Hindu Villagers of India

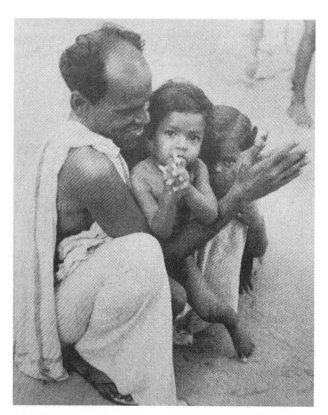

Figure 6.1. An Indian father shows his child how to fold his hands in greeting. *From Notes on Love in a Tamil Family, by Margaret Trawick. Copyright © 1990. Courtesy of the University of California Press.*

FILMS ABOUT THE VILLAGE
INDIAN WAY OF LIFE

These films will enable you to more accurately imagine Indian families as you read this chapter.

"I Lived in an Indian Village" (2019). Karl Rock walks us through an Indian home and village, discussing daily life there. Produced by Karl Rock. 22:25 min. youtube.com/watch?v=EF63yggtiRg

"Why Dalit?" (~2010). In a village setting, Dalit and higher-caste people discuss their relations. Published by Nordic Anthro. Film Assn. 29:51 min. boap.uib.no/index.php/jaf/article/view/1323/1211

"Desi Life in India" (2021). With no narration, we watch villagers' daily work, including making cow dung patties. Real Life India series. 10:14 min. youtube.com/watch?v=a6-pTFrSxu0&t=165s

On YouTube, a search for "real life India" or "villages in India" yields many films made in India, mostly in villages, that depict outdoor work and cooking. Many of these films have no narration.

Hot links to all films and videos are at
howotherchildrenlearn.info/films

Based on anthropological fieldwork carried out primarily between 1950 and 2000.

If you already know something about India, you're probably aware that it's the home to extraordinary diversity. Take languages. They almost certainly number over 700, including some you might have heard of—Sanskrit, Tamil, and Hindi—and some you probably haven't—Dogri, Odia, and Tulu. The anthropologist who has done the most extensive fieldwork in India began by gaining fluency in Odia.[1]

All those languages signal that India harbors numerous disparate tribes and cultural groups, some characterized by strongly held religious beliefs. The names of the largest religious groups probably are familiar to you—Hindu (by far the largest), Sikh, and Muslim. But the names of some of the tribes and cultural groups might not sound familiar, such as Chakma, Nagpuria, and Pahadis.

Almost certainly, you associate India with the caste system, and rightly so; it's responsible for more day-to-day differences among Indian villagers than either tribal or language diversity. In India, three terms are in use: caste, *varna*, and *jāti*.² Caste is a European term for the grouping of people into ranked classes. *Varna*, an Indian term, refers to the notion, based on Hindu scripture, that society is composed of people in four hierarchically ranked classes according to their occupational roles. We'll revisit the varna concept later. *Jāti* is the term commonly used by Indians and will be the term used throughout this chapter. It refers to thousands of fine distinctions among people that Indians make to rank themselves and others in relation to each other.

The population of India includes millions of citizens who are economically and socially disadvantaged. Some of them are known as "untouchables" because their occupational roles—for example, toilet cleaning—are viewed as sources of contamination by those who are more fortunate. Others have low occupational roles, too, but ones that necessarily bring them into contact with people, such as barber, cook, housekeeper, and midwife. Terms that Indians often use to refer to their fellow citizens in these lowly roles include *Dalit*, which means "one who is oppressed," and *Harijan*, "children of God," which was introduced by Gandhi.³ Throughout this chapter, I will use the term *Dalit*.

Friends who knew I was drafting this chapter said, "Given India's huge size and diversity, how can you write just one chapter on child-rearing?" Good question.

IN AN OCEAN OF DIVERSITY, CHILD-REARING SIMILARITY

During my research for this chapter, I studied anthropological reports on family practices in ten widely scattered Indian states.⁴ I found that the guiding values and patterns of child-rearing are remarkably similar across India. Yes, there are differences, mostly involving practices such as details of ceremonies that welcome newborns into families. In the southern state of Kerala there's a group called the Nayars that, unlike others in India, traces family lineage through the mother's side rather than that of the father. Nevertheless, Nayars raise their children according to values and patterns similar to those of most other groups in India.⁵

I also discovered that respected anthropologists had published articles about "child-rearing in [all of] India." One observed that . . .

> Accounts *from all regions* speak of joint families, multiple caretakers, and rules of restraint on parent–child interaction in front of elders. Even where joint families do not predominate, nuclear families are reported to locate near relatives in order to approximate joint family participation in child rearing.⁶

How can the similarities in child-rearing across India be explained? One clue comes from around 300 BCE, when the Greek ambassador in India wrote about the way in which Indian society had long been organized: People divided themselves into occupationally specialized groups; an individual could marry only within his group; and no one could change his group membership.[7] That's a good description of India 2,300 years later, that is, during our own 20th and 21st centuries.

So 23 centuries ago, the Indian subcontinent was home to a society that was stable enough to be exchanging ambassadors with other, far away, societies. Even then, venerated religious scriptures were informing the daily behavior of citizens who followed Hindu teachings, just as they do now. These scriptures are thought to have originated more than *12 centuries prior to* the ambassador's note.[8]

Prevalent in all sections of Indian society is a sense of needing guidance from gods and goddesses; in traditional Hindu families, one's day starts with prayer.[9] It's not surprising that India's rich repertoire of ancient scriptures is a source of pride for the Indian people—even if many Indians can't actually read them.

For us, what's important is that the scriptures contain extended discourses about, among other things, various aspects of family life including ideal patterns of parent–child relations. Another set of ancient texts with prescriptions for child-rearing is *Ayurveda*, the traditional system of medicine. For example, traceable directly to Ayurveda is the common practice of giving oil massages to infants.

What I am suggesting is that the surprising similarity in parenting practices across India is the result, at least to some extent, of the widely revered legacy of the scriptures. Their appeal and influence, generation after generation, proved able to withstand a determined effort to undermine and replace traditional ways during more recent times. I'm referring to the British "Raj" (rule) over India, which lasted from 1858 until 1947, and which was preceded by a century when the British East India Company held sway over a large swath of India.

The Raj introduced to Indians unfamiliar types of political, economic, religious, legal, social, and educational institutions.[10] British colonialists conveyed a belief in their cultural superiority in ways that were both conspicuous and subtle. For example, one of the conspicuous ways was that Christian missionaries branded most Hindu worship as idolatrous and barbarian.

An example of the subtle ways was that the colonialists, simply by the way they lived and conducted their affairs, promoted *individual-centered values*. One of their deepest values was personal integrity, that is, steadily maintaining one's own principles despite how others think and behave. This directly clashes with Indians' traditional reliance on *context-oriented values*, which lead people to be mindful of—and responsive to—the nuances of their social situations.

Here's a metaphor that captures this fundamental difference: As everyone goes through life, a wide range of social situations and people are encountered. Through it all, Westerners have gyroscopes that guide them according to their pre-determined values, enabling them to keep steadily on course. Indians (and other Asians) have radars, which continually enable them to be sensitive to the social situations and people they encounter, and to adapt their thoughts and behavior to conform harmoniously to their current context.[11]

But here's the thing: Only rarely during the Raj did Western values make their way into villages and rural areas. Yes, some villagers heard about them; those who felt beguiled departed for the cities. The British did not transform all of India. They did create an urban intelligentsia. Largely untouched were the village and rural masses that constituted nearly 75% of India's population.[12]

COMMUNITY AND FAMILY IN VILLAGE INDIA

What mental images should "village India" bring to our minds? Here's a colorful description of one village in the southern state of Tamil Nadu:

> Most houses are constructed of mud and thatch, so they are impermanent and must be rebuilt frequently. Some are less wide than a reclining person is long. Exterior walls are crumbling; the narrow pathways that wind among the houses are filled with rubble. Doors and windows are almost always open. Dogs, cats, rats, crows, monkeys, insects, and reptiles enter through these permeable borders to receive the household refuse or steal their share of grain. People depend on them for cleanup, sometimes eat them.
>
> Mobs of children surge through courtyards, restrained only, if at all, by the invisible walls of their elders' antagonisms—spats between families, caste prides and fears. There occurs a perpetual daily ebb and flow of people through each other's living spaces, including fluctuations caused by kinspeople's visits. Such close, tumultuous merger of lives is taught and learned as a value, and this makes all the difference.[13]

If you are an Indian villager, you identify with your village; after all, it's likely your father's forbears lived there for generations. More tenaciously, though, you identify with your hierarchical group. India is about hierarchical distinctions, finely if informally calibrated, constantly guiding one and all.

Let's think about hierarchy.[14] You and I know the American version: *Some* relationships—for example, at work—include hierarchical distinctions. We participate in them willingly, assuming that the superior and the subordinate persons are, at base, equals, but for practical purposes are temporarily fulfilling these roles. Indians assume that virtually every relationship is shaped by hierarchy, and that superior or subordinate status is inherent in individuals, not in the roles they fill.

As noted earlier, the broadest set of hierarchical distinctions (varna) assigns people to one of four ranked occupational roles; from the top down, these are priests and scholars, warriors and rulers, tradesmen, and cultivators.[15] There are also millions of Dalits filling the lowest occupational roles.[16] But for most Indian villagers, a far more persistent daily reality is the jāti system of rankings. Every day, every villager uses the local jāti system to make infinitely fine hierarchical distinctions among those with whom they encounter. If you ask a villager, "Who are you?," their response will always identify the jāti to which they belong.

A jāti is a group into which one is born.[17] Each jāti is historically associated with an occupation. A village contains several. Within it and neighboring villages, the members of one's jāti are actual and potential kin who earn a living in similar ways, share characteristic behavior and attitudes, and maintain a certain lifestyle. Each jāti is informally ranked in the local hierarchy by the villagers, based on their beliefs about the relative degrees of pollution and purity associated with a jāti's occupations, practices, wealth, and influence. A jāti's rank can shift. Each jāti has rules of behavior about eating, drinking, touching, and so forth driven by members' fear of being "polluted" by the members of a lower-ranked jāti. The higher your jāti is ranked above mine, the more restrictive are the rules by which you abide when you're in my vicinity.

Jātis are not rigidly exclusionary. Men of different jātis may work side by side without keeping their usual physical and social distance. Sporting events often involve contestants from different jātis. Friendships may cross jāti boundaries, though they usually don't endure. A jāti's traditional occupation does not restrict its males only to that work, and agricultural work may be undertaken by everyone. Marriages, however, must unite a bride and groom of the same jāti.

Each family depends for various goods and services on the families of other jātis in its village and beyond.[18] For example, a family's washerman might live in one village and its carpenter in another. The family itself similarly provides goods or services to others in a circuit of villages. Even high-ranking landowners employ the services of Dalits. In turn, the Dalits' families depend on their patrons for their livelihood, emergency help, and support for religious rites.

The center of family life is often the central courtyard. As related by anthropologists who worked in the state of Uttar Pradesh, the courtyard is where you find the women and children. The men's platform, a short distance away, is for the men and adolescent boys. In the courtyard the women sleep, take care of children, and cook for the men and boys, who come to the house for meals. Sharing a courtyard is often the household's oldest woman plus her unmarried daughters and young sons, her married son's wives, and those wives' young children—three generations related through the male line. It's not unusual for the women to be quarrelsome. Tempers have no chance to cool off in the close quarters of the courtyard. One woman said that if *purdah* restrictions [which require female seclusion] did not prevent a woman from taking a walk, most minor irritations would not escalate.[19]

Some homes are larger, as depicted in this account from the state of Orissa:

> Because space is scarce, homes are built physically contiguous to one another. The only way to expand is upward. Prosperous families have homes that are two or three stories high, with stucco walls, cement floors, and reinforced cement ceilings, rather than mud walls, dirt floors, and thatch roofs. In interior décor, however, there is little difference between homes. Furniture is scarce—most eating, sleeping, and working is done on the floor—and there are few decorations. No home has electricity or running water. Families depend on kerosene lanterns for light in the evenings and on public wells for water. Some have wells in their backyard. The life of the household goes on in the interior courtyards and verandahs and is invisible to the outside world.[20]

A key distinction between American and Indian families is that ours typically are "nuclear" while theirs are often "joint."[21] This term designates a household in which three or more generations linked through the male line live together, raise children and crops together, and pool incomes and expenses. When key decisions are to be made, the senior male's authority prevails. These living arrangements are also called "single-kitchen households" because each meal is prepared for everyone in residence. For a youngster, "my joint family" comprises his or her

- mother, whose love for her child is thought to be the strongest of all loves but who must never visibly express her love when anyone else is present.[22] (Strong pair-bonds, including husband–wife, pose a threat to a joint family.) Even when she gives the child her breast, she must treat it as merely a practical activity. In company, a child shouldn't receive even a furtive smile from his mother. But until her next birth, the child sleeps with her at night. Somehow her love shines through; adults deeply appreciate and revere their mothers.

- father, characterized by physical and emotional distance.[23] No one expects him to contribute to his children's care; most fathers are content to leave them to the women. Some daughters see their fathers solely at mealtimes, when they serve but do not eat with him. One anthropologist wrote that, to his children, their father "has the subtle authority of a stranger." Fathers will punish a child who repeatedly disobeys his mother; many are feared as well as respected.

- brothers and sisters, who have special relationships with a young sibling.[24] Older brothers are ritually superior but often show interest in the child. An older sister and a child can form a lifelong bond if the sister is given caretaking duties after their mother gives birth again. The sister tends to all needs, punishes bad behavior, treats the youngster as a playmate, and is *not* constrained from caring for her younger sibling in a loving way. Sisters with some schooling often coach their brothers for exams and take their parents' place in meetings with primary school teachers.

- uncles and aunts in the household, the fathers' siblings, are expected to serve as the child's substitute adult parents.[25] Paternal uncles are father-like authority figures but often are less aloof and more approachable than the father. Uncles and aunts *not* in the household, the mother's siblings, characteristically indulge their beloved nephews and nieces without having any responsibility for their upbringing. Occasions for them to spend time together are limited.

- grandparents, the father's parents, play a significant role in child-rearing.[26] They typically develop a feeling of familiarity with their grandchildren, and might even indulge them, but they also guide and discipline them. A recently weaned child often switches to sleeping with one of the grandparents. And the distant relationship between fathers and children is counterbalanced by the openly affectionate grandfather on the father's side. It's a common village sight to see an aged gentleman keeping watch over, and playing warmly with, his grandchildren.

One's family is no exception to the assumption that every relationship is shaped by hierarchy.[27] The ordering principles are age and sex. Between an older woman and a younger man, maleness prevails. Men have formal property rights, which ranks a male's authority greater than that of his older sister or even his mother. However, authority confers responsibility. Men must care for aged parents; brothers must protect sisters. Coloring all this is the temperament and dynamism of various individuals. In some families, the senior female rules the roost.

A related feature of family life, especially among the upper-status jātis, is the system of *purdah*, which refers to a graded variety of measures that require a woman to conceal the shape of her body from the public. At a minimum, purdah requires a woman to cloak her body and, often, her face when away from her home and its courtyard. Many women living under purdah are further barred from leaving their homes at all except in the company of their husbands and only for very special occasions. These and related restrictions[28] apply to the younger women; the movements of widows with grown children are not as circumscribed.

In the United States, 20-something children often move away from their parents and each other; distances then make visiting an expensive project. In India, when married sons leave the parental household, it's rarely because they've reached a certain age; it's because their father has died.[29] When a joint family separates, each married son sets up a separate home near the others; nevertheless, the family remains, for most purposes, joint. Family members are in and out of each other's homes daily and easily combine for life-cycle rites and holidays. Their social circle doesn't change, villagers still regard them all as one family, and the children continue being raised by multiple caretakers. But each son and his wife do have their own kitchen.

It's no surprise that youngsters learn kinship terms early.[30] In many families, a child is addressed by a kinship term, not his name. Being called "first," "second," or "third" son or daughter emphasizes the importance of kinship, gender, and birth order, and deemphasizes individual identity. Adult talk with young children often centers on their learning and properly pronouncing kinship terms and—this is crucial—applying them to the correct individuals. One researcher listed 21 kinship terms including unique words for these kinfolk: mother of any parallel cousin,[31] son of one's opposite-sex sibling, and kinswoman of one's grandparents' generation.

HOW NEWBORNS ARRIVE AND RECEIVE CARE

How infants come into being is no secret among the villagers. But mystical and supernatural forces are thought to play a determining role in both conception and safe delivery.[32] A couple's horoscope readings might signal a benign or adverse conjunction of their planets, or that they might have good or bad *karma* (destiny).[33] A difficult birth also could follow the mother-to-be's doing something that is taboo such as visiting cremation or burial grounds, or witnessing an eclipse.

Household women usually refuse to assist in a birth because blood is deemed unclean, that is, a source of ritual pollution.[34] When labor begins, the local midwife, usually a Dalit woman, is sent for. Mothers in labor sometimes squat with each foot on a brick to provide greater elevation from the floor. The umbilical cord is cut with any available knife; it and the placenta go to the rubbish heap. In some villages, children are allowed to watch these proceedings, wide-eyed.

Because both mother and newborn have been in contact with blood, they are viewed as polluted and therefore are ritually isolated during a period lasting up to two weeks. Each day, the midwife returns to clean the bed, wash all soiled clothes, remove excrement, and clean the room with cow dung. When the period of ritual pollution ends, mother and child are bathed and purified. The newborn is then introduced to the family but often not yet named, the first of many indications that he or she is not regarded as a separate individual.

Ceremonies of welcome for the infant differ widely. Here's an example from the state of Kashmir.[35] It occurs when mother and child emerge from isolation after six days. The father's eldest married sister waves a burning piece of birch bark over the heads of mother and infant, ensuring the child's safety and the mother's continued fertility. Some jātis perform a hair-cutting ceremony. In the state of Uttar Pradesh, this occurs for both boys and girls at about age one.[36] A barber accompanies family members to a local shrine and there cuts the child's hair, which is offered to a goddess to protect the child from harm.

A baby's mother is but one of several caregivers; the only responsibility that's uniquely hers is to nurse him. Consider this vignette from the state of Orissa:

> Older Sister returned carrying one-month-old Bapu. Two neighbor girls came in and sat down. Older Sister lay Bapu on his back on a wooden platform. Bapu urinated and began to cry, but Older Sister ignored him. One of the neighbor girls picked him up and held him for a moment. Then she passed him to the other neighbor girl. They took turns bouncing him on their laps. Bapu's mother came in and took Bapu and held him for several minutes. Then she handed him to one of the neighbor girls and left. Grandmother came in with Bapu's young brother Rabi, but they soon departed.[37]

Although Indians regard adult feces with disgust and insist they be removed by the lowliest of the Dalits, the sweepers, they seem unperturbed by an infant's excrement.[38] Babies are not diapered; most wear only a shirt. If an infant urinates while being carried, it's held away so the urine is absorbed by the earthen floor. If the person holding the infant is slow to react and gets wet, no problem. Women learn to anticipate a baby's need to have a bowel movement, then rush to hold him over the courtyard drain or a trash heap in the cattle compound. If infant feces end up on the floor, they are cleaned up at once with little fuss, no sweeper needed. By the way, everyone seems perfectly relaxed around cow dung, which children routinely collect and adults use daily for practical purposes.[39]

Now you might suppose that, with women and girls around throughout the day, an infant would be shamelessly indulged. That's what some commentators were saying—until anthropologists devoted hundreds of hours to patiently observing daily life in joint households. That earlier supposition turned out to be false.

An infant in India is never alone.[40] It's also true that *an infant is virtually never the focus of sustained attention.* Village women all grew up in households in which births were a common occurrence. Before they were 10 years old, each of these women most likely had already been fully responsible for an infant. So after the most recent birth activities are over, all the females of the household return to their normal routines. The tiny human in their midst occasions neither anxiety nor fascination. It's just another infant.

Yes, the mother must feed the infant. But don't imagine a nursing mother who is seated and gazing lovingly at her suckling child. Indian mothers artfully hold their child on their hip in such a way that it can suckle while they do their household tasks. When other females carry the infant, they also prop it on their hip and get on with their work. Childcare is practical and impersonal. It's rare for anyone to actually focus sustained attention on an infant; when this does happen, it's likely an aged grandfather, a visiting uncle, or a neighbor girl.

Nursing occurs "on demand"—but not as we usually understand that term. When her infant cries, the mother does *not* drop everything and rush to offer her breast. She responds when she finishes whatever she's doing, which can be minutes later. Mothers rarely nurse an infant to satisfaction; rather, they nurse it incompletely, wait for it to cry again, then finish whatever they're doing and nurse it again—often incompletely again.

An infant is never isolated in a separate room or cradle; rather, it passively witnesses ongoing courtyard activities. When it fusses—and only if it fusses for a while—it is comforted. When it isn't fussing, it's left alone. The goal is to keep the baby quiet, not to stimulate it. It has no stimulating toys, either. Babies learn that, if they want attention, entertainment, or food from others, they must make multiple requests—a pattern of interest to anthropologists, as we'll soon see.

LEARNING TO BE INDIAN: THE EARLY CHILDHOOD YEARS

When youngsters are ready, they figure out how to walk; no adult encourages this process.[41] Toddlers aren't allowed to venture beyond the home's threshold, but they're sometimes taken on visits. A grandmother might bring a child along to a neighbor's home, or a fond father or uncle might take them to the men's platform. After children learn to walk securely, they tag along with siblings and cousins into the street or to a nearby pond, where they play with other village children, jāti distinctions notwithstanding.

Inside the household, toddlers spend most of their day observing, poking into things, and being distracted if they're headed for danger. The only imaginative play of girls is to mimic women's cooking (making mud bread) and infant-tending (using rag dolls). For boys, it's farming; they might play with miniature bullock carts or make imitation fields and then irrigate them. Otherwise, most play is toy-free random activity that adults ignore unless a loud quarrel erupts. Note this, however: All children are taken to the numerous extended-family events such as weddings and religious ceremonies. Baby-sitting isn't even a concept.

Early childhood experiences vary depending on a child's jāti. I'll consider the upper- and middle-status jātis first, then the economically disadvantaged ones.

Early Childcare among the Upper- and Middle-Status Jātis

Among the higher-ranked jātis, the care of younger children has a relaxed, laissez-faire quality.[42] There is no expectation among adults that youngsters should learn self-reliance or a skill, should significantly contribute to household chores, or should comport themselves in any particular way.

In some Indian languages, there are no words for "to toilet train" or "to wean."[43] In many families, children who can walk may defecate anywhere, ideally in an isolated corner, after which they present themselves to a female to be washed. Weaning often is delayed until the mother is well on with her next pregnancy; a mother's final child often is allowed to nurse until it loses interest, as late as age six. (Late-weaners have long been eating a variety of solid foods, too.)

One explanation for this casual approach is that joint households have an inhibiting effect on adult–child interaction.[44] Adult males are infrequently in the courtyard. Instead, it is populated by women and older girls, none of whom is eager to take responsibility for the youngsters. And as previously noted, young mothers must very largely ignore their own progeny when both are in the company of others, including close relatives.

A second explanation is that a youngster's future family roles, occupational expectations, and marriage options are known to all in advance. So it's assumed that children don't need explicit guidance; there's plenty of time for them to pick up adult ways. They're immersed in a sea of role models who, day by day, enact what membership in an interdependent family looks like.

One Indian put it this way: "You Westerners bring up your children. We live with ours."

Finally, there's also a philosophical reason for laissez-faire child-rearing: the Hindu perspective on children.[45] This teaches that a newborn arrives with inborn tendencies to enact certain types of behavior, which parental rearing cannot alter in any major way. Nature is key; nurture has limited efficacy. The Hindi term for rearing someone, *palna-posna*, means "protective nurturance," not deliberate training or shaping. Rearing needs to be a process in which children are subtly induced to renounce their internal inclinations and adapt their attitudes and behavior to the indirect and implicit signals of those around them. Mothers often signal displeasure not by making demands, but by changing their mood. Through this upbringing, Indians learn heightened sensitivity to situational nuances and nonverbal signals—"radar" instead of our "gyroscope."

Casual rearing phases out between ages three and six, depending on the region in which the family lives and the practices of the family's jāti. Sometimes it occurs when the next child is born; it always occurs after the child has basic facility in the local language. This transition does not mean that children begin learning how to contribute to the family's economy and well-being. Rather, it means that adults begin insisting on the children's compliance with family and jāti norms, on obedience, on respect for elders—and on peace and quiet. Older relatives encourage children's obedience in several ways.[46]

On the positive side, body-to-body physical affection is much preferred over both tangible rewards (very rare) and direct verbal praise for a specific achievement. For example, a young child is likely be hugged and shown big smiles by his mother because he was obedient to her wishes, but rarely because he carried out a specific act well. Verbal praise is used sparingly; it is seen as inflating a child's ego, which spoils one's character by building self-esteem and pride. Adults do their best to avoid encouraging self-centeredness in children because it short-circuits their development of "radar," keen alertness to the sentiments of others so that the child can be guided by *their* reactions. One anthropologist put it this way: "The sense of self-worth comes from fulfilling expectations of important others."

On the negative side, the most common form of discipline is verbal scolding, often consisting of a curse or insult. These range from a simple "Go away!," through "Sister-seducer!," and on to "Go to hell!" Or a child might be called by the name of a low jāti (e.g., *"Scavenger!"*), which is effective because it cites an absence of jāti-appropriate behavior, implying a humiliating loss of status. Other strategies include teasing and ridicule, threatening blows (but rarely landing them), and warning of the child's kidnapping by ghosts, animals such as jackals—or even by Americans.

When children are constantly surrounded by family, shaming or the threat of shaming is another way by which adults persuade them to behave. But what happens when school attendance begins, or when joint families split into small households, so that children aren't always under surveillance by kinfolk? One anthropologist found that adults employ shaming techniques less often than in children's early years and, instead, begin appealing to a child's internal controls.[47] In other words, adults less often warn, "Do this because it's *how we do things* around here" (penalty: being shamed by others); they more often advise, "Do this because it's the *right thing* to do" (penalty: experiencing internal guilt).

Early Childcare among the Economically Disadvantaged Jātis

Among poverty-stricken families (not only the Dalits), the care of younger children differs sharply from that described above.[48] This difference occurs mainly because mothers must contribute to the family's income.

After the youngest child turns three, the mother as well as the father leaves home daily to earn a living. (The restrictions of purdah are ignored when your family is fending off starvation.) Even in joint households, all the adults are away except possibly the aged ones. The children must fend for themselves. Who looks after the youngest ones? Their older siblings. And that's not all. Describing life in West Bengal, two anthropologists write that poverty-stricken families depend to a great extent on their girls for the daily gathering of protein, vegetables, and fuel.

> Girls help from the age of five or six by collecting cow dung to make fuel cakes. Girls of seven or eight collect snails and fish from paddy fields, and gather potatoes, onions and, for fuel, twigs and wood. The girls mix cow dung and straw, then plaster the mixture on the wall as round cakes. After drying, these cakes are collected and sold as fuel.[49]

As early as age six, a girl can be running her household, including cooking and childcare. Boys are thought to need a few more years before they can take on male tasks such as fixing lanterns, ironing clothes, and herding animals to their pastures and back. Boys lacking older sisters might care for younger siblings but try to avoid female tasks such as cooking, hauling water, and tending fires.

Infants and toddlers in these families spend more time with their own mothers than occurs in upper-status households. Mothers sometimes take their babies with them to work, whether in the fields or homes of better-off villagers. When an anthropologist followed a mother and her four daughters into a field one day, she observed the mother working and a one-and-a-half-year-old girl sitting on the grass eating green peas; her five-year-old sister stripped the peas from growing stalks and handed them to her. When the mother and two older daughters had finished cutting fodder, the five-year-old put the baby in a position to defecate. The two older sisters and mother did not wait for the baby to finish but set out for home, each carrying a large bundle of fodder on her head. The five-year-old was considered quite competent to care for the baby and bring her home later.[50]

Because parents and children as young as five share their family's economic burdens, parents have an egalitarian relationship and the children often enjoy warm bonds with their parents. Parents sometimes even praise their children.

Six-year-old Chinta cares for her two-year-old brother and two sisters, one age four, one an infant. Chinta's mother said, "She looks small, but she can work like a big girl. When I go to work, she is responsible for feeding herself, her brother, and her sister. She also carries her infant sister and feeds her milk." While her mother spoke, Chinta went to her father and rubbed her head on his chest. He smiled at her approvingly.[51]

You and I are prone to react along the lines of, "It's not even conceivable that a six-year-old could actually care for three younger siblings *all day, every day*!"

But it's not forced child labor; it's everyday life for Indian families that are constantly fending off starvation. One outcome is the children of such families gain a dynamic capacity for assuming full responsibility for vital family functions far sooner than we Americans even imagine possible.

How do they learn responsibility?[52] There is little overt training for self-reliance or responsibility. When the mother returns to work, older siblings aid the youngest one to learn to care for him- or herself and, a few years later, to learn to assist the next newcomer. Rarely are tasks assigned; rarely is one child put in charge. The siblings simply begin doing tasks as they have seen others doing them.

LEARNING TO BE INDIAN: THE LATER CHILDHOOD YEARS

As Indian youngsters progress into the middle years of childhood, the contrast between the upper- and middle-status jātis and the economically disadvantaged ones continues.

Later Childcare among the Upper- and Middle-Status Jātis

The expectations of higher-status families regarding their school-age children vary considerably, depending on their jāti's customs and the region in which they live. An anthropologist who lived with a family in southern India writes that its children

> were rough-and-tumble, disobedient, competitive, mysterious. None of them had any duties or chores in the household except to learn lessons, which they did poorly. When they were out of school, they would tear around the house wildly or play in the dust of the temple yard across the street.[53]

But anthropologists whose fieldwork was in the north write that, following virtually task-free early years, older girls wash dishes and clothes, tend babies, serve men food, pick vegetables, and more.[54] Some boys routinely take care of the cattle and assist in the fields; others are expected to focus on their schoolwork and help in the fields only during weekends and harvests. Despite this work,

> adults tend to belittle children's contributions because they are aware of their inept performance. Perhaps for this reason, most children are not notably self-reliant or conscientious. When schoolwork is challenging, they are likely to consult another student instead of figuring it out themselves. And outside of school, children seldom undertake a task beyond their ability. They get someone else to do the work.[55]

On the other hand, from the same northern locality we also have the following account of a child's self-reliant perseverance in spite of adults' discouragement:

> A six-year-old girl was trying to embroider a little piece of cloth. Her aunt and grandmother were nearby but did not help her. She threaded the needle after many tries and then followed the lines of the design, carefully counting the stitches and correcting her mistakes. After five minutes, her aunt and grandmother inspected her work and told her to take it all out because she was ruining the cloth. But the girl continued to work and correct her mistakes.[56]

The child-rearing objective of higher-status parents is not preparation for a productive adulthood, nor is it the building of capacity for self-reliance.[57] Those are American concerns. Rather, upper-status Indian parents foster in their children a strong sense of family unity, of "we-ness," grounded in empathic sensitivity by each toward all the others. The focus is on relationships. A child entering puberty already is, and remains, enmeshed in interdependent family life. Absent are the tumultuous years of "adolescence" that many in the West have come to expect.

As a boy advances in age, his relationship with his father changes.[58] When he was a child, he and his father might have been affectionate toward one another. But as the son attains middle childhood, he and his father become emotionally distant because the father is expected to be a disciplinarian and the son is now accountable for his actions. The father's decisions are never questioned. After a son marries, he might gain some responsibilities. But as long as the father remains sentient, his sons are not accorded full adult status.

To a researcher's query about his responsibilities, a 35-year-old father replied, "I am only a young boy, madam! My father is alive; what is my responsibility?"

Between mothers and sons exists a tender, dependable bond that is celebrated and romanticized in traditional and popular culture.[59] One's mother is respected, revered, and loved. When a son's childhood is past and the custom that required her to ignore him in the courtyard has weakened, a mother is never aloof toward her son. But their relationship is jostled when he marries, as we'll soon see.

Let's consider the middle-childhood years of girls by first gaining a historical perspective. In a book published in 1910, a woman recalls her late-1800s childhood:

> The girls of our family were carefully guarded from any modern ideas. No females over eight years were allowed to appear before the men, or even to come outside the house. We knew nothing of reading, and the word "writing" had no meaning for us. As long as my father's mother was living, she had ruled the home. Her grandchildren were never allowed to speak to their father in her presence; they lived in terror of him. After she died, my father was freed to follow his own desire. He made much of his baby daughter, playing with and petting me. I took liberties with him—within limits. One of my sisters was married in her fifth year, the other in her seventh. I had no one to play with. I had friends among our neighbors but couldn't play with them often. My father didn't like his girls to go elsewhere to play; neither would he endure the noise and commotion we made when the other children came to see us.[60]

By the mid-1900s, the experience of most upper-status girls was different.[61] Around the age of six or seven, a girl's parents begin to be motivated by concern over her eventual marriageability. Her father might pamper her or remain aloof, but her mother must ensure that she will become an admirable daughter-in-law—demure, obedient, and skillful in the domestic arts. The girl begins to assist in the care of others, especially her junior siblings, which includes expressing authority over them. As she approaches puberty, her mother usually draws closer to her, knowing that soon she'll disappear into her husband's household, a thought that softens discipline with compassion. We'll continue this story in the next section.

Later Childcare among the Economically Disadvantaged Jātis

"Later childcare" is misleading. By the time children in economically disadvantaged households reach age six or seven, they are routinely *giving* the childcare—which attracted the attention of two anthropologists. From their accounts of children at work in the state of West Bengal, here are excerpts from two:

> One day, eleven-year-old Milan collected a large basket of cow dung for fuel; she also gathered large palm fruit and a medium-sized basket of greens. Two days later she collected more cow dung and greens, plus a small basket of crabs and snails for sales and home consumption. Also for her family's meals, she's always alert for other edible plants such as mushrooms. Every day, Milan herds ten cows and buffaloes for six hours. She cleans the cow shed, prepares the fodder, and collects milk to supply to a high-caste home. Often when she returns from herding at about 4:00 PM, she takes her little brother with her to play with some friends. Her parents express to Milan their appreciation for her contributions; to others, they might even praise her openly.[62]
>
> Ten-year-old Santosh cooks for and feeds his two siblings while his parents are at work. When Santosh must leave for cow herding, he leaves his siblings for a few hours with a neighbor. Santosh's parents, like others, hope to have their son become a *mahinder*,[63] thus ensuring additional food for the family. In West Bengal, an untouchable boy starts at around age nine as a domestic servant for a high-caste landowner. He receives three meals a day (some of which can be taken home), a fixed monthly salary, and clothing twice a year. A *mahinder* works all year round, cultivating land and performing other services inside and outside the house. Many *mahinders* enjoy a life-long relationship with their respective families, receiving gifts during their own family's ceremonies.[64]

TEENAGE GIRLS' MOMENTOUS TRANSITION

Here's a thought experiment: You're an Indian girl who has just experienced her first menses. As you well know, this event signals to everyone that you're now marriageable. You have *seen* boys in your age-group, but the concept of "dating" is absent from your mindset. You are scarcely even acquainted with any young males other than those in your extended family. And now that you're a nubile maiden, adults in your household make doubly sure that you never, ever leave the premises alone. Yet *now* is the time to marry. What do you do?

Nothing. It's your parents' concern, primarily your father's. Just wait.

For Hindu parents, giving a virgin daughter in marriage is a highly meritorious act.[65] So parents usually get the process moving with little delay. The process centers on negotiations between two households, potentially leading to their establishment of affinal ties. But step one isn't a father-to-father declaration of interest, but the arrival of a priest at the boy's home to request a copy of his horoscope. The identity of the girl's family is not revealed.

The factors considered by negotiating fathers are beyond the scope of this book. But two deserve attention.

The first is the dowry: cash and in-kind valuables given by the wife-sending household to the wife-receiving one. Dowries often are extravagant, and the necessity of funding one presents the girl's parents with a dilemma. They'd prefer her to "marry up," which would be prestigious. But a high-status boy's family will expect an over-the-top dowry, which can bring the girl's family to financial ruin. And what if they have three or four daughters?

The second is the role of the boy and girl. We Americans worry that romantic love will be lacking. Correct. In India's traditional villages, *that* kind of love is not a concern. Consider this discussion between an anthropologist and two teenagers:

> Today Mita and her sister Sita and I discussed marriage in India and the U.S. They asked about divorce. "Why would anyone want to leave one's spouse?" I explained that husbands and wives are sometimes unhappy with each other. "But you are part of a *joint family*," they said, noting that in Indian homes a woman's relationships are mainly with other women; the source of unhappiness is more likely to be *them*, not one's husband. It made little sense to the sisters that the husband–wife relationship could be central to one's happiness. The father-in-law's joint household is central. I asked Mita if she'd have input to her father's choice of a groom. She replied that she *could* object to the potential groom when they had an "interview," a visit by the potential groom and his relatives to see the girl, which Mita described as "having to stand up and be examined." On what grounds could she object to the groom? Mita could not think of any.[66]

Indians raised in traditional villages rarely experience "love" as an intense, aching desire generated by a specific individual.[67] Rather, love is a deep sense of emotional connectedness with one's entire extended family. Love is about familial interdependence and a sense of duty to the group. Within an extended family, a husband–wife bond is incidental.[68]

In the life of every girl, there's a Great Divide: that fateful day when she leaves home to begin the rest of her life in her new husband's household.[69] As one scholar said, "In story, proverb, and song, the society has from her earliest years reminded her of the sharpness of the transition at marriage, and of the possible hostility of the mother-in-law and sisters-in-law." Onlookers' hearts are stirred by the poignant scene of the bride being driven away while members of her family grieve.

Depending on the region of India and the groom's jāti, a bride's reception in her new home varies.[70] Two examples: She might be obliged to wear her bridal clothes and jewels for several days. Her in-laws scrutinize her for any lapse of etiquette or skill; if these persist, they send her parents a message of reprimand. Alternatively, she and her dowry might be put on display every afternoon for several days so that the women of the husband's lineage may come to look. The bride, the end of her long scarf over her head, sits huddled on the floor while the visitors voice comparisons with previous brides and dowries. No one speaks to her.

The new bride doesn't delay contributing to her new household.[71] She's given the most onerous chores. She must constantly be busy and self-effacing. Whatever misfortunes come to the household may be blamed on her: *The pot was golden if the daughter-in-law broke it, but earthen if the mother-in-law broke it.*

Mothers-in-law tend to be taskmasters, not comforters; most other women in the household are poised to be critical. Communication with her husband's father and elder brothers is minimal; they sometimes cough before entering a room where she is so she can leave. On the bright side, brides may develop joking relationships with her husband's younger siblings or with another brother's wife, though these take time to establish. Her husband? He never openly shows regard for her, which she must reciprocate. (Don't despair: At night they sleep together.)

Her burdens lighten when she becomes pregnant, for she's fulfilling her raison d'être. Matters significantly improve after she gives birth—especially if it's a boy.

Young married women may go home for extended visits. Customs differ. In the state of Uttar Pradesh, a woman visiting her parents is dealt with as a guest, free from tasks.[72] She need not observe purdah and may visit old friends. Some women even deliver their first child in their parents' home.

Women's emotional ties to their natal villages are so strong that they persist throughout life, no matter how well they adjust to their in-laws' villages. But a wife's paramount loyalty is expected to always be to her husband's household.

INFORMAL LEARNING BY VILLAGE INDIAN CHILDREN

Most Indian adults grew up in homes where there were many children, most of whom made it to adulthood despite having parents who were not worrying about how best to "raise" them.[73] For reasons that we've already explored in the section on the early childhood years, child-rearing is laissez-faire and impersonal. In fact, it's been suggested that the whole concept of "child-rearing" scarcely exists.

Yes, infants and toddlers are caressed and amused. But the idea of taking a break specifically to play with an older child is rare among villagers. Adults have little awareness of older children's activities. Two mothers put it this way:

Why should I make myself small by getting into their quarrels?

I have so much to do. I don't mind whatever they play. I just pray to God they'll go out and play.[74]

It's common to see Indian children quietly observing events and conversations unfolding in their courtyards. Increasingly, boys watch older males and girls watch older females; in this way they begin internalizing the expectations of their jāti and family regarding for their future gender roles. If the courtyard includes a grandmother, the youngsters might hear recitations of proverbs, folktales, and myths from Indian epics, which—as the youngsters come to understand more and more—give meaning to what they're seeing, such as everyone's unfailing deference to hierarchy.

When youngsters aren't silently observing others, they're being talked to by others. Occasionally they receive instruction, including patient demonstrations, about how to carry out simple tasks. Here's an example from near Delhi:

A two-year-old girl would be instructed by her mother to hold the tail of her shirt in such a way as to be able to carry lentils to a nearby container, into which she slowly and carefully poured them. She might spend half an hour working with her mother on this task whenever her mother cleaned lentils. She would, as soon as she was able, be asked to lift and carry various objects to her mother or any adult in the household.[75]

Almost all youngsters learn the proper use of the left and right hands.[76] Use of the left hand to clean oneself after defecating becomes a habit by age three. More skill is required to eat only with the right hand. Imagine using *solely* your right hand to tear off a small piece of bread, then use it to pick up cooked food. Mothers and older sisters usually need to manipulate small hands before a child masters this.

But the big picture is that youngsters are largely left to their own devices. As the mother quoted above said, adults pray to God they'll go out and play.

At the end of the section about newborns' arrival, I noted that if young children want attention, entertainment, or food from others, they learn to make multiple requests. As they grow older, the lesson they learn shifts to "expect others to do things for you." (Keep in mind that we're considering the middle- and upper-status jātis here, not the disadvantaged ones.) One anthropologist concluded that Indian children are *actively dependent*,[77] a tendency observed and written about by anthropologists working in three regions. In the northern state of Uttar Pradesh:

> Little work is expected of children aged four and five. The few chores that are assigned are irregular and brief (e.g., little girls might occasionally wash a dish or two). Self-reliance training is almost as scarce as training in responsibility. Mothers still dress, bathe, and feed children of this age. If the children want something, they ask their mother instead of trying to solve the problem by themselves.[78]

In the eastern state of Orissa:

> If the children attempted to feed, bathe, or dress themselves, mothers frequently interfered. Many forcibly fed their children up to the age of seven or eight.

> Following weaning, a mother might retain full control by insisting upon hand-feeding her child. She will most likely insist on bathing her child as well. Thus, children are kept physically dependent until about ten years of age.[79]

And in the southern state of Kerala:

> Children were expected to await assistance from others rather than do things on their own. It was not unusual to find a six- or seven-year-old being carried on someone's hip. Shyness was considered natural, especially for girls. A child who asserted himself too much or gave signs of originality was derided as "too forward and bold."[80]

The question is why? Most likely, the answer is that learning to rely for just about everything on family members lays the foundation for a key cultural trait of village Indians: an unshakable expectation of familial interdependence.[81] What a growing youngster informally learns is how to avoid self-*anything* and instead fit smoothly into, and unfailingly prioritize, the effective functioning of the household.

FORMAL LEARNING BY VILLAGE INDIAN CHILDREN

Primary schools were available in most areas during the mid-1900s, but in many traditional villages, interest among parents in sending their children to school was low. Let's imagine ourselves in the sandals of the father of young children:

You never attended school.[82] The skills that you use, and that you see other adults using, are not due to school attendance. (The single exception is the Hindu priest.) You know that going to school *might* enable your child to attain a paying, nonagricultural job. But that's *years* from now, on top of which you've never been convinced that schools teach anything useful about the essentials of living.

Then there's the question of which child to send. Could schooling help one of your daughters marry up? Not likely—and it's a dubious investment because a daughter ends up benefitting another family. If you're going to send anyone, it'll be a son. Sons are future household heads and care for aged parents—you! If a son can get a job with a steady income, that will benefit *your* extended family.

Can your sons succeed in school? It's a mystery to you that pupils are expected to study at home even though they spend hours each day in school. Where is homework going to occur? Your home is crowded; everyone goes to bed after dark. And what's the point? If a child must do homework to succeed, then he wasn't born with the right innate predisposition. He shouldn't even be in school.

Nothing in your experience has prepared you to grasp that school learning is cumulative. You assume that pupils simply memorize passages as directed by teachers. So you won't hesitate to keep your son home whenever he's needed to work in the fields, to run errands, or to care for an infant when no girl is available.

If you're leaning toward "yes" for one of your sons, you must face the certainty of out-of-pocket costs for books, uniforms, exam fees, and so forth. Well, one thing's for sure: If you do send a son to school, you will diligently monitor his performance. Should he begin to falter, you'll pull him out at once. Why waste time and money?

All those hurdles having been cleared, one of your sons is sent to the village primary school. What does he experience there?[83] His classes are held outdoors on a platform as well as in adjacent rooms; the boys sit on the ground or on their own mats and write on slates. Reading, writing, and numbers are taught during the first two years; other subjects such as history and geography after that. (If the village has a primary school for girls, it might be obscured behind high walls.)

The crucial fact about schooling in India during the mid-1900s was that everyone in the community accepted without question that memorization was the path to learning. Much of each school day was devoted to memorizing—questions and their answers, problems and their solutions, poems, multiplication tables, even lengthy essays. Children worked individually or in pairs. The teacher checked for accuracy by asking a pupil to recite; absence of accurate recall could yield a beating with a cane. Thus, fear of making errors was instilled early. The whole ethos of learning-to-perfection-via-memorization inhibited original thinking.

Teachers distinguished between "memorization" and "rote" even though pupils attain both through multiple repetitions.[84] When asked to recite, if a pupil recalled the repeated material imperfectly, his teacher claimed he had tried to learn it by rote, a mindless process. But if the pupil recalled the material accurately, his teacher said he had "memorized" it, implying some degree of comprehension.

You and I might think that "learning" resulting in word-for-word reproduction of a text is pointless. But hold on. We're talking about pupils being raised at home to assume that they are indistinguishable (other than bodily) from, and dependent on, their families. Attending school weakens that assumption because there, each pupil is dealt with as a separate individual. Even if he shows no more learning than rattling off a memorized text, *it is he who accomplished this*. He is demonstrating "agency," the ability of *an individual* to intentionally act to produce a result. If you are a child from a traditional Indian family, that's huge.

FROM AN ANTHROPOLOGICAL PERSPECTIVE

More than any of the societies dealt with in the previous four chapters, Indian society has its ethical foundation in a body of ancient spiritual texts. The discourses found in those scriptures on ideal family living have plenty to say about parent–child relations. These ideals have long remained persuasive in thousands of traditional Indian villages, which the culture-disrupting British Raj largely ignored.

Fundamental to those ideals is the all-encompassing unity of one's extended family, that is, one's forebears and relatives through the male line. Yes, an individual identifies with his village and his jāti, but nothing eclipses his commitment to blood relatives. For Indian parents, children's growing maturity is demonstrated by their acceptance of familial interdependence: expecting to be fully cared for by their parents and older relatives while acknowledging that they will care for their parents in their old age.[85] For middle- and upper-status extended families, the main goals for up-and-coming children are *social*: to fit harmoniously into the extended family by mastering its relationship patterns, and to develop interpersonal "radar" that enables them to adapt to whatever interpersonal situations they encounter.

For lower-status families, it's also important for children to harmoniously fit in. But due to the necessity of bringing in enough food and money to avoid starvation, *every able family member* contributes to that goal every day, including even five-year-olds. Unlike their peers in higher-status jātis, lower-status children gain self-reliance and take on adult responsibilities—with virtually no parental guidance.

Summary of Village Indian Children's Learning and Socialization

Based on anthropologists' findings, I believe that five key features of how village Indian children are socialized into adulthood are the following. Village Indian children . . .

- experience a learning curve driven by their families' social status.
- are looked after by many; no child is the focus of one adult's attention.
- learn social skills in a context of hierarchy and interdependence.
- grow and develop despite scant parental interest in their activities.
- begin adapting to their gender-linked roles gradually after age six.

Children experience a learning curve driven by their families' social status. Of the five societies presented in this book, Indian society is by far the most diverse—and the most difficult about which to offer a generalization about how children learn. However, anthropological findings reveal that there's an enduring contrast between the experiences of children from the upper- and middle-status jātis, and the experiences of children from the economically disadvantaged jātis.

There are differences in detail among the hundreds of different ethnic groups that call India home. Nevertheless, it seems that among members of the upper- and middle-status jātis, adults have little or no expectation that young children should pitch in on household chores or begin learning any practical skill other than key politeness norms such as proper use of the left and right hands. The Hindi term *palna-posna* means "protective nurturance," not deliberate training. Even when children reach the age of five or six, adults' expectations are limited to their children's figuring out how to comply with family and jāti norms, how to show respect to their elders, and how to maintain peace and quiet.

Middle- and upper-status parents in several regions of India are determined that their children will develop a powerful sense of family unity, of "we-ness," grounded in empathic sensitivity by each toward all the other members. So important is this objective that children are deliberately conditioned from infancy to become what one anthropologist termed "actively dependent," meaning that they learn to rely for the fulfillment of virtually every need—including even putting food into their own mouths—on other family members and are discouraged from gaining more than minimal self-reliance.

In low-status households living on the brink of starvation, a youngster's early years could hardly be more different. The mother must work outside the home, so she leaves each child who's just turned three in the company of his or her older siblings. Parents provide virtually no instruction in responsibility or self-reliance, and they neither assign tasks nor designate one child as the leader. Their children have no choice but to figure it out by themselves. By all accounts, they do. As well, they find ways of directly contributing to their family's economy every day.

Children are looked after by many; no child is the focus of one adult's attention. From day one, newborns are constantly in the company of women, leading some to assume that infants are shamelessly indulged. The reverse is true. Infants arouse neither fascination nor anxiety—which is easy for the women because they all have previously cared for at least one youngster. A child's mother isn't supposed to so much as smile at him when anyone else is nearby. She nurses him in an impersonal manner, completing her tasks all the while. When another woman picks up the child, she props him on her hip and gets on with her work. Childcare is a *practical* concern. Never alone, a child is not the focus of anyone's affectionate attention except, occasionally, that of a grandfather, neighbor girl, or visiting uncle. As one Indian put it, "You Westerners bring up your children. We live with ours."

Children learn social skills in a context of hierarchy and interdependence. In Indian villages, the attention to hierarchies—higher–lower distinctions among jātis, occupations, neighborhoods, and families—extends into intrafamily relationships. Woven through familial hierarchy rules are traditional customs about household relations (e.g., strictures governing a new bride in her in-laws' household). As if all that weren't enough, there are also personality factors (e.g., the mother-in-law who rules her household). In middle- and upper-status jātis, relationship skill-building begins by age six, initially facilitated by children's learning to read their mothers' moods and later becoming fine-tuned as they adjust their behavior to relatives' scolding and shaming—every persuasive tool except praise. Young people eventually gain social "radar"—sensitivity and adaptability to every sort of interpersonal situation. If deliberate training occurs, it's when someone ensures that children are mastering kinship terms and correctly using them to address relatives—far more kinship terms for far more categories of relatives than most speakers of English ever imagined.

In low-status homes, there's little time for the niceties of relationship skill-building. Every able family member must get out and work, leaving children aged three and up home alone. The result? It's not unusual for a child of six or seven to be running a household *and* contributing to the family's nutrition and its finances.

Children grow and develop despite scant parental interest in their activities. Our American passion for planful "child-raising" is virtually nonexistent among village Indians. They share none of our eagerness to talk with, play with, and buy toys for children, and they don't arrange team sports or learning excursions for them. They pay very little attention to whatever activities children themselves devise, and they refuse to referee their squabbles. But before you conclude that Indian youngsters have a bleak childhood, consider this: They are literally *never alone*. During their waking hours, they have other children to play with in the courtyard and, later, in the street. They do not sleep alone. Babysitters are unknown because whenever the adults in a household leave to attend any event—many of which, such as weddings and Hindu rituals, are family-oriented—the children go, too. Bottom line: Nothing is done to enhance a child's development as a self-reliant individual; everything is done to draw him or her ever more tightly into the enveloping bosom of his or her interdependent extended family.

Children begin adapting to their gender-linked roles gradually after age six. Few male–female distinctions are made, at least overtly, when children are born and into their years of early childhood. Youngsters in middle- and upper-status homes sometimes devise gender-linked ways of playing—boys mimic farming, girls imitate cooking and tending children—but rarely are chores that promote family welfare expected of them. When children turn six, they gradually begin helping in gender-appropriate ways: girls wash things, pick vegetables, look after babies, and serve men food; boys help in the fields and care for cattle, less so if they have schoolwork to complete. In middle childhood, one's relationships with parents shift. A boy begins to experience his father as a disciplinarian, while he and his mother lay the foundation for lifelong deep affection and high regard. A girl increasingly is drawn under her mother's wing. It's her mother who is responsible for ensuring that she will be perceived as a worthy bride, and for conditioning her to withstand and adapt uncomplainingly to the rigors of her early years in her in-laws' household—until she proves her worth by becoming a mother.

SUGGESTED FURTHER READING

Each of the readings below is profiled at howotherchildrenlearn.info/profiles.

The Rajputs of Khalapur, India, by Leigh Minturn & John Hitchcock (1966); 155 text pages.

Women, Family, and Child Care in India: A World in Transition, by Susan C. Seymour (1999); 291 text pages.

Notes on Love in a Tamil Family, by Margaret Trawick (1992); 258 text pages.

BIBLIOGRAPHY

Chaudhary, Nandita. (2012). The father's role in the Indian family: A story that must be told. *Fathers in Cultural Context*, David Schwalb, et al., eds. Taylor & Francis: 68–94.

Edwards, Carolyn Pope. (2005). Children's play in cross-cultural perspective: A new look at the Six Culture Study. *Faculty Publications: Department of Child, Youth, and Family Studies*. University of Nebraska–Lincoln, 1–23.

Freed, Ruth S., & Stanley A. Freed. (1981). Enculturation and education in Shanti Nagar. *Anthropological Papers of The American Museum of Natural History, 57* (2), 49–156.

Gideon, Helen. (1962). A baby is born in Punjab. *American Anthropologist, 64* (6), 1220–1234.

Gough, Kathleen. (1956). Brahmin kinship in a Tamil village. *American Anthropologist, 58*, 834–853.

Hossain, Ziarat, & Giovanna Eisberg. (2020). Parenting and academic socialization of young children: Sociocultural context for early childhood development in South Asian families. *Parents and Caregivers Across Cultures: Positive Development from Infancy Through Adulthood*, Brien Ashdown & Amanda Faherty, eds. Springer, 89–104.

Isaac, Rita, I. K. Annie, & H. R. Prashanth. (2014). Parenting in India. In *Parenting Across Cultures: Childrearing, Motherhood, and Fatherhood in Non-Western Cultures*, H. Selin, ed. Springer Media, 39–45.

Kennedy, Beth C. (1954). Rural–urban contrasts in parent-child relations in India. *Indian Journal of Social Work, 15*, 162–174.

Kurtz, Stanley. (1992). *All the mothers are one: Hindu India and the cultural reshaping of psychoanalysis*. Columbia University Press.

Madan, T. N. (1989). *Family and kinship: A study of the Pandits of Rural Kashmir*. Oxford University Press.

Mandelbaum, David G. (1970). *Society in India. Volume One: Continuity and Change*. University of California Press.

Mencher, Joan. (1963). Growing up in South Malabar. *Human Organization, 22*, 54–65.

Minturn, Leigh, & John Hitchcock. (1966). *The Rajputs of Khalapur, India*. John Wiley & Sons.

Narain, Dhirendra. (1964). Growing up in India. *Family Process, 3*, 127–154.

Opler, Morris. (1958). Spirit possession in a rural area of Northern India. *Reader in Comparative Religion*, W. A. Lessa & E. Z. Vogt, eds. Row, Peterson, 553–566.

Paiva, Nupur Dhingra. (2008). South Asian parents' constructions of praising their children. *Clinical Child Psychology and Psychiatry, 13* (2), 191–207.

Raj, Stacey P., & Vaishali V. Raval. (2013). Parenting and family socialization within a cultural context. *Socialization: Theories, Processes, and Impact*, Ethan Anderson & Sophia Thomas, eds. Nova Science, 57–78.

Ranade, Ramabai. (1938). *Himself: The autobiography of a Hindu Lady*. Translated from Marathi by Katherine Van Akin Gates. Longmans, Green & Co. [Originally published in the Marathi language during 1910.]

Rohner, Ronald P., & Manjusri Chaki-Sircar. (1988). *Women and children in a Bengali village*. University Press of New England.

Roland, Alan. (1988). *In search of self in India and Japan: Toward a cross-cultural psychology*. Princeton University Press.

Sarangapani, Padma M. (2003). *Constructing school knowledge: An ethnography of learning in an Indian village*. Sage.

Saraswathi, T. S., & Shefali Pai. (1997). Socialization in the Indian context. *Asian Perspectives on Psychology*, Henry Kao & Durganand Sinha, eds. Sage Publications, 74–92.

Seymour, Susan. (1975). Child rearing in India: A case study in change and modernization. *Socialization and Communication in Primary Groups*, Thomas R. Williams, ed. Mouton, 41–58.

Seymour, Susan. (1976). Caste/class and child-rearing in a changing Indian town. *American Ethnologist, 3* (4), 783–796.

Seymour, Susan. (1980). Patterns of childrearing in a changing Indian town. *The Transformation of a Sacred Town: Bhubaneswar, India*. Susan Seymour, ed. Westview Press, 121–56.

Seymour, Susan. (1983). Household structure and status and expressions of affect in India. *Ethos, 11*, 263–277.

Seymour, Susan C. (1988). Expressions of responsibility among Indian children: Some precursors of adult status and sex roles. *Ethos, 16* (4), 355–370.

Seymour, Susan C. (1999). *Women, family, and child care in India.* Cambridge University Press.

Seymour, Susan. (2004). Multiple caretaking of infants and young children: An area in critical need of a feminist psychological anthropology. *Ethos, 32* (4), 538–56.

Seymour, Susan C. (2013). The Harvard–Bhubaneswar, India, project. *The Asian Man, 7* (1–2), 1–8.

Sharma, Dinesh, & Robert A. LeVine. (1998). Child care in India: A comparative developmental view of infant social environments. *New Directions for Child Development, 81* (Fall), 45–67.

Trawick, Margaret. (1992). *Notes on love in a Tamil family.* University of California Press.

Tuli, Mila. (2012). Beliefs on parenting and childhood in India. *Journal of Comparative Family Studies, 43* (1), 81–91.

Ullrich, Helen E. (2017). Conclusion: Transition in totagadde from 1964 to 2011. *The Women of Totagadde: Broken Silence*, Helen Ullrich, ed. Palgrave Macmillan, 227–242.

Whiting, Beatrice B., & John W. M. Whiting. (1975). *Children of six cultures: A psycho-cultural analysis.* Harvard University Press.

Whiting, Beatrice Blyth, & Carolyn Pope Edwards. (1988). *Children of different worlds: The formation of social behavior.* Harvard University Press.

Yasir, Sameer. (2022). Documenting the scope of India's linguistic riches. *The New York Times*, 11 June 2022, A4.

Chapter 7

How Do Other Children
Learn Responsibility?

Chapter 8 will contain my summary of what traditional societies tell us about how other children learn and other parents parent. But first I want to summarize what those societies tell us about how other children readily learn to be responsible.

I'm using "responsibility" to refer to an individual's taking the initiative, without being reminded, to carry out a task that benefits the entire group to which he or she belongs, usually a task repeated on a daily or weekly basis. A person with a "sense of responsibility" is one who willingly completes group-oriented tasks.

In the Introduction, I looked askance at recent books that identify a problem experienced by American parents, then explain how parents in another society deal successfully with it: "We've got a problem; *they've* got a solution!" I admit that this chapter will proceed similarly—but with this difference. I am not going to propose a solution from a single society, devoid of background and context. This chapter occurs near the end of a book that explores five traditional societies, including a discussion of each one's background and context. In addition, I'll be drawing on a body of related findings from anthropological fieldwork. So what I'll share with you is collective wisdom about how other children become responsible—or, more accurately, *the circumstances under which* they become responsible.

One more thing. Two of the societies focused on by this book turn out to not be useful for our present purpose. Following weaning, Aka youngsters may do pretty much whatever they want all the way to young adulthood; they may even ignore their parents' requests for assistance. And among the middle- and upper-status *jātis* of India, there is no expectation among adults that youngsters should learn self-reliance or a skill, or should significantly contribute to household chores. These two are not representative of traditional societies in general.

THE ROOTS OF RESPONSIBILITY

Traditional peoples sustain themselves by relying on the land (or sea).[1] Pastoralists live on the products of domesticated animals. Foragers hunt for edible animals and plants. Farmers sow seeds and harvest crops. These labor-intensive ways of sustaining life are most effectively carried out by many workers coordinated by an experienced, respected leader. Extended families are well suited for such work.

An extended family is well suited in another way. Additional foragers, farmers, or pastoralists are always welcome, and each family generates its own. And that's not all. As workers grow old and become infirm, they need to be supported. Again, children are the ideal solution; those aging workers are their own parents.

In traditional societies, *children are needed.* They are not reckoned as "costs," for they soon become producers and caregivers whose contributions yield practical benefits for their parents, younger siblings, and extended family members.

However, infant and young child mortality is high.[2] Parents look forward to having many children, which will ensure that a sufficient number survives to assist them in their daily labors and to care for them in their old age. Anthropologists have termed as "quantitative" this set of values about family size because parents have many children but, following weaning, they do not strive to improve their children's quality of life.[3] Instead, beginning at age five or even younger, it's the children who help to sustain their parents' lives.

The circumstances of modern societies are completely different. The typical family does not sustain itself through labor-intensive foraging, farming, or grazing. Instead, at least one member works at a distance from home, or in a home office, and earns a wage or salary that sustains the family. His or her employment is as an individual; little helpers are not welcome at the job site. They must remain at home.

The home itself has cold—and hot!—water on tap. Cooking fires are instantly lit. Food is readily obtained in quantity and stored safely; day-long toil to acquire it is not necessary. Clothing also is readily obtained and need not be handmade. Heat, cold, and rain are kept at bay. The flick of a switch illuminates the night; the flick of another yields entertainment or enlightenment. And it's all made possible by the wage or salary earned by one or more adult family members.

What is there for children to do?

Roles, Responsibilities, and the Qualitative Approach to Child-Rearing

The reality of most modern children's lives is that they simply are not needed in any practical sense. Yes, many modern couples *want* children, and when children come most couples *love* them—but now we're talking about emotional satisfaction, not practical assistance and support. Unless a modern couple is living off the land to some extent (e.g., farming),[4] their children have no role to play in contributing to the family's sustenance or otherwise helping to maintain its economy or lifestyle.

In fact, the parent–child relationship is 180° reversed. Modern nonfarm parents sustain their children: give them food, buy their clothes and toys, hire child-minders, pay the costs related to their learning (e.g., school fees, music lessons), provide enrichment opportunities (e.g., family excursions, league sports, summer camps)—this list goes on and on! It's expensive and constantly demanding, so most couples limit the size of their brood. This set of values about family size has been termed "qualitative" because parents continually give their relatively few children benefits and advantages that increase the quality of their lives.[5]

The differences between the background and context of traditional societies on the one hand, and modern societies on the other, generate a fundamental contrast in how parents and children relate to one another:

In traditional societies, practical benefits flow *to parents* from children.
In modern societies, practical benefits flow *from parents* to children.[6]

In traditional societies, most extended families have visible practical needs for additional hands to help wring food from the land and care for aged and infirm relatives. Children supply those hands. Neither time, energy, nor (what we call) disposable income is available with which to enhance all those children's lives. Rather, they are needed to pitch in on the never-ending labor, which yields for them a sense of belonging and pride in their own burgeoning abilities. Children become accustomed to the role of carrying out tasks on a daily, weekly, or even seasonable basis for the benefit of the household and the entire family. *What I want is what we need.* For them, a children-to-parents benefit flow is normal. In short, they become responsible.

In modern societies, few middle-class families have visible practical needs, thanks to all those modern conveniences. Instead of multiple repetitive chores, many have, to some extent, disposable income. What is the role of a child in such a family? In place of any specific practical role—"Here, raise your just-weaned little brother"—children are vaguely expected to prepare for adulthood. This is understood to mean going to school to learn the prerequisite skill of adult life—the recognition and manipulation of symbols—plus other knowledge that adults need. A massive undertaking, but it doesn't use up children's time and energy.[7]

What I believe happens in many middle-class families goes something like this: A child is born. He or she is gorgeous, beloved, and priceless, spurring parents to feel highly protective of their little one, and to provide the best upbringing that their budget can afford. Parents with tight budgets sometimes deny themselves to free up funds to provide more than bare necessities for their child. They spend a great deal of time in their child's company, buy stuff that entertains and begins to educate him, take him to fun and fascinating places, inflate his self-esteem by responding with effuse admiration to all his performances, and much more. A precious child seems delicate to his parents, so besides being protective they make few demands on him except to ensure that he learns the basics of polite behavior. Their goal is a happy child who is getting a head start on schooling.

Modern parents give, give, give to their child, expecting very little in return. As a result, *the child has no practical role to play*. Instead, he or she gets, gets, gets.

As the years go by, more demanding career opportunities might be offered to one or both parents. Perhaps another infant or two arrives. A nicer home might necessitate a longer commute. Aging grandparents might need more attention. The child himself needs ferrying around. *Daily life gets busier*. It occurs to the parents that their family actually has at least one additional sets of hands to get chores done. So they ask the child to assist, to take responsibility for some tasks.

What is likely to be that child's response?

FINDINGS FROM ANTHROPOLOGICAL FIELDWORK

Reports of anthropologists' fieldwork in traditional societies are overflowing with accounts of children's practical contributions to their families' sustenance and well-being. Perhaps you recall examples from this book's five main chapters. Here are six more from a wide range of other societies. The first is from the 15th century, the second is from the 19th century, and the other four are recent:[8]

Germany. Children's fingerprints on the surface of Siegburg stoneware vessels of the 13th to 15th centuries have confirmed the employment of children (probably family members) in the unskilled task of transporting freshly thrown vessels from the wheel to the drying area.[9]

France. Jean de Brie, at the age of seven, was responsible for the care of the geese and goslings; at eight, minding pigs; at nine, helping a cowherd; by eleven, in charge of eighty lambs; at fourteen, 200 ewes.[10]

Liberia. I [anthropologist David Lancy] was led into the bush on a mushroom-hunting expedition by a group of Kpelle children barely out of toddlerhood. The atmosphere was entirely playful, yet the children were able to locate and gather edible mushrooms that were completely invisible to me.[11]

Papua New Guinea. On Ponam Island, children help to build and then learn to handle various size canoes, and they work various sections of the reef with different tools and techniques. They learn to make rope; work with wood; make a variety of traditional ornaments and costumes; and make various nets, spears, and other fishing gear.[12]

Samoa. The tiniest little staggerer has tasks to perform—to carry water, to borrow fire brands, to fetch leaves to stuff the pig. These slighter tasks are laid aside for harder ones as soon as the child becomes strong enough or skilled enough.[13]

Guatemala. The earliest task for which children are given actual responsibility is the running of errands. Considerably more difficult are the errands to the maize fields or others that require the child to go outside the community. Selling various items may include the cognitively complex task of soliciting buyers and making change.[14]

Also found in anthropologists' fieldwork reports are their observations about how the children themselves reacted to their roles and responsibilities.

Peru. When we were observing young children at home, it was evident that they felt proud of the things they could do, and when we were working with them in group sessions, they enthusiastically listed and drew all the things they were able to do to help at home. They were aware that the activities they participated in were duties they had to perform for the collective well-being of their families.[15]

Kenya. Giriama children understand that the tasks requested are necessary to the well-being of household members; they recognize that task assignment has a wider legitimacy than their parents' personal prerogative. Many care for small children, which develops strong bonds and has a significant long-term impact on the quality of children's relationships.[16]

Mexico. From an early age, Mayan children demonstrate a desire to be included in the dominant work activities of the household. They take pride in newly developed skills and the confidence that the adults come to place in them to do new tasks independently. Children three to five years old volunteer to do 40% of the work that they do. They are eager to become contributing members of the household.[17]

It's difficult to find anthropological studies that deliberately try to answer the question posed by this chapter's title. Fortunately, an excellent one does exist. Two researchers looked at how parents get children to accept responsibility in three societies. Two of the societies were traditional—one in the Amazon, one in Samoa[18]—and one was in Los Angeles, where 30 middle-class families participated. Here's how the authors summed up the West Coast families:

> Middle-class parents are highly accommodating starting from infancy. Adults use toys to stimulate children, intervene when children face difficulties, and anticipate possible harm through elaborate safety devices and placing dangerous objects out of reach. They strive to understand children's thoughts and emotions, and give children sole credit for accomplishments in which parents provided considerable assistance. Children are often praised for unsuccessful efforts ("Good try!") and sometimes are allowed to "win."
>
> Across the 30 families, parents made effortful appeals for help with practical matters, relying on "please," offers of rewards, or veiled threats. Directives were often phrased as suggestions. Children in 22 families frequently resisted or flatly refused. In the other eight families, children contributed little to the practical running of the household.
>
> Many parents remarked that it takes more effort to get children to collaborate than to do the tasks themselves. Parents did not systematically apprentice children into chores nor routinely delegate chores to them.[19]

Like all good American parents, the 30 in L.A. had been giving their children things, advantages, comfort, protection from danger and disappointment, and self-esteem-enhancing credit whether or not credit was deserved. But when they asked for assistance in return, their children had no listening. Sound familiar?

Understanding Children's Responsibility-Rejection; Often-Tried Solutions

You might be relieved to learn that responsibility-rejection isn't only an American problem. Anthropologist David Lancy has collected examples from European societies. In Rome, a father doesn't even bother to get his daughter to make her bed; he does it himself while grumbling. In Geneva, children scream, bang doors, sulk in their rooms, or agree to submit if their parents can prove their demands are well-founded. In Sweden, a four-year-old is "shepherded" to bed, a major undertaking consuming her mother's time and energy every evening.[20]

How can we make sense of this traditional–modern contrast? We can make sense of it by reviewing the two sharply contrasting value constellations that animate and regulate family relationships: *communitarian* and *individualistic*.

The value constellation of traditional families is communitarian, encapsulated by *What I want is what we need.* "What we need" is whatever will best serve the interests of the entire family. No member's unique needs or desires have greater weight. In a communitarian family, each newborn is raised among loved, trusted others, young and old, who expect from each other behavior characterized by respect, collective alignment, and timely fulfillment of obligations to the group.

The value constellation of middle-class WEIRD[21] families is individualistic, in which each member's unique needs and desires have substantial weight. For a variety of historical and cultural reasons, children's needs and desires have come to take precedence whenever possible. Each newborn is raised by loved, trusted parents whom the child experiences daily as giving goods, services, and emotional benefits to them. The child gets used to—*and likes!*—the role of receiver.

When it comes to routine chores around the house, some parents share the burdens with their children. Hats off to them! But there are many anecdotal and research-based reasons (see the Los Angeles findings above) to believe that most parents are not routinely sharing these burdens. When parents do get around to asking a child to do a chore (i.e., *to give*), the child doesn't recognize that as his role, which from the day of his birth has been *to receive*.

So what solutions are available for responsibility-rejection? Surely the answer is that parents need to be more persuasive! Here's a short review of ten often-tried ways in which middle-class parents have attempted to be more persuasive. Each one is followed by my suggestion about its likely weakness:

1. Talk about one's obligations as a family member. However, communitarian homilies are unlikely to draw a positive response from a brash young individualist.

2. Talk about how essential the chore is to the family's well-being. Examples of chores that are essential to a family's well-being include taking its herd of sheep to pasture or helping to bring in the wheat crop at harvest time. Your child knows darn well that taking out the garbage is not essential to family well-being.

3. Talk about the wisdom of gradually getting used to adult responsibilities. Alas, rarely persuasive; the responsibilities you have in mind are laughably trivial.

4. Phrase the request as though it were a spontaneous suggestion. "Hey, know how you could help right now? Take the garbage out. Would you

like to do that?" No, she would not. And even if she does, it's just this once. Every week? No way.

5. Play the authority; demand compliance and/or issue threats. These very well might work, but they introduce a corrosive element into parent–child relations. Plus they contradict your high-minded talk about how your family operates democratically.

6. Bolster self-esteem. Minimize the chore's difficulty and portray the child as entirely competent to complete it; stay away while she finishes it; then, ignoring the quality of the result, compliment her performance ("Good job!").[22] This gambit might be effective for a time with young children. However, chores very often are poorly completed and youngsters learn to be proud of slapdash work.

7. Negotiate. This strategy holds more promise because you, the parent, have established yourself as the Giver of Good Things. "OK, you take out the garbage this week and we'll get McDonald's burgers on Saturday!" This is likely to work in many cases—but it sets a bad precedent. Do you really want to raise the specter that your every responsibility-request could trigger hard bargaining?

8. Offer cash. This often takes the form of a weekly "allowance," money given to a child on condition of certain chores being completed. No chores, no money. However, by paying the child to perform, this strategy implicitly proclaims that "We, the parents, are responsible for the completion of all chores here; we choose to do some of them ourselves and hire our children to do the others." This undercuts the communitarian spirit, which is for each family member to *voluntarily* perform responsibilities commensurate with his or her level of ability.

9. Portray it as a personal favor; say "please." How many times will this work?

10. Go on strike. No joke! It's been done. Anthropologist Lancy "distinctly recalls a news item relating how a suburban couple in Florida, the Barnards, had gone on strike and moved into a tent in their driveway, refusing to cook, clean, or otherwise care for their teenage children until they agreed to help out with household chores."[23] Unfortunately, I don't know the outcome.

THE CIRCUMSTANCES UNDER WHICH CHILDREN LEARN RESPONSIBILITY

The societies in which children willingly carry out responsibilities are those in which children began helping with household tasks *beginning when they were toddlers*.

Also, the societies in which children willingly carry out responsibilities are those in which the routine lives of most families are shaped by communitarian values. The crucial factor, of course, is that *the family* embraces communitarian values, not that its containing society tends to be communitarian. It is possible for a society that tends to be individualistic to include families that are guided by communitarian values. Many American farm families provide examples.

In short, it's all about two things: timing and values.

The researchers in Los Angeles reported that the parents there "did not systematically apprentice children into chores nor routinely delegate chores to them." Instead, they:

- Waited until it was too late—middle childhood or even later—to begin expecting their children to contribute to running the household (timing); and
- Had not been aligning their families to any significant extent with the communitarian ethic of *What I want is what we need* (values).

That much seems clear. But I expect that some of you are doubting that toddlers can be persuaded to assist in running their household. With toys and other distractions all around, are little ones really going to get interested in work?

Turns out that an American researcher looked into exactly this question using as her subjects American parents and their little children. The researcher was not an anthropologist but a developmental psychologist, and she used what technically are laboratory methods, not participant observation. Here is what she did:[24]

She studied 80 children in three age groups—18, 24, and 30 months—chosen on the basis of age from local hospital and county records. The 18- and 30-months-old cohorts each included 20 parent–child pairs, while the 24-months-old cohort included two sets of 20 parent–child pairs. Most parents were college-educated.

The "laboratory" was a set of three connecting rooms furnished to simulate a home environment. In the rooms were nine typical household tasks including a table to be set and a basket of laundry to be folded. Toys, children's books, and other potentially distracting items were also available in the three rooms.

Each child and his or her parent were studied separately. The parent was told that they could do the tasks in any order, that they did not need to do them all, that they could take breaks to read to or play with their child, and that they were to maintain their usual way of interacting with their child. They were encouraged to talk about the tasks but asked to not tell their child what to do.

Each parent–child pair was given 25 minutes while the researcher and others watched and videotaped behind one-way windows.

The principal findings of this study include the following:

- Of the 18-month-old children, 63% helped on half or more of the tasks.
- Of the 24-month-old children, 78% helped on half or more of the tasks.
- Of the 30-month-old children, 89% helped on half or more of the tasks.
- In some cases, before the parent turned her attention to a task, the child either spoke of doing that task or actually began to work on it by themselves.
- The videotapes show that, in many cases, the children carried out their efforts with quick and energetic movements, excited vocalizations, animated facial expressions, and evident delight in the finished task.
- Some children spontaneously went beyond completing a task, for example, after laundry had been folded and placed in the basket, they stored the basket under the table; and after the table had been set, they brought chairs from another room to ensure that all settings had a chair (no parent thought of this!).

By the way, every child to some extent was distracted from the household chores by the toys, books, and other distracting items in the rooms. There were cases, too, in which the parents paused to play with or read to the child.

* * * * *

So how do other children learn responsibility?

The research with the 80 American toddlers and the findings of anthropologists in dozens of traditional societies combine to demonstrate this: *During their first two or three years of life*, children are ready, willing, and increasingly able to participate in doing whatever chores need to be done for the benefit of the family. They want to do what the big folks are doing. They want to be involved with their group. They seem to recognize that being involved will give them a sense of belonging and identity. After they begin participating, they begin to bask in awareness of their burgeoning competence and rising status as an increasingly valued group member. Their self-esteem grows—organically.

If harnessed by being put to use, these communitarian impulses can become internalized as a settled expectation that *we all contribute to keeping this place running*.

But the window of opportunity for solidifying toddlers' communitarian impulses doesn't remain open indefinitely. I'll guess that, in an individualistic society such as ours, that window is swinging shut around age three.

At the beginning of this chapter, I promised that I would share collective wisdom with you about the circumstances under which other children become responsible. Children are likely to learn and internalize responsibility in any situation in which:

- Toddlers are routinely expected to make small, practical contributions to their families' essential needs. Ignoring their initial clumsiness, parents continue over the years to expect contributions suitable for each child's growing level of ability, to monitor the quality of the results attained, and to encourage improved performance.
- The background and context of the society are such that families routinely have tasks that children can perform beginning at an early age, tasks that are genuinely essential and contribute visibly to families' daily and long-term sustenance, prosperity, or security.

Genuinely essential tasks are readily available in traditional societies but scarce in modern middle-class communities, thanks to our many labor-saving devices. Does this mean there's no way for *our* youngsters to contribute?

It does not. Our middle-class homes actually *do* have many important tasks to be done. Let's see what the research team that studied the 80 toddlers arranged in its three laboratory rooms:

> Five tasks were distributed around the main room: a table to be set with tableware stored nearby; a scattered dock of playing cards to be inserted in a box; magazines scattered on the floor to be placed on a table; a litter of paper bits to be swept up; and two dust cloths on the floor nearby. Two tasks in one small room were a cot to be "made up" and children's books to be placed on a table; the other room contained a basket of laundry to be folded and a pile of crumpled papers to be put into a wastebasket.[25]

Every home has routine cleaning, washing, arranging, and straightening up that need to be done. Every home has a kitchen with food to be prepared, which largely involves simple procedures followed by routine clean up. Some homes have indoor plants that need tending. Many have a lawn and even a garden, where there's gloriously dirty work to do. Many parents have pastimes and special projects; a friend just told me that, from the age of three, she was helping her father do carpentry. My father, over a decade, constructed an ever-larger table-top layout for model trains; boy, did I get involved in that![26]

Many often-repeated activities around the home include veritable "tasks for toddlers." Yet we adults don't often think of asking our toddlers to *routinely* join us in doing them. If such a thought happens to cross our minds, we dismiss it with the rationalization that "she can't do *that* yet," or "if I involve him, it'll take *way* longer." Because we Americans put a high value on efficiency, we look for ways to distract or corral our youngster while we zip through the tasks. We continue in that mindset year after year—until one day we're crazy busy and ask for a helping hand.

Too late. The window of opportunity has closed.

SUGGESTED FURTHER READING

Each of the readings below is profiled at howotherchildrenlearn.info/profiles.

"Responsibility in childhood: Three developmental trajectories," by Elinor Ochs & Carolina Izquierdo. *Journal of the Society for Psychological Anthropology, 37* (4), 2009; 18 text pages.

"Learning to be responsible: Young children's transitions outside school," by Patricia Ames. *Learning, Culture, and Social Interaction, 2*, 2013; 11 text pages.

The Bibliography at the back of this book includes all publications cited within Chapter 7.

Chapter 8

How Do Other Children Learn? And How Do Other Parents Parent?

The tables in Appendix A will aid your understanding as you read this chapter.

One of the principal conclusions of anthropologists of childhood has been this: The ways children are dealt with in any given society are rational and adaptive, given that society's particular background and context. This is so even if that society's adults are unable to explain why they deal with children as they do.[1]

In this second summary chapter, we will address the related questions of how children learn and how parents parent in traditional societies. To do that well, we need to remain conscious of the background and context factors that characterize most such societies. In the first summary chapter, Chapter 7, we reviewed some of those factors, including that child mortality is high, that children genuinely are needed, and that parents do not expect to give benefits to their children but rather to receive benefits from them throughout their lifetimes.

Before we consider how children learn and how parents parent in traditional societies, we will review additional factors that characterize those societies. In particular, we'll explore the nature of what traditional children need to learn, the role that formal education (i.e., classroom instruction) plays in any society, and the profound repercussions that a traditional society and its children begin to experience soon after the arrival of formal education.

One more thing: Despite their differences, the Aka, Quechua, Navajo, village Arab, and village Indian societies qualify as "traditional" based on the criteria stated in the Introduction—small settlement size, low literacy, low mobility, past oriented, strong extended families, and economic reliance on the land. However, these five are only a tiny sample of the hundreds of small, traditional societies. In this summary chapter, I will draw on what anthropologists have learned about the full range of traditional societies, and about modern or WEIRD[2] societies as well—especially American middle-class society.

WHAT TRADITIONAL CHILDREN
LEARN AND HOW THEY LEARN IT

Although "work" can refer to mental effort, its classic reference was to people's physical efforts to wrest life's necessities from the land and use them productively. Physical labor is a major component of the daily lives of foragers, farmers, and pastoralists. But they are not as quick as we are to distinguish between work and whatever might be its opposite. One anthropologist reminded her fellow scholars that their frequent distinction between "work" and "play" was *their* idea, not that of the children they had been observing.[3]

The same could be said for "learning." In traditional settings, learning how to contribute to the family economy is a by-product of children's ordinary activities. It is neither separated from other parts of their lives nor specified by adults in any sense as a set of objectives. It's been termed "the chore curriculum," laid out for all children to observe and imitate, in sharp contrast to the "core curriculum" of schools, which is sequestered in classrooms, textbooks, and formal lessons.[4]

Children are frequently in proximity to adults as the latter go about their typical work routines. The workers are usually older relatives who are well known and implicitly trusted; the youngsters want to fit in with them. The work is semi-skilled or unskilled, so it can be observed and imitated with little or no explanation. Children strive to contribute to the common good through work, just as the adults are doing. Are tools in use? No problem; all tools are available for practice; none are kept hidden because they are "dangerous." Safe, child-size, machine-made replicas are unknown.[5] As children gain know-how and strength, they increasingly pitch in. The family genuinely needs their contributions to its economy, so their early efforts are welcomed even if they are a bit bumbling.

One of the most significant findings about children in traditional societies is that their freely chosen activities—whether called "play" or not—often are attempts to replicate what they see adults and older children doing. Recall the two Aka boys climbing a tree to get "honey"; the three-year-old Quechua, Anali, acting as her family's hostess for Inge Bolin; and a young Navajo girl explaining that, "when my mother puts up a loom, I watch and learn, and when she gets up to cook, I get in there and try to do it." Such activities don't only build the know-how needed for useful labor; they also instill their group's values, roles, emotions, and quality standards.

Because of the physical nature of the work and the constant opportunities for youngsters to observe, imitate, and pitch in, parents and other adults in most traditional societies see no need to deliberately teach work skills and processes that their growing children can very well pick up on their own.

If children are going to fit in smoothly, they need to learn more than how to work. Important are group members' manners, morals, myths, and symbols, which are cerebral, interpersonal, and often emotional in nature. The child who delays in adhering to them is criticized—along with his parents. Parents know that they cannot rely on observation and imitation; instead, they must instruct, direct, and insist. Village Indian adults pointedly teach children to learn and correctly pronounce kinship terms, and to apply them to the correct people. An adult Navajo recalled that, "They used to get us together at campfires and tell us what to do and what not to do." Young Arabs have been heard reciting five generations of their genealogies on both sides, and older Arab daughters have drummed into them that, outside the home, they must behave with conspicuous modesty, according to local standards. And let's not forget that parents in many traditional societies very deliberately—even manually—train their youngsters to always use their left and right hands in socially appropriate ways.[6]

There's one more capability that traditional children absolutely must acquire: how to communicate. Consider language first. Except for kinship terms and phrases for respectful behavior, traditional parents show scant interest in their children's language-learning progress.[7] Interpersonal communication also occurs by nonverbal means, the principal way in which humans reveal inner emotions: facial expressions, eye and eyebrow use, gestures, postures, tone of voice, and nonverbal sounds (e.g., humming). Dress and self-decoration carry meaning, too; compare the message an Indian bride conveys to others by draping the end of her scarf over her head, with the message an Aka girl's pointed teeth convey to young males visiting her camp. Except perhaps for matters of dress and self-decoration, there is little reason to imagine that traditional parents are intentionally teaching nonverbal behavior skills to their children.

FORMAL INSTRUCTION AND THE
TRANSITION TO MODERNITY

Experts believe that, until maybe ten thousand years ago, every human was living more or less as hunter-gatherers live today. So why aren't we all still living as folks did way back then?[8]

Why Aren't We Still Living as Hunter-Gatherers?

Once upon a time, an ancient human in a hunter-gatherer or nomadic group had an idea about an improved way to get something done. Let's say the weather had been favorable and edible plants were abundant. The group had started to store plant material for lean years. Perhaps it would be useful to keep records of what had been stored: when, how much, and so on. His—or her—unique idea was *how* to keep such records. OK, that's a story I created out of whole cloth, but the key point is this: Someone came up with an innovative way of getting work done that could benefit the entire group—*if* other group members learned how to use it. So he or she decided to show them how.

This was the origin of what we now call education: the first time that someone intentionally and consciously transmitted a new skill or idea to another person.

This skill or idea was completely new; it was not familiar to any of the group's other members. And it was complex, not readily mastered via observation and imitation. Let's say you're helping your uncle at the granary and notice him making dents in soft clay tablets,[9] something utterly strange to you. If you're going to learn to do *that*, he'll need to explain it to you.

"He'll need to explain it to you" indicates that your uncle must set aside time for the specific purpose of intentionally and consciously helping you learn his new technique. *Here we have a fundamental distinction that separates modern from traditional societies.* Learning by observation, imitation, and participation occurs in both types of society. Learning through direct instruction, planned and formally delivered, is a defining characteristic of modern—and modernizing—societies.[10]

In traditional societies, learning occurs because youngsters grow up among trusted models of behavior and come to understand that the way to become part of the group is by acting like the others. To benefit from learning opportunities that occur serendipitously, they maintain open attention to their surroundings. Adults and older youth who possess useful abilities rarely bother to instruct the younger ones; instead, they go about their business, willing to be watched and able to respond if a little observer/imitator has a question.

In modern societies, much learning occurs in similar fashion. But in our highly technological times, in which painstakingly gained mental skills such as math and reading are indispensable, we have consciously emphasized deliberately organized formal instruction. Instruction doesn't occur solely because those who already have knowledge are willing to organize and teach classes. It also occurs because the state insists that at least some of this knowledge be taught to every one of the society's youth—whether those youth want it or not.

Formal instruction and modern society are inextricably linked. What links them is the volume and cognitive complexity of what children need to learn. Technologically advanced societies would not exist today in the absence of formal instruction by adults.

That children in traditional societies learn on their own is greatly admired by some modern folks, who advocate that we should rethink schools so that children can learn what they like, when they like, and how they like. This works if the skill is to herd llamas, grind corn, or care for your just-weaned sibling, thereby doing as your elders do and visibly contributing to your family's well-being. But suppose the skill is to multiply fractions, correctly use gerunds, or distinguish endothermic and exothermic chemical reactions.[11] A modern child rarely, if ever, observes elders doing such things, none of which has any visible effect, positive or negative, on her family's well-being. Whom would a child observe and try to imitate? Why?

What Are the Repercussions of Formal Instruction in Traditional Societies?

It's commonly believed that bringing the benefits of modernization to traditional societies is a Good Thing. This attitude solidified in the American mindset during the late 19th and early 20th centuries, when we proudly viewed our civilization as superior and were determined to introduce modern progress to "less fortunate" others.

But for the people being introduced to technological and other forms of modern progress, the reaction has been mixed. Sure, it's appealing to think that one of your repetitive tasks could be performed by a machine, or that your son might obtain a wage-paying job able to sustain your family when harvests are poor. But wait. What if the repetitive task was washing clothes in the river, a pleasant outdoor social diversion for you and other women? Machines will change the social aspects of wash day. What if the wage-paying job your son gets is in the city? There he'll encounter alluring options for spending his wages, not to mention manners, morals, and maidens beyond your comfort zone.

Along with modernity come schools with formal instruction in the three R's and more, said by many to bring transformative long-term benefits. Maybe so. But in the short term, what exactly is the effect that schools might have on your family and your village or camp?

First of all, what the heck's going on in that school? If the whole idea of schooling is new to you, formal instruction is an enigma. Isn't it enough that children are in school for hours at a time each day? But they return with "homework" to do, which competes with their economic contributions to the family. During the planting and harvesting seasons children are essential to a family's economy, yet when they're kept out of school the parents get push-back: They're told that, "If your children miss three weeks in a row, they'll never catch up." Catch up? With what? It's really hard to fathom this if, during *your* childhood, you gradually absorbed everything you needed to know via casual observation.

Occasionally the instructors encourage parents to come to the school for a meeting. Many parents are reluctant. Some have a language barrier; some work multiple jobs and cannot afford to take time off. Even if those two hurdles are not applicable, school people often seem unapproachable; they almost always are outsiders with much higher social status. Most parents know virtually nothing about schooling and prefer not to put their ignorance on display. If parents do show up, grasp some of what's discussed, and combine that with what they've been hearing from their young scholars, they begin to realize that the basic purpose of schooling is antithetical to their time-honored values.

Traditional societies inculcate in children the know-how and mindset of past generations, thereby maintaining social continuity. Traditional adults assume that youth of sound mind are those who fulfill obligations, overtly respect authority, maintain harmonious relationships, and contribute to their family's economy.

With schooling comes a new reality. Schools aren't hostile to the past but relentlessly pursue their mission to prepare youth to seize opportunities in the future, in the cities, and in types of work requiring mental acuity more than stamina or manual dexterity. School people view "intelligent" youth as those who are curious, creative, assertive, articulate, and independent-minded— very, very different from traditional adults' view of youth of sound mind.

Which brings us to the final repercussion. Schooling often leads to fissures in traditional families: parents' old-fashioned versus students' new-fangled. In Chapter 4, a Navajo student just back from boarding school felt called upon to apologize to his Anglo friends about his parents' bizarre behavior: "These Navajos are kinda funny."

What Are the Consequences of Formal Instruction for Traditional Children?

The first schools to be established in traditional villages often are pretty dreadful. The teachers tend to be poorly prepared and paid, the buildings and materials at their disposal are substandard or worse, and their methods often rely entirely on rote memorization.[12] Children who attend such schools in anticipation of moving into the modern labor force often are too poorly educated to fully realize their dream. Those who persist occasionally are able to advance to better schools in nearby urban areas. (An exception to this generalization is the Quechua. Why many rose to the top of the class in better urban schools isn't well understood.)

The learning process of formal classroom instruction is sharply different from the ways in which traditional children were learning how to learn. In camps and villages, children learned alone or in multi-age groups, unobtrusively observing the practices of those with fully developed skills. Rarely did children have reason to view themselves as being in competition with one another; on the contrary, they routinely collaborated. The partial knowledge of a slightly older mentor often was at just the right level for a fledgling learner, whereas an expert adult might have overwhelmed her with unnecessarily elaborate details.[13]

In school, children usually find themselves separated into groups of age-peers. They learn what, when, how, and how much their teacher directs. Topics involve cognitive abilities—recognition and manipulation of symbols, and memorization of facts. Whereas in their villages, youngsters had grown adept at following observation with trial-and-error imitation, all in their own good time and with friends, they are now expected to follow classroom lessons with solo "study," attempts to comprehend if not memorize the new material, often overnight.

Consider evaluation. In a classroom context, evaluation determines the relative worth of students based on their correct or incorrect answers to questions that test their cognitive abilities, which in turn usually leads to the public identification by adults of children who are deficient. This approach to children's learning has no counterpart in traditional societies where, as this book documents, children learn alone and together with little direct input from the adults.

In traditional settings, it's rare for a child to be *publicly* labeled as deficient based on his or her errors, with one exception: parents do call out infractions of behavioral norms (e.g., an Aka child who fails to share).[14] In fact, it's rare for a child's purely *cognitive* abilities to be openly judged, again with one exception: in some societies youngsters must memorize, and correctly apply, dozens of kinship terms. Teachers' public denigration of individuals' cognitive shortcomings discourages some students from trying at all. Furthermore, teachers' insistence on individual performance negates the collaborative ways that children have learned how to learn.

Consider, specifically, testing. Sometimes it is a paper-and-pencil test, with everyone's score made public later. Sometimes it's a "recitation," in which each child, in front of his mates, is called upon to stand up and demonstrate mastery. *Testing involves competition and the ranking of individuals.* Each student is overtly matched against their relatives and friends, leading to public knowledge of who is best and worst. The focus on individuals means that during tests, collaboration is labeled "cheating" and punished. These practices clash with traditional values.

The most profound and lasting repercussion of formal instruction is its ability to undermine the fundamental value proposition of a traditional extended family: We are one social entity, not a group of voluntarily cooperating, but ultimately self-serving, individuals. Yes, extended family members inhabit separate bodies, but their mindset is one of indelible relatedness, shared purpose, and mutual obligation—"communitarian" values. *What I want is what we need.*

That value system is profoundly disturbed whenever one learns in a classroom, where each student is treated daily as a separate person who has "agency," the ability of an individual to intentionally act to produce a result. The teacher gives material to you to understand or memorize. Your classmates receive it, too. Each of you will be tested separately, not as a group. If you perform well, the credit is yours alone. If you perform poorly, it is you who did not study enough. Even if you don't end up at the head of the class, you are repeatedly having the experience of receiving a cognitive challenge, of engaging your own mind to learn something new, and then of having to separately demonstrate how well you, and you alone, learned it. It's all in the service of preparing you, *on your own*, to attain your personal ambitions by exercising your agency and seizing future opportunities.

Welcome to the methods, the mindset, and the values of our modern world.

SO HOW DO OTHER CHILDREN LEARN?

Other children learn, alone and together, with very little direct involvement by adults.

In traditional societies, where infant mortality is high, newborns receive the dedicated attention of their mothers until weaning. Then each just-weaned child, mobile and beginning to talk, is released into the care of an older sister and/or their community's multi-age group of curious and spirited little explorers. Mothers don't want just-weaned children underfoot; they are focused on the next child. So the children's group does whatever it wishes in the vicinity.

Doing whatever it wishes in the vicinity could be endlessly aimless. It's not. The youngsters are spending their time among older people—not only adults but also older children and aged old-timers—whom they know and trust, who they want to emulate, and who model both essential skills and acceptable behavior. If the youngsters can maintain open attention, observe inquiringly, imitate patiently, practice with peers, and gradually pitch in on the adults' ongoing activities and relationships, all will be well.

While the boys and girls are discovering how to work, they're also discovering how to behave, communicate, relate to others, and what to believe. One scholar holds that years of unstructured exploration during childhood enables children in any society to

> (a) develop intrinsic interests and competencies; (b) learn how to make decisions, solve problems, exert self-control, and follow rules; (c) learn to regulate their emotions; (d) make friends and learn to get along with others as equals; and (e) experience joy.[15]

As we have seen in the five societies discussed earlier in this book, parents ensure that social essentials are mastered (e.g., how to respect elders). Beyond that, adults rarely focus their attention on the children's progress toward maturity. The children learn, alone and together, with little direct involvement by adults.

What Does This Tell Us about *Our* Children's Learning?

How *our* children learn is highly similar in most ways, but totally different in one way.

Writing this book has given me a fresh perspective on children's learning in any society. Instead of attending to the *whats* (i.e., the various new capabilities to be acquired by children), I'm now more interested in the *hows* (i.e., the mental means by which children acquire new capabilities). My principal distinction is between capabilities acquired *subconsciously* and capabilities acquired *consciously*:

1. Capabilities acquired subconsciously, that is, outside of conscious awareness
2. Capabilities acquired in part subconsciously, in part consciously
3. Capabilities acquired consciously, often intentionally and with effort, including
   a. Functional, culinary, artistic, and other manual skills (practical competencies)
   b. Factual information including traditions and beliefs (cognitive knowledge)
   c. Symbol-decoding, analytical, and scientific abilities (cognitive manipulation)

Category 1 (capabilities acquired subconsciously) comprises multiple elements of nonverbal behavior, almost all of which are learned below the level of conscious awareness. The ability to communicate verbally is similarly acquired—which is why we adults envy children when we try to learn a new language! There is very little difference between how traditional children learn to communicate verbally and nonverbally, and how modern children learn to communicate: All children do this subconsciously. Therefore, knowing how *other* children learn Category 1 capabilities tell us nothing useful about *our* children's learning.

(When it comes to verbal skills, however, many middle-class American parents are not content to allow these to be acquired wholly subconsciously. We have proto-conversations with infants, read to them, buy them books, put them in front of vocabulary-oriented programs, and more. We'll revisit this topic soon.)

Category 2 (capabilities acquired in part subconsciously, in part consciously) includes a wide range of interpersonal skills, many of which incorporate nonverbal behavior.[16] I'm thinking of capabilities like how to make a friend, behave modestly, talk to a toddler, show respect for elders, gain cooperation as a leader, act angrily without going overboard, conduct a performance appraisal, board a bus together with many others,[17] flirt, take the next step after flirting, and countless more. These are gained at the margin between consciousness and subconsciousness, often by imitating the ways of more experienced others.[18] Behavior associated with manners and morals, as locally defined, is likely to be explicitly taught to children. Behavior learned subconsciously can become conscious if a social gaffe leads to a parent's scolding, a friend's upset, or an opportunity denied. Again, there is very little difference in how children in *any* society acquire Category 2 capabilities.

Category 3a (consciously acquired functional, culinary, artistic, and other manual skills) comprises practical skills that are learned while consciously alert but do not involve numbers, letters, or verbalized knowledge: how to till soil, get honey, set a snare, erect a hut, weave a rug, deliver a baby, make fuel cakes from dung, paint with watercolors, use a lawn mower, prepare toast or tiramisu, and countless others. These practical, culinary, and artistic competencies are alike in that they can be learned by observation and imitation. In the old days, apprenticeships were a means for acquiring such skills.[19] Nowadays, manuals, recipes, and formal instruction often are available, but they are not essential. Category 3a competencies can be, and very often are, learned by children in all types of societies by means of observation and imitation. Once more, knowing how other children learn them tells us nothing useful regarding *our* children's learning.

But hold on. Research has revealed that there *is* a difference in the quality of traditional and modern children's observation. Earlier in this chapter, I referred to "open attention," which actually is a technical term used by anthropologists of childhood. It turns out that traditional youth pay close and sustained attention to a wider range of activities and cues than do modern youth. They've become aware that, if they're going to acquire all they need to know, they must carefully watch and learn from anyone exercising a useful skill, and from any situation that includes subtle clues to what will happen next. Their in-the-moment alertness has been likened to mindfulness, to extra antennae, or even to a kind of sixth sense. Researchers have termed it *open attention*, contrasting it with "school-inspired models of attention that narrow one's focus and apply it selectively, sequentially—and sporadically—to a series of objects and events."[20]

Unfortunately, it's not plausible to imagine that modern children can be taught to develop open attention. Everyone with whom they interact is a product of schooling; everyone around them attends to events selectively, sequentially, and sporadically—and with frequent interruptions. It's the modern mindset.

Category 3b (consciously acquired factual information including traditions and beliefs) is about deliberately learned, mostly verbalized knowledge that people have about their extended family, their tribe or ethnic group, and (nowadays) their nation; it includes matters such as history, genealogies, symbols, and verbal traditions including origin stories and poems, religious beliefs, taboos, sacred texts, and the like. In some contexts, children are obliged to absorb prodigious amounts of such information, while in other contexts little is required. Contrast village Arab children memorizing the entire Koran with Aka boys and girls being initiated for a few days in the forest. We modern parents also care about the beliefs and traditions our children learn; some of us expect little, others expect a lot. For millennia, this kind of knowledge was passed down from generation to generation verbally, by "oral tradition." Now we use written and other visual materials, but they are not essential. Once again, knowing how other children learn such things tells us little that seems useful for our purposes.

Category 3c (consciously acquired symbol-decoding, analytical, and scientific abilities) brings us, finally, to something completely different: knowledge mediated by invented written symbols, symbols that must be taught, formally and directly, to those not familiar with them. Easy familiarity with numbers and letters, and skill in mentally manipulating them to attain certain results, is indispensable in modern society. So we oblige each and every child to begin learning symbol use at a young age. Their learning will need to continue, almost full time, for a minimum of eight or nine years.

Neither Category 3c knowledge nor how adults transmit it to children has any counterpart in a traditional society that has not begun to modernize.

Is there a Take-Away from these Insights into How Other Children Learn?

Yes, but it's not about contrasts in how traditional and modern children learn. It's about contrasts between the backgrounds and contexts where their learning occurs.

Like traditional children, modern ones have a natural capacity to learn a great deal on their own by observation, imitation, and pitching in on productive work, participating in social relationships, and engaging in a wide variety of activities repeatedly occurring in their vicinity.

But how do their *opportunities* to observe, imitate, and pitch in compare with those of traditional children? The differences are major and they are many.

Consider traditional children first. Unless and until they start going to school, traditional children grow up among the members of a group, often numbering at least ten, that infrequently changes and always includes close relatives and in-laws. Youngsters soon become highly familiar with these people, whose behavior is animated by a spirit of collective alignment.[21] Realizing that they belong to this group, they are motivated to play an active role in its daily activities. In their village, camp, or compound, they have daily opportunities to witness everything that's going on; no scene or tool is denied them. Especially when they are younger and expected to carry out family chores infrequently, they have hours every day to observe, imitate, and pitch in—or not—on the activities of older community members.

Equally important is the fact that traditional children are regularly in the company of other children—often in a multi-age group—that is unrestricted in its choices of where to roam, what to explore, and how to go about doing whatever members want to do. Note that (a) many activities are conducted outdoors; (b) group membership changes very slowly; (c) adults are in the vicinity but never supervise any activity; and (d) any child may temporarily leave the group and spend time alone—or even with his parents! (Let's not forget that, in some societies, pubescent girls might not be allowed as much freedom as boys.)

Modern children grow up in a nuclear family that rarely numbers more than five.[22] Its members are the closest of relatives; other relatives typically live too far away to become highly familiar. For some modern children, there is only one adult whose daily rounds they have multiple opportunities to observe. When both parents work away from home, this option vanishes. In that case, and whenever both parents wish to go somewhere alone, they're replaced by a hired minder who initially is a stranger and might be replaced from time to time. If both parents do office work at home, a child observing them can become bored very quickly.

Modern youngsters' observational opportunities only sporadically include adults who are exercising their functional, culinary, artistic, or other manual capabilities, except in the kitchen. They are denied opportunities to use implements deemed dangerous, or even to observe activities deemed morally suspect or age-inappropriate. Instead, most parents provide their children with a handheld media device, which instantly transforms into a captivating, almost bewitching, presence that largely eclipses whatever interest they had in real-time, real-life observations of adults.

Nowadays, it is exceedingly rare for a modern urban or suburban child to have an opportunity every day to roam, explore, and do whatever comes to mind in the company of a group of other children whose membership rarely changes and whose activities are free of adult supervision.[23] One historian notes that the high plateau of children's unstructured activity encompassed the first half of the 20th century, diminishing after the mid-1950s because adults began exerting ever-increasing control over children's daily lives.[24]

Scholars of childhood are now pointing to a concerning trend: As American children's occasions for unstructured group activity have steadily decreased since the late 1950s, the occasions in which they are diagnosed with depression, anxiety, and other psychological disorders have steadily increased. To take just one statistic, between 1950 and 2005, the suicide rate for children under age 15 quadrupled.[25]

Unlike traditional children, modern children spend time alone. How do they occupy themselves? Electronic media have become the pastime of choice. I won't repeat the usual concerns about their constant media use. My concern is that when children are alone and mesmerized by electronic media, they are *not* observing, imitating, or pitching in on activities or social interactions of adults, nor spending unstructured roaming and exploring time with peers. Much of their remaining time and energy is devoted to classroom learning of symbol manipulation, which is indispensable. But is it also indispensable for us to rarely, if ever, give them opportunities for screen-free self-guided exploration and serendipitous learning?

That's one of the issues we'll tackle in the final section, about parenting.

AND HOW DO OTHER PARENTS PARENT?

With one or two significant exceptions, other parents parent as little as possible.

The underlying driver for the way traditional parents think and behave is that children are needed, initially as laborers, later as caretakers. Tender affection may blossom between parent and child, and often does; that's fine.

But that does not change the fact that the role of parents is to *receive* benefits from their children.

Consequently, the characteristic activities of traditional parents do not include many roles that American middle-class parents consider normal. They do not play with their children. They do not buy toys for, or arrange play dates on behalf of, their children. They never accompany children to a play area. The idea of a youth sport league never occurs. They don't curate or even set aside special children's areas indoors or outdoors.[26] They don't provide special food to cater to children's tastes, nor arrange activities so children can have fun, nor do anything to accelerate their children's cognitive development. Traditional parents do not put "dangerous" items out of reach, nor alter their schedules to align with those of their children, nor protect children from participating in activities they believe to be unhealthy, sinful, upsetting, or not age-appropriate such as childbirth, sex, death, salty foods, or foul language. "Self-esteem" and "quality time" are not in their vocabularies.

What traditional parents do *not* do, however, is only half of the story.

On the positive side of the ledger, let's begin by acknowledging the significance of the mother's role. She is engaged 24/7 with each child until weaning. She is constantly active at the core of her large family's life. Traditional adults revere their mothers; many maintain a warm, close relationship with her. Fathers are appreciated, too, but the feelings seem to lack the same ardent quality. Aka fathers might be "intimate,"[27] but they are not representative of traditional fathers generally.

It is often noted that a traditional child is never isolated. But except for the period before weaning, that fact cannot be attributed to either parent. Rather, it's because in the traditional child's household are multiple siblings (some with spouses) and, under the same roof or nearby, multiple cousins, and perhaps an aunt and uncle, and even a grandparent or two. To the extent that a weaned child is minded at all, minding is shared by members of the extended family—Exhibit A for why it's possible for traditional parents to "parent as little as possible."

That traditional children are never isolated also cannot be attributed to the care of a nanny, babysitter, or day-care provider. Child-minding by a hired outsider is an idea that does not occur in the premodern world. The notion that the two parents might want to slip away for time by themselves also rarely occurs. In traditional cultures, "love" is not understood as an aching, dewy-eyed desire for a specific individual. Instead, people experience an abiding sense of emotional connectedness with their extended family members. So if the parents go on an excursion, the children come along: weddings, funerals, seasonal fairs, religious festivals, whatever. Often, other extended family members will be there, too.

The culture of traditional extended families is one in which obedience, respect, collective alignment, and fulfillment of obligations are highly valued in precept and example. A child's personal needs and interests have no standing in comparison with those of the family as a whole. Each family member's reigning value is: *What I want is what we need.* This value constellation is termed "communitarian."[28] Given their extended family's communitarian mindset, it's understandable that parents are willing and able to "parent as little as possible."

What Does This Tell Us about *Our* Parenting?

With few exceptions, we parent as much as possible—or think that we should. We belong to the society in which the noun "parent" became a verb.

But our parenting occurs within a totally different background and context. We find ourselves participating in a society where communitarian values have been largely overshadowed—although not entirely, thank goodness—by a constellation of "individualistic" values. Focusing on one's self-interest is normal, expected, and reinforced daily by the overt and covert messages we receive from institutions, media, and people around us. I won't offer a litany of examples, but a catalog just arrived in my post sporting the slogan, "my time, my place, my self."

Thanks to myriad scientific and technological advancements, our background and context is such that we need to devote only a fraction of our time and energy to provisioning our families. We have time to pursue opportunities that respond to our personal interests and/or—if we're fortunate enough to have the means—that enable us to amass wealth and resources. For most traditional people, the idea of competitively amassing wealth far beyond day-to-day requirements either does not occur, or is too farfetched to be considered, or is seriously bad behavior. For us, the acquisition and display of wealth is a signal to others that, as individuals and nuclear families, we're living an especially Good Life.

Everyone understands that, to enter this society-wide competition with any hope of success, certain measures are necessary. Education and training. Long hours of work. Seizing advancement opportunities wherever, geographically, they might arise regardless of where our family has its roots. Prudent application of income and resources as they are acquired. Care with respect to expenses and savings. Savings? Not only to amass resources and wealth, but also to retire in comfort without "burdening" our grown children—that is, to avoid their needing to give practical benefits to us. In our individualistic society, we admire self-reliance and pity those forced to depend on others, even their children, for their needs.

That's a lot of hectic striving! So why become a parent? Let's face it: Children are, as they say in business, a major cost center.[29] They take careful managing and bring huge responsibilities—time and effort away from pursuit of the Good Life.

But there's an insistent emotional, seemingly instinctual tug. For many of us, *the Good Life is incomplete without children*. People "get" that child-rearing is a voluntary activity with huge costs and responsibilities but believe the game is worth—more than worth—the candle. And thanks to one of those scientific advances, we modern folks can limit our brood to three, two, or even just one.

Modern, middle-class parents shepherd newborns into material, human, and cultural surroundings that scarcely could be more different from those awaiting the children of traditional parents in villages and camps. Given this yawning gap, can "other" parents have anything useful to tell us? Let's see.

Is there a Take-Away from these Insights into How Other Parents Parent?

Yes. The ways we deal with our children in our modern society today actually *are rational and adaptive*, given our society's particular background and context.

For example, the biggest difference between our world and the "other" one is that day-by-day, hour-by-hour, life in our world is mediated by written symbols and their manipulation. In the worlds of foragers, pastoralists, and farmers, there is nothing comparable that children *must* learn in order to participate productively in adult society. Our society tries to ensure children's mastery of symbols through years of instruction in schools. That's rational and adaptive. Of course, our schools could be doing a better job. That's why the effort some parents devote to helping their youngsters master symbols is equally rational and adaptive.

But it's not all about symbols. We can gain other insights by contrasting our modern parenting patterns with those of traditional peoples. Alerted by these contrasts, we will become aware of big-picture attributes of modern parenting to which we weren't paying attention, enabling us to pause and reassess them. Doing this might motivate us to make changes in dealing with our children. It definitely *will* provide us with a more informed perspective on certain features of how we do things around here.

Join me in reassessing these six attributes of modern American parenting:

- We are child-centered in dealing with children instead of modeling adult ways.
- We erect a boundary around our adult world and keep children out.

- We constantly shield our children from danger, stress, and iniquity.
- We insert ourselves and our preferences into our children's activities.
- We assume almost total responsibility for the raising of our children.
- We continue being responsible for our children after they attain puberty.

We are child-centered in dealing with children instead of modeling adult ways. American education was swept decades ago by the supposed virtue of child-centeredness,[30] and the same is true of American parenting. The ways we deal with children are driven by our adult notions of how young children view the world. The books we read to them, the media we sit them in front of, the toys and games we buy for them, the excursions on which we take them, and our readiness to be their playmates all reveal our belief that childhood ought to be a time of fun, fantasy, and innocence of serious cares.

Consider fantasy.[31] Traditional children's fantasy is more accurately termed "make-believe." That's because it is anchored by adults' activities, which children imitate as the keystone of their process of gaining maturity. They scavenge props, create scripts, invent scenes, divvy up roles, and impersonate adults—all with no adult input except as models. Some of this occurs in our world, too. But much of modern children's make-believe is pure fantasy, invented by adults whose aim is to entertain—and reap profits. Modern fantasy, epitomized by Disney theme parks, has scant anchoring in the real world. We even call it "never-never land." Does it serve as a keystone of children's process of gaining maturity? Debatable.

In this book, the ways of parenting in five traditional societies were portrayed. *In none of these societies was anything remotely like child-centeredness common among adults.* Children were raised by older children while parents consistently remained in their adult roles, modeling mature behavior, skills, and perspectives.

How can we make sense of this huge disparity between traditional and modern parenting? Here's my take: Our ways of parenting are rational and adaptive. We have very few roles for our children other than preparing for the economic rigors of adulthood—the mission of schools. We love our children, an emotion that leads us to want to see them happy. So we become, part of the time, childish, joining them at their presumed lower level of comprehension. Hey, it's fun for us, too!

We want our children to become adults at *some* point. Many of us believe sooner is better. Could we advance that goal by becoming less child-centered?

We erect a boundary around our adult world and keep children out. I have noted that traditional adults pay little or no attention to children's activities—and that traditional children are never alone. Have I contradicted myself?

No. The confusion arises for two reasons: When we modern folks think of children, we envision *supervised* children. And in traditional settlements, children are constantly in the vicinity of adults, but they are not being supervised by those adults. The adults are going about their business. The children are going about theirs. And here's the thing: *The children often are paying attention to what the adults are doing.* Their proximity provides the opportunity for them to learn.

Modern urban society presents a stark contrast. Most of us support our families by working miles away from our home. Some of us now work in our homes, which in most cases obliges us to sit still, look at a screen, tap keys endlessly, and discuss arcane topics with others on that screen. A crashing bore for little observers.

Of course, our adult world and our children's worlds do intersect to some extent. But the two worlds pull apart regarding parents' bread-winning roles, adult activities deemed unsuitable for children's participation, and times when parents simply want a break from their 24/7 obligations. So children's opportunities to observe, imitate, and pitch in occur sporadically, replaced by adult-designed toys we give them in abundance (many of which encourage fantasizing), and by supervised athletics. We also give them mesmerizing electronic gadgets that facilitate communication with absent friends and— wait, who are those people they're sharing photos with?

Modern urban children are not needed in practical or economic terms, have few interesting adult activities to observe and imitate, and lack a nearby group of children with whom to roam and explore. With high energy but no economic or social role, and high capacity for getting into mischief to relieve their boredom and satisfy their burgeoning curiosity, our children *must* be given diversions after they're weaned and walking. We divert and entertain them with toys, electronics, media, athletics, and excursions. "Bread and circuses."[32] What else can we do?

Another factor is at work as well: We're prone to compartmentalize interactions with our children.[33] We want to give them "quality time," which we usually conceive as time when we involve ourselves in what our child wants to do—visit the zoo, build a model, play in the yard. All good. What if we could also conceive of quality time as being when we involve the child *in a project the family needs doing.* Fresh food needs preparing; a wall needs painting; the garden needs weeding. Could such tasks be done together? In many cases, the answer is yes—*if* we put aside either-or thinking: I have an hour to either devote to my child or efficiently get chores done.

One of our society's economic segments preserves many of the opportunities available to traditional children: family farms that raise livestock. There, youngsters are genuinely useful—Jenny, go get us some eggs, please—and they have daily opportunities to observe older relatives doing productive work suitable for imitation and pitching in. The distinction between "work" and "play" is weak; learning occurs via everyday activities; and the boundary between the worlds of adults and children is low.[34]

Traditional societies demonstrate that, *with almost no parental effort*, children willingly learn the skills and norms of adulthood. It's difficult for similar learning to occur in our society because we tend to compartmentalize the way we think about using our time, and because of how most of us work to support our families. We can control our thinking about time use. But most of us have few options for how we support our families. Thus, this situation will remain resistant to change.

We constantly shield our children from danger, stress, and iniquity. Continuous, all-encompassing protectiveness has become a hallmark of American middle-class parenting. Dangerous tools are kept out of reach. Unhealthy foods are kept out of cupboards. Children are very rarely allowed beyond the scope of our vision.[35] Play areas set aside for their use are carpeted in rubber. Scenes and activities we deem emotionally upsetting, morally corrupting, or age-inappropriate are kept out of their sight. Lately, some of us are extending our protectiveness to children's books and textbooks.[36] We even try to protect youngsters from disappointment and grueling effort by voicing opposition to homework and high-stakes tests, and by giving a trophy to every child who participated in each organized sport.

We treat children as though they are mentally fragile. While researching my 2013 book, *The Aptitude Myth*, I discovered that this notion emerged in 15th-century Europe because Church leaders became eager to preserve youngsters' miraculous innocence. People began regarding children as precious, which came to imply that their minds—especially girls' minds—were harmed by more than modest effort.

Don't worry, I'm not going to advocate for pornography, tobacco use, or even salty snacks. I do advocate that we step back and reevaluate our protective stance in anthropological perspective.

Children in traditional societies receive virtually no adult protection, save during the 18 to 24 months between birth and weaning. During those pre-walking months, children are positioned so they can observe everything going on nearby; they're not isolated in a room or crib nor left on their backs facing the ceiling, and they're generally carried facing to the front. After weaning, youngsters join the group of local children, after which their activities receive little adult attention. Can we somehow become less enmeshed in our children's lives? For possibilities, consult *Free-Range Kids: How Parents and Teachers Can Let Go and Let Grow*, and/or *The Self-Driven Child: The Science and Sense of Giving Your Kids More Control Over Their Lives*.[37]

To what extent have you erected a protective shield around your children? How much of their lives does it encompass? Could some of it be relaxed, or even discarded entirely?

We insert ourselves and our preferences into our children's activities. Another reason we find child-rearing exhausting is that we are activist parents. We hold pretend conversations with our infants, select their playthings and play partners, and buy them toys and electronics that allegedly will spur early symbol use and creativity. We read to them, choose materials for their artistic efforts, thoughtfully schedule their screen time, and take them to events that entertain and educate. We join other parents in arranging athletic contests, often in organized leagues, coach youngsters who barely can run to practice their ball-handling skills, buy them pint-sized equipment, and drive them to distant locations for contests where some of us try to help them win by arguing with sight-impaired referees.[38]

Traditional societies are characterized by laissez-faire parenting, with this caveat: Laissez-faire applies when weaned children are not contributing to the family's economy. The degree to which children contribute varies, as we have seen, from nearly zero in the case of the Aka to quite a lot in the cases of the Quechua, the Navajo, and the Arab villagers. And let's not forget the daily toil of youngsters in economically insecure Indian families. But what's going on when children are *not* contributing economically? Encouraged by parents' laissez-faire stances, they create their own childhoods. Limited only by community norms, natural environments, and work responsibilities, traditional children are self-reliant.

We like to say that modern children have nearly unlimited choices, suggesting that they, too, are self-reliant. Not true. Adults past and present have imagined, designed, engineered, and manufactured nearly all of the options from which our children may choose. And some parents steer their youngsters toward certain types of choices—sports, arts, intellectual pursuits—that align with their family's habits and values. Technically, modern youth have virtually unlimited choices. In practice, though, their options usually are bounded by adults' prior choices, current prohibitions, and future planning. Are modern youth self-reliant? No. Their childhoods are provided for them— furnished, curated, supervised, circumscribed, and guided—by parents, educators, and other adults.

Some of our prior choices are counterproductive. For example, to encourage creativity, we buy our youngsters precision-engineered building sets that can be assembled in only a few ways—as the instructions specify. Can any toy that is manufactured and comes with detailed instructions really promote creativity? For contrast, consider those five Quechua youngsters who collaborated to fashion a model of their ayllu using only found objects: dirt, sticks, stones, grass, leaves, branches, water, mud, flowers, and tufts of wool.

How much of our parenting is necessarily adaptive to the background and context of our extraordinarily complex, symbol-driven modern lives? How much unnecessarily denies our children opportunities they could create on their own?

We assume almost total responsibility for the raising of our children. There is no counterpart in the historical or anthropological records for the isolation of modern parents. We live in nuclear families, in one-family households, often far from extended family members. We often lack close relationships with our neighbors. Our individualistic values impel us to feel insulted if anyone else dares discipline our child or even offers us advice. Parenting is the ultimate D.I.Y. project.

Do first-time American parents have useful experience to apply to raising their first-born child? Rarely. What passes for experience is baby-sitting when we were teenagers, which frequently involved doing our own thing while the baby slept. So when our own Number One Infant emerges, it's a whole new world. To whom do we turn for help? Experts.[39] For those who distrust experts, there are always the "mommy blogs" on the Internet.

In a traditional society, when Infant Number One emerges, the mother already will have attended births, observed her own mother nurturing younger siblings, and served as the full-time caretaker for at least one just-weaned child. If a first-time mom still needs support, nearby are her own mother, an aunt or two, and maybe even a grandmother.[40] After her child is weaned, she can rely on several others. Recall that a Navajo mother can count on an average of 6.5 nearby helpers.

Modern parents operate at a huge disadvantage: Little experience; extended family far away; a feeling that they must constantly shield their youngster from danger, stress, and iniquity; and a belief that they are solely responsible for providing a memorably happy childhood and fashioning a well-adjusted, successful adult. Fortunately, in some cases mothers with similar-age children form informal local groups for support in child-rearing and relief from isolation, in effect creating substitute extended families.

If you are, or soon will be, in this predicament, consider revisiting your options for sharing the responsibilities, even if for just some of the time. (As a child I was packed off each summer both to summer "sleep-away" camp and then to my aunt and uncle's farm. Great memories!)

We continue being responsible for our children after they attain puberty. Puberty is the process of physiological change by which a child's body becomes able to reproduce. It is the same for children everywhere, although the age at which puberty arrives is known to vary. How parents react to the arrival of puberty—especially their girls' menarche[41]—is cultural, driven by values.

Chapters 2 through 6 portrayed traditional parents' responses to the arrival of their children's puberty. Generally, they accept that the arrival of sexual maturity brings with it social maturity. In other words, they accept that their nearly grown children are responsible for making their own decisions.[42] That's a generalization with one qualification and one exception.

The qualification is that, in traditional societies, the whole process plays out within a communitarian value system. This increases the likelihood that the nearly grown child's choices will align with the interests of the extended family.

The exception occurs in societies in which the tracing of descent lines—usually through the male line—is highly valued. Accordingly, it is imperative to safeguard the premarital chastity of pubescent daughters, which can be assured only by tightly constraining their behavior until they are married. Pubescent sons face few restrictions[43]—but they've been steeped in communitarian values, making it likely that their behavior will be pleasing to their elders.

American children encounter and contend with puberty's physical changes within a different background and context. Many of our cultural values and social norms originated during earlier eras and were passed down to us, evolving as time passed. Among those was Puritanism, which strongly condemned any sort of sexual relationship outside of marriage, even any temptation to that end.[44] Pubescent youth are well known to experience exactly that temptation. So, historically, close supervision of youth has been deemed indispensable until they become adults.

During our lifetimes, this "puritanical" attitude has undergone rapid change among much of the population. Nonetheless, our forefathers considered parental responsibility for children and adolescents essential. It became enshrined into law, and there it remains. Thus, this situation will remain resistant to change.

* * * * *

The fundamental contrast between "other" parents and ourselves is simply stated:

Traditional parents parent as little as possible.

Modern parents parent as much as possible.

But please do not think of this contrast as being merely an expression of alternative ideas about parenting. This contrast reflects vast differences in the backgrounds and contexts in which traditional and modern parents deal with their children. Their minimalist parenting is adaptive to their circumstances. Our maximalist parenting is adaptive to ours. So even if we feel envious of their laissez-faire approach, it won't work for us to cut and paste it into our modern environment.

An unintended consequence of maximalist parenting is that our children have few opportunities for self-guided exploration and observation—the very process that traditional children use to learn virtually everything they need to know.

We have no choice about our children's years of instruction in symbol use; it is indispensable. But we *do* have choices about the extent to which we dominate their lives, ignoring their burgeoning capabilities. Can we take a step or two back, thereby releasing opportunities for them to explore and learn on their own?

That's the issue I encourage you to tackle now that you've finished reading this book.

SUGGESTED FURTHER READING

Each of the readings below is profiled at howotherchildrenlearn.info/profiles.

An Introduction to Childhood: Anthropological Perspectives on Children's Lives, by Heather Montgomery (2009); 238 text pages.

Raising Children: Surprising Insights from Other Cultures, by David F. Lancy (2017); 170 text pages.

Learning Without Lessons: Pedagogy in Indigenous Communities, by David F. Lancy (2023).

Appendix A, which supports Chapter 8, follows the Postscript.

The Bibliography at the back of this book includes all publications cited within Chapter 8.

Postscript

Of all the quotes in this book, one has lingered in my mind. When an anthropologist asked a young Aka about his plans for the future, he replied simply, "I am Aka."

What we know about the Aka makes it likely that this hunter-gatherer had a secure sense of self—his identity—anchored within the context of a closely familiar, stable group of people with shared values, beliefs, and practices.

Plans for the future? The Aka youth must have been perplexed by this query. His forthcoming adult roles and responsibilities were familiar to all, respected by all, *needed by all*. Like other young Aka, his future was as predictable as sunrise.

If this Aka's certitude and stability fail to excite a little envy in you, it's most likely because you sense that he doesn't have any choice in the matter.

As Americans, we expect choices about every aspect of our lives. This paramount value is most tangible in our markets, where we can choose from a staggering variety of products, and even one product type (e.g., toothpaste) is available in multiple sizes, tastes, and so forth. We are accustomed to having choices in countless intangible ways, too, from the life-defining (study science or humanities?) to the inconsequential (use Android or iOS?). We alert our youngsters to the normalcy of choice by often asking them to choose, for example, "What do you want for breakfast?"

The opportunity for each of us to make choices every day is what defines ours as an individualistic culture. For it is by making choices that each of us establishes our individuality, our identity—not only for those around us *but also for ourselves*.

Writing this book has alerted me to a contrast between the teenage/young adult years of American middle-class and traditional youth. It's about choice.

In societies yet to be penetrated by formal education, youth come of age aware of the direction their lives will take and what adulthood will require of them. Their identities are awaiting them, known to others as well as to themselves. This is a defining trait of a communitarian family culture. Security and continuity are valued.

In American society, middle-class youth coming of age foresee little about the direction their lives might take or what their adult roles might be. Yes, for some, the expectations of family, community, or faith point the way. But for most, ready-made identities do not await. Instead, they face dozens of self-defining options. This is a distinctive trait of an individualistic family culture. Liberty to make self-determined choices is valued. Hopefully, security will follow.

The range of options are of two types. One concerns, "What will I do with my life?" Beginning with "What am I good at?" and "What do I enjoy?," this type comprises choices about courses, extracurriculars, summer activities, SAT prep, student loans, further education, apprenticeships and internships, and more.

The other type concerns, "Who am I?" My preoccupation decades ago involved religious faith. Others wrestle with relationships and dating, use of leisure time, political alignment and activism, dietary options, social media use, dress and self-presentation (tattoo?), and a recently newsworthy one, sexuality and gender.

I asked the late-twenties son of a friend to share "the fundamental questions he struggled with between ages 15 and 25." Among the items on his list were:

- How can I handle growing apart from a friend due to different lifestyle choices?
- Which activities are worth giving my energy to, and which ones can I let go of?
- What will the people I want to be friends with think about my doing *this*?

It's hard to imagine that an option like any of those above ever worries a young Aka hunter-gatherer. But in the cases of the Quechua, Navajo, village Arabs, and village Indians, awareness of different paths through life might exist for youth who have attended school. As we have seen, classroom learning alerts the children of communitarian families to their own agency, and thus to individualism and choice.

To live a satisfying life, is it better to start by receiving a secure sense of your future anchored within the context of a deeply familiar, stable group of people with shared values? Or is it better to start by receiving many options, from the trivial to the life-defining, from which you must make choices to shape both your future and your identity in the context of transient relationships and fluctuating values?

Simply put, is it preferable to realize early in life that a secure role and identity awaits you, or to realize that you are responsible for figuring it all out on your own?

I see pros and cons to both. I also wonder if there might be an option midway between those two extremes, and what that might look like. What do you think?

Appendix A

These five tables are provided as potential aids to your understanding of Chapter 8, "How Do Other Children Learn? And How Do Other Parents Parent?" The tables generalize what anthropologists have discovered through fieldwork in many traditional societies, and in our own society. As always, each generalization has exceptions. These tables are not intended as a summary of Chapters 2 through 6.

The Bibliography at the back of this book includes all publications cited within Appendix A.

Appendix A, Table 1: Background and Context of Other Children and Our Own[1]

1. Background and Context of Other Children and Our Own

	Traditional & village societies	Middle-class American society
Family type and size	Extended; usually 10 or more in household.	Nuclear; usually 5 or fewer in household.
Parents' availability	Mother is always available until weaning; father is irregularly home and away.	One or both parents might be infrequently available; in their absence, caregiver hired.
Identity of other caregivers	Caregivers other than a close relative or long-trusted neighbor are extremely rare.	Caregivers in the home or at day care are often strangers, and they change often.
Extended family availability	Extended family members of all ages live near the family, interact often with children.	Few or no extended family members live near the parents and children.
Familiarity with neighbors	Neighboring families reside in the vicinity for long durations; most are well known.	Turnover among neighbors is frequent; relatively few neighbors are well known.
Items for children's attention	Found objects, adults' tools. A few parents will fashion a child-size tool for their child.	Parentally supplied, manufactured items are abundant, many irrelevant to adult life.
Areas where children gather	Areas only for children are rare; they gather in all the same areas frequented by adults.	Areas solely for children are curated; some encourage physical play, some fantasy play.
Young children's companions	Siblings, cousins, familiar neighbor children, often in freely associating multi-age groups.	Siblings & parents; other children, usually selected, planned, & supervised by adults.
Children's time use	Freely chosen, unsupervised activities; some involve imitating adults' typical activities.	Play supervised by adults, encouraged for fun & learning. Some play involves fantasy.
Visibility of adults' daily work	Often or constantly visible to children.	Infrequently or never visible to children.
Available activities when alone	Children are very rarely alone; adults or other children are always in the vicinity.	Electronically enabled activities, including fantasy play, contact with distant others.
Opportunity for child to assist	Children's assistance with the family's work typically is expected, encouraged, required.	Opportunities for children to substantively contribute to the family's work are rare.
Important for children to learn	How to fit in supportively throughout life, contribute to family's well-being & honor.	Knowledge & skills, academic & social, to enhance child's later life away from family.
Older children's social context	If no school, little difference from earlier years; many familiar faces and activities.	Schooling brings many different settings, people, activities, hierarchies, anxieties . . . .

Appendix A, Table 2: Contrasting Models of Parenting and Families[2]

2. Contrasting Models of Parenting and Families

	Traditional & village societies	Middle-class American society
Major environmental realities	Children needed to labor for family income and to support aged parents. High infant mortality. Little or no formal preparation needed for agrarian adult life and work.	Children not needed to labor for family income or support aged parents. Infant mortality low. Long formal preparation needed for modern adult life and work.
Basic child-rearing goals	Bear many children. To increase chance of survival, carefully nurture and protect each till weaned. Involve each in family economy from a young age. A "quantitative" goal.	Restrict number of children. Prepare each very well for success in modern economy and ability to establish own separate, self-sufficient families. A "qualitative" goal.
Basic stance of parents	Raising children is a practical necessity that brings long-term benefits to this extended family, while costing little.	Raising children is a voluntary activity with high costs and heavy responsibilities that must be borne by this nuclear family.
Practical parenting strategy	Mother intensively nurtures, protects each new-born till weaning. Then releases child to care of older sibling or other family member, or into the neighborhood children's group.	Mother engages one-on-one with each child to provide mental stimulation and build awareness of separateness, agency. Father often involved to some extent.
Characteristics of interactions	Parents expect from child polite behavior and conformity to family role obligations. Child's desires are low priority. Interactions dispersed throughout extended family.	Child is the primary driver of interactions. Parents are responsive to child's desires & needs, supervise most of child's activities. Interaction concentrated in nuclear family.
Desired psychological profile	Child acquires "hierarchical relatedness": Views self in terms of roles and obligations within a hierarchically organized family.	Child acquires "psychological autonomy": Views self as acting independently while influenced by others on some decisions.
Assignment of responsibilities	Child's labor vital to family welfare; taking on responsibilities compatible with ability enables child to share the family's culture.	Child's labor rarely vital to family welfare; parents use various strategies to persuade children occasionally to take on a chore.
Sources of support for mother	Extended family such as mother's mother, sisters, aunts; occasionally, child's father.	Mother's mother, friends who are mothers, father; experts not personally known.
Direction of resource flow	Parents get resources from their children.	Parents give resources to their children.

Appendix A, Table 3: What Traditional and U.S. Parents THINK about Childrearing[3]

3. What Traditional and U.S. Parents THINK about Childrearing

	Traditional & village societies	Middle-class American society
Understanding of parental role	Responsibility for child's protection and development shared with extended family.	Parents have almost total responsibility for child's protection and development.
Source of mothering know-how	Apprenticeship as full-time caretaker of a sibling; years observing mother, aunts.	Rarely any opportunity to learn before own first child born; experts and/or own mother.
Extent of the mother's role	Mother expected to be main caregiver until weaning; caregiving then distributed.	Mother is a principal caregiver throughout each child's early and middle years.
Inculcated re self and others	Early upbringing emphasizes extended family members' interdependence, loyalty.	Early upbringing inculcates individualism, e.g., self-expression and self-advancement.
Characteristic of parental love	Main emotional bond is with one's extended family, to which spouse & children belong.	Main emotional bond is, or should be, with one's spouse; children also are loved.
Goal for early development	Child senses self in enduring relation to others in extended family and community.	Child senses self as a separate being who exercises agency, contends with others.
Goals for child's intelligence	Relational: respectful of authority, dutiful re obligations, loyal to extended family.	Cognitive: curious, quick-witted, articulate, creative, assertive, independent-minded.
Goals for long-term future	Relational competence with extended family, whose members fulfill obligations.	Education leading to secure employment, upward mobility, eventual independence.
Importance of child's needs	Child's needs rarely eclipse adults' needs.	Child's needs should dominate use of family's resources and parents' schedules.
Concern for child's innocence	Concern for child's innocence is rare.	Child's innocence should be maintained by barring access to many details of adult life.
Hoped-for child characteristics	Increasingly contributes to family well-being but expects to receive little from parents.	Precocious, well rounded, creative, doing well in school & sports, popular with peers.
Attitude re arrival of puberty	Highly variable across traditional societies.	Wariness due to parental responsibility for curbing anticipated excesses of puberty.

Appendix A, Table 4: What Traditional and U.S. Parents DO about Childrearing[4]

4. What Traditional and U.S. Parents DO about Childrearing

	Traditional & village societies	Middle-class American society
Obtain child-rearing assistance	Older siblings, extended family members, other trusted adult women in the village.	Usually baby-sitters, nannies, and day-care staffers previously unknown to the family.
Involve child with wider family	Extended family females often are nearby and will actively participate in childcare.	Extended family often is too distant for more than sporadic direct involvement.
Involve self in child's play	Involvement in child's play is very rare.	Frequent play with child and arrangement of child's external play opportunities.
Support make-believe play	Adults not involved; child often uses found objects to replicate adults' real-life work.	By providing manufactured toys, adults foster fantasy and work-replication play.
Involve child in adults' work	As capabilities improve, child increasingly expected to contribute to family economy.	Child's world is kept almost totally separate from adult maintenance of family economy.
Assign child responsibilities	Growing responsibilities almost all visibly contribute to maintaining family economy.	The few responsibilities requested usually have little relevance to family's economy.
Regulate child's environment	Regulation of environment is very rare.	During early years, environment curated to maximize fun, minimize stress, danger.
Regulate child's schedule	Regulation of schedule is very rare.	During middle years, schedule regulated to maximize opportunities for learning, fun.
Enhance child's self-esteem	Concern for self-esteem is very rare.	Cultivate child's high self-regard by praising output when quality is both good and bad.
Enhance child's intelligence	During early years, strive to hasten growth of child's relational (emotional) intelligence.	During early years, strive to hasten growth of child's cognitive (scholastic) intelligence.
Methods of child socialization	Child is largely self-socialized; if needed, shaming, frightening, issuing directives.	Reasoning; issuing directives; promising to give or threatening to withhold resources.
Respond to arrival of puberty	Highly variable, from complete autonomy to tight control of females' behavior.	Parental responsibility for child continues unabated until his or her 18th birthday

Appendix A, Table 5: Learning and Schooling in Traditional and U.S. Societies[5]

5. *Learning and Schooling in Traditional and U.S. Societies*

	Traditional & village societies	Middle-class American society
Principal purpose of learning	To maintain continuity by inculcating youth with received wisdom of past generations.	To maintain continuity and to enable youth to real-ize their unique inborn potential.
Important abilities learned	Practical, manual: homemaking, farming, forag-ing, hunting, making arts and crafts.	Abstract, mental: recognizing, analyzing, manipu-lating, generalizing using symbols.
Difficulty of what is learned	Low: largely manual skills requiring stamina, dex-terity, know-how, but rarely analysis.	High & increasing: cognitive skills at ever-higher levels, driven by global economy.
Principal modes of learning	Observing in-progress work; trial-and-error imita-tion; increasingly contributing to work.	Receiving formal instruction, reading, memorizing, rehearsing, reciting, testing.
Ideal conditions for learning	Autonomous children alone and in groups sponta-neously observe, imitate, contribute.	Organized same-age groups of children learn in tandem under teacher's direction.
Identity of knowledge-bearers	Well-known others, mainly respected and loved relatives senior in experience & age.	Adult strangers professionally trained and formally certified to carry out instruction.
Identity of fellow learners	Siblings, cousins, neighbor children in adult-free, multi-age, randomly formed groups.	Strangers, neighbors, relatives organized by instructors into same-age groups.
Mode of learner's attention	All-inclusive attention to one's surroundings and their context (similar to mindfulness).	Narrowly focused analytical attention to one thing at a time, often without context.
Understanding of intelligence	Relational: respectful of authority, dutiful re obli-gations, loyal to extended family.	Cognitive: curious, quick-witted, articulate, cre-ative, assertive, independent-minded.
Parents' view of education	Education leads to desirable wage earning but also might undermine cherished values.	Indispensable for employment, but is only one ele-ment of child's well-roundedness.
Parents' school involvement	Hands-off due to respect for high-status teachers, perplexity re classroom learning.	Prefer teachers to take lead; will intervene if values refuted or expectations unmet.
Schooling's impact on learners	Children from interdependent families gain new sense of individuality, personal agency.	Entire culture inculcates individualism, so school-ing rarely alters children's self-view.
Schools' impact on community	Viability of community can be undercut as chil-dren sensing agency seek new horizons.	A school, especially via sports, can become rally-ing point of a smaller U.S. community.

Appendix B

SOURCES OF INFORMATION FOR
THE FIVE MAIN CHAPTERS

To write each of the five main chapters of this book—about the Aka, Quechua, Navajos, Village Arabs, and Village Indians—I relied entirely on books and journal articles, the majority completed by anthropologists or other researchers using the method of participant observation. This appendix overviews how I acquired these documents and which ones I found especially useful. It will also explain why this book cannot be about the current situation in these societies but instead discusses parenting and children's learning during the recent or not-so-recent past.

When I decided that I wanted to write a book of this nature, my first step was to identify, within the worldwide literature of anthropology, those traditional societies in which at least some research on childhood had been done. This preliminary step required three months because separate Internet searches had to be done for each world region and country, and records had to be kept regarding each traditional society that initially seemed promising.

This initial exploratory effort enabled me to eliminate most societies because too little research had been completed in them regarding childcare and children's learning. For the few societies that seemed promising, leads had to be pursued to determine the type and extent of the research that had been completed. Document titles alone rarely reveal clearly whether the research team used anthropological participant observation methods or psychological survey techniques; I have little interest in the latter.[1]

How I Acquire Books and Journal Articles

During my doctoral dissertation days decades ago, I spent many hours in libraries. Nowadays virtually everything can be done by tapping the keys on my computer. Academic scholarship has undergone revolutionary change in half a lifetime!

Books: To search for books by title, topic, or author, and to obtain information on what each one is about, I start with books.google.com, which is helpful but has significant limitations.[2] Equally or more valuable is barnesandnoble. com, which is superior to amazon.com for this purpose. The B&N website includes the table of contents for virtually every nonfiction book it carries, which is valuable to me. I've never found a table of contents on amazon.com.

So when I decide to purchase a book, I use B&N's more useful website, which carries most books I want. But not all. Some books I need were published decades ago and are kept in stock only by small, specialized booksellers. B&N has relations with some of these specialized sellers, but Amazon has relations with far more.

Journal articles: In the case of journal articles, scholar.google.com is both excellent and indispensable. One can search for articles by title, topic, or author. You are immediately taken to a list of articles that match your request (thus, a search for a specific article title usually yields a list of one). Each item in the list is a link to an article on a website maintained by a journal publisher such as Brill, JSTOR, Sage, ScienceDirect, Springer, Taylor & Francis, Wiley On-Line, and many others. On that website, you can read the abstract of the article and, almost always, arrange to purchase it.[3] Upon purchase, the article in PDF format is immediately available for downloading, saving, and printing.

Some journal articles that seem to require purchase also might be available at no charge, in two ways: (1) On scholar.google.com, to the right of an article's main link (to a journal publisher) you might also see an alternative link; it almost always is free. (2) An article's author (or each author) is almost always a university faculty member. On that university's website, find the author's faculty-member page, on which you might find no-cost links to most of the journal articles he or she ever wrote.

Bibliographies: The most useful method of identifying books and articles about my topic of interest—for example, about the Navajos—is to consult the bibliography of each journal article and book on that topic that I already own. This method sometimes yields citations of old and obscure journal articles or books that I have not found on either books.google.com or scholar. google.com.

The Aka Hunter-Gatherers of Africa

Some of the anthropologists who have studied the Aka used *quantitative* research methods. In other words, they counted things.[4] I mention this because their penchant for counting things complicates my job. What works far better for me is the kind of information provided by anthropologists who use the participant observation method,[5] which yields narratives rather than numbers. (This type of research is termed "qualitative.") This is why the Aka chapter includes fewer stories, vignettes, and insider quotes than the other four main chapters.

The leading scholar of the Aka hunter-gatherers is Barry Hewlett of Washington State University, whose book *Intimate Fathers* (1991) was an important source for me. Hewlett was the dissertation advisor for, and later a collaborator with, Adam Boyette, a second key figure in Aka research. Another of Professor Hewlett's graduate students was Bonnie Bentz, who became Bonnie Hewlett and a Ph.D. anthropologist in her own right. Fortunately, Bonnie doesn't count things! Instead, she gave us her warmly humane book about the lives of Aka and Ngandu women, *Listen, Here Is a Story* (2013a), which is the source of most of the stories, vignettes, and insider quotes in Chapter 2.

Other scholars on whom I relied include Courtney L. Meehan, Sheina Lew-Levy and her collaborators, and—regarding the Aka–Ngandu relationship—Kiyoshi Takeuchi.

The Quechua of Highland Peru

The Quechua of Peru presented me with an ideal resource: a recently published book focused on children and child-rearing, completed in one high-altitude Andean community by an anthropologist using participant observation methods over multiple visits.

So I was enthusiastic about Inge Bolin's engaging work, *Growing Up in a Culture of Respect* (2006). Bolin's book was everything I had hoped for: stories, vignettes, insider quotes, and many evocative photographs that portrayed the Quechua as welcoming and warm in spite of their environmental challenges. But, as always, I was unwilling to rely entirely on a single source.

It turned out that other anthropological studies of the Quechua were in short supply. I found only one other useful book, *Pastoralists of the Andes* (1968), by Jorge Flores-Ochoa. Useful journal articles were penned by Fernando García (a native Quechua), Guillermo Salas Carreño, Catherine Allen, and— especially for understanding the supernatural world of the Quechua—Juan Núñez del Prado. After I drafted the Quechua chapter, I was fortunate indeed to have Inge Bolin herself read and comment on my draft, and she has been helpful in other ways since then.

The Navajo of the U.S. Southwest

During the mid-20th century, the Navajo tribe was one of the most heavily studied of all traditional peoples. Researchers quipped that a typical Navajo family included a mother, a father, several children, and an anthropologist.[6] This reputation was gained primarily due to the extensive work by the team led by Clyde Kluckhohn and Dorothea Leighton; especially useful for me was their second book, *Children of The People* (1947), which focused entirely on Navajo children and their upbringing.

Leighton was not an anthropologist but a psychiatrist; her research used a battery of psychological tests including some that involved projective techniques such as the Rorschach "inkblot" test. These did not interest me at all. Fortunately, in both of their coauthored books, the chapters written by Kluckhohn are clearly identified.

Another useful source of information about Navajo childhood was the work of James Chisholm. *Navajo Infancy* (1983) was his published Ph.D. dissertation, which he undertook largely to determine whether cradleboards undermined mother-child "attachment" (discussed in Chapter 1). In 2014, Chisholm wrote a journal article, "Learning 'respect for everything,'" which also proved relevant to my work.

Concerning the other sources that I unearthed about the Navajo, I particularly want to mention two authors. Three useful articles, all written during the 1990s, came from Donna Deyhle (as either lead author or solo author); these explored the Navajos' fraught relation to schooling. And in the mid-1930s, Walter Dyk recorded the extensive reminiscing of an aged Navajo man who had been born during the tribe's internment near Fort Sumner. Dyk's published transcript provides us with a fascinating if rambling autobiography, *Left Handed, Son of Old Man Hat* (1938).

The Village Arabs of the Levant

At first, I hoped that I could focus this chapter on the child-rearing practices of the Bedouin nomads. I soon became aware that much has been written about the Bedouins but little about their child-rearing. For example, the most comprehensive book about the Bedouins is 670 pages long; only one page is about "Boys and Girls."

A problem was that no book stood out as my "anchor volume." Eventually, I found a few mid-20th-century books by anthropologists who had focused on child-rearing in the Levant. Most useful were those by Hamed Ammar,

Hilma Granqvist, and Judith Williams, plus a book of readings compiled by Abdulla Lutfiyya and Charles Churchill. And one cannot study the Levantine Arabs without encountering the works of Dawn Chatty; I made use of two of her publications.

The oldest source I consulted was the two-volume desert travel memoir, *Bedouin Tribes of the Euphrates* (1879), by Lady Anne Blunt. I thought, "Great! She'll have lots to say about the Bedouin children she encounters." Wrong. She took only a cursory interest in the children.

One of the most recent sources I consulted was by another Western woman who found herself among the Bedouins: Marguerite van Geldermalsen. A nurse from New Zealand who was touring Jordan during 1978, she met and married a Bedouin souvenir-seller, moved into his cave, bore three children, and wrote a book about it: *Married to a Bedouin* (2006).

I am leaving for last the book that impressed me greatly: *Within the Circle: Parents and Children in an Arab Village* (1997), by Andrea Rugh. An independent scholar with extensive experience in the Middle East, Rugh has a discerning eye for the nuanced differences between Arab and American child-rearing practices and their underlying values. Her final chapter is outstanding.

The Hindu Villagers of India

India quickly became more challenging to research than the other four societies, but not because there was too little information. There was a great deal of information—from all around India. Participant observation research on children and parents had been completed in the northern Indian states of Kashmir, Punjab, and Uttar Pradesh; in the western state of Gujarat; in the southern states of Karnataka, Kerala, and Tamil Nadu; and in the eastern states of West Bengal and Orissa. And two studies had been completed in the vicinity of Delhi, the capital city.[7]

I had hoped to be able to focus on one locality. The greatest volume of research in one location had come from the east coast state of Orissa, where a modernizing town had been studied longitudinally by Susan Seymour.[8] But her work didn't adequately fulfill my needs.

As I perused research reports from all around India, I realized that the regional differences among family organization and child-rearing ways were fewer than I had imagined—as long as I kept my focus on rural villages.[9] Several anthropologists had written about children from an all-India standpoint.[10] One summarized research from all around India, then concluded that

> accounts from all regions speak of joint families, multiple caretakers, and rules
> of restraint on parent–child interaction in front of elders. Even where joint

families do not predominate, nuclear families are reported to locate near relatives in order to approximate joint family participation in child rearing.[11]

So I became convinced that I could write Chapter 6 as a composite, drawing on research completed in all ten Indian states. Among the books I relied on most were those by T. N. Madan, David Mandelbaum, Margaret Trawick, Leigh Minturn and John Hitchcock, Ronald Rohner and Manjusri Chaki-Sircar, and especially Susan Seymour's *Women, Family, and Child Care in India* (1999). Also useful was the monograph by Ruth and Stanley Freed. Among the most useful journal articles and book chapters were several by Susan Seymour as well as Stacey Raj and Vaishali Raval's "Parenting and Family Socialization within a Cultural Context" (2013).

Ten thousand years ago and through the early Middle Ages, all societies were traditional. Today, some societies are WEIRD: Western, Educated, Industrial, Rich, and Democratic. How and why did that momentous transformation occur? For a fascinating explanation, read Joseph Henrich's 2020 book, *The WEIRDest People in the World: How the West Became Psychologically Peculiar and Particularly Prosperous*; Farrar, Straus and Giroux, 489 text pages. Grounded in history, psychology, sociology, and anthropology, Henrich's hypothesis is both meticulously researched and patiently explained. I highly recommend this book.

The Bibliography at the back of this book includes all publications cited within Appendix B.

Notes

INTRODUCTION

1. Robert LeVine himself relates this story in LeVine (2021a), 17.

2. Blum, 27; in turn, Blum cites ZeroToThree.org, 2004; shortened.

3. One expert holds that "Vocabulary is the best single indicator of intellectual ability and an accurate predictor of success at school." Blum, 26; in turn, Blum cites W. B. Elley.

4. I say "most" traditional societies because, as Chapter 2 will reveal, the children of Aka hunter-gatherers are not expected to share in the completion of any chores and may refuse if requested to do so.

5. I have been informed that some people feel that "traditional" borders on being derogatory. I agree that "primitive" had come to imply that a society's inhabitants are subhuman, so I *never* use "primitive." If you believe that my use of "traditional" is derogatory, I apologize—and ask you in return, "What term would you recommend I use?" Reach me using the "contact" page of www.howotherchildrenlearn.info.

6. I am confident that those who coined the term "WEIRD" were disappointed that it did not also include a "U" for Urban. Virtually all WEIRD societies are highly urbanized (and suburbanized): WEIRDU.

7. Henrich, Joseph, Steven J. Heine, & Ara Norenzayan (2010). The weirdest people in the world? *Behavioral and Brain Sciences, 33* (2/3), 1–75. The lead author, Joseph Henrich, went on to write *The Weirdest People in the World* (Picador, 2021), which explains how Western societies became weird over the past 1000 years. For a brief overview, visit henrich.fas.harvard.edu/files/henrich/files/sciencefull.pdf.eiH.

8. Henrich et al., 3.

9. Kluckhohn & Murray (1948), 35. I have substituted "human" where they used "man" or "men."

10. The information about fathers is inspired by Hewlett & MacFarlan, 424.

11. Reliance on the sea (i.e., fishing), would be a form of hunting or gathering. I am not personally acquainted with anthropological studies of societies that sustain themselves through fishing.

12. *Bringing Up Bébé: One American Mother Discovers the Wisdom of French Parenting* (2012), by Pamela Druckerman, a journalist. To raise wonderful children, follow the example of French parents.

How Eskimos Keep Their Babies Warm: And Other Adventures in Parenting (2012), by Mei-Ling Hopgood, a journalist. Superior parenting is found in Lebanon, Polynesia, Mexico, China, and other locations.

The Mindful Parent: Strategies from Peaceful Cultures to Raise Compassionate, Competent Kids (2015), by Charlotte Peterson, a psychologist. Animated by her concern about violence in the United States, Peterson explores parenting in three "peaceful cultures," those of the Tibetans, Bhutanese, and Balinese.

Hunt, Gather, Parent: What Ancient Cultures Can Teach Us about the Lost Art of Raising Happy, Helpful Little Humans (2021), by Michaeleen Doucleff, a journalist. Distraught over her "battles" with her young child, Doucleff seeks wisdom among Mexican Maya, Canadian Inuit, and Tanzanian Hadzabe.

A World of Babies: Imagined Childcare Guides for Eight Societies (2016), by Alma Gottlieb, a professor of anthropology, and Judy DeLoache, a professor of psychology. Here the focus is on the approaches of parents under duress, such as Palestinians under Israeli occupation and Somali immigrants in the United States.

Do Parents Matter? Why Japanese Babies Sleep Soundly, Mexican Siblings Don't Fight, and American Families Should Relax (2016), by Robert A. LeVine & Sarah LeVine, Harvard professors. (Robert LeVine is one of the world's leading authorities in the field of the anthropology of childhood.) Their message for American parents is, "Relax; don't try so hard!" An especially useful contribution of this book is its review of "the psychiatric perspective" in its first chapter, "Parent-Blaming in America."

13. The general finding of anthropologists has been that whenever one tries to take a solution from one culture and apply it in a different culture, problems inevitably occur. One anthropologist likened the process to that of an organ transplant, which works only if special, lifelong measures are taken to ensure that the recipient's body doesn't reject it.

14. *Raising Children: Surprising Insights from Other Cultures* (2017), by David F. Lancy, a professor of anthropology at Utah State University. Billed as a book about parents and children, not a prescription for how to be a better parent, *Raising Children* was written as a "baby version" of Lancy's truly encyclopedic scholarly work, *The Anthropology of Childhood: Cherubs, Chattel, Changlings*, now in its third edition.

15. My 2020 book, *A Mirror for Americans*, explored preschools and primary schools in East Asia. One of the researchers on whom I heavily relied was James Stigler of UCLA, who used qualitative methods and identifies professionally as a psychologist.

16. During the autumn of 1972, I briefly visited a center of the Aka-inhabited region of Africa, the town of Bangassou (a.k.a. Bangandou) at the southern edge of the Central African Republic. None of the information in this book is based on that visit.

17. In Chapter 6 (Village Indians), this section is followed by a unique section, "Teenage Girls' Momentous Transition."

CHAPTER 1

1. Anthropology's focus is broader and more holistic than I'm suggesting in the text. Anthropology takes a "four field approach" to studying humans. The four fields are prehistoric archeology, biological (formerly physical) anthropology, anthropological linguistics, and social/cultural anthropology. What the text is describing is social/cultural anthropology. Thank you to Willa Hallowell and Laila Williamson, both anthropologists and both my close friends, for prompting me about these four fields.

2. Whiting & Edwards (1988), 10.

3. For example, 160 definitions of "culture" were discussed by Alfred Kroeber & Clyde Kluckhohn (1963), in *Culture: A Critical Review of Concepts and Definitions*. New definitions have appeared since then.

4. These two paragraphs were inspired by LeVine (2021), 84.

5. This crossing-the-street example is drawn from my own experience as a father. My choice was to apply corporal punishment instantly—in the middle of the street.

6. In his book *Sapiens* (2015), Yuval Noah Harari emphasizes that human behavior is not the result of instinctual drives but rather is learned. He writes (p. 163), "Myths and fictions accustom people, nearly from the moment of birth, to think in certain ways, to behave in accordance with certain standards, to want certain things, and to observe certain rules. They create artificial instincts that enable millions of strangers to cooperate effectively. This network of artificial instincts is called 'culture.'"

7. For an up-to-date review of discoveries, including chimps sticking blades of grass in their ears to appear more alluring, see https://www.nytimes.com/2021/05/07/science/animals-chimps-whales-culture.html.

8. The scientific process sometimes involves more than forming a question. Scientists usually have some awareness of the domain in which they are interested, which enables them to be specific about what they believe their fact-finding will discover. This *hypothesis* guides their research efforts, which conclude when the scientists can report whether their hypothesis was found to be accurate or erroneous.

9. Determined eugenicists favored measures such as sterilizing women from "inferior races." The most despicable outcome of eugenicist thinking was the Nazi death camps of World War Two.

10. Tracking (a.k.a. streaming) occurs when students who are presumed to have similar academic abilities are kept together for their classes, and apart from students presumed to have different academic abilities. When I taught high school during the 1960s, my school had four tracks: Honors, Superior, Middle, and Essentials. For a fuller discussion of the influence of G. Stanley Hall and other thought-leaders on American education, see my book *The Aptitude Myth*, Part II, especially Chapter 15.

11. For a detailed historical discussion of these events, see King (2019), especially Chapter 7 (entitled "A Girl as Frail as Margaret").

12. After gaining his Ph.D., Hall spent about a year in Germany in academic pursuits.

13. The first major publication to come from the Six Cultures Study was *Children of Six Cultures: A Psycho-Cultural Analysis*, by Beatrice B. Whiting & John W. M. Whiting (1975). Many other books and articles have come from the Six Cultures

Study, and countless others have been inspired by it. One of my sources for Chapter 6, on the Hindu villagers of India, was an original Six Cultures study.

14. LeVine (2007), 253.

15. Hewlett, Bonnie L., 4–5; lightly edited.

16. Anthropologists are aware that their mere presence among the group being studied over a period of months is bound to introduce some changes into that group. Most do their best to keep their non-native impact on the group to a minimum.

17. King (2019), 165; lightly edited.

18. Induction—from the Latin *in* + *ducere*, "to lead in"—is the mental process of gradually attaining a generalization about how a portion of the world works after using the five senses to carefully observe many individual cases of the relevant phenomenon. The resulting generalization is viewed as "very probably true" because if new observations find contrary evidence, the generalization will be revised. Observation-based induction is the principal method of science. For a fuller discussion including the distinction between inductive and deductive reasoning, see my book *The Aptitude Myth* (2013), 23–24.

19. For example, anthropologist Derek Freeman (1916–2001) devoted most of his career to relentlessly criticizing Mead's Samoan research and its findings. Freeman's accusations ignited fierce controversy but failed to bring many other anthropologists around to his perspective. For a fuller account of Freeman and the controversy, see King (2019), 368 note 166.

20. My account of "attachment theory" in these two paragraphs relies substantially on LeVine & Norman (2008), 127–155. See also Lancy (2017), Chapter 3. I prefer to call it the "attachment hypothesis."

21. The British psychologist who introduced "attachment theory" to the scholarly community was John Bowlby (1907–1990). He devoted much of his career to researching and publishing on attachment and closely related topics such as separation anxiety. Bowlby gained a wide following during his lifetime.

22. The American psychologist was Mary D. Ainsworth (1913–1999). At Baltimore's Johns Hopkins University during 1962–63, I took Ainsworth's course on "Maternal Deprivation," which was fascinating. I might be writing this book now because of an interest kindled by Professor Mary D. Ainsworth then.

23. Marey-Sarwan et al. (2016), 320. Ainsworth had previously completed fieldwork in Uganda, where young children have multiple caregivers. In *Infancy in Uganda* (1967), Ainsworth developed the concept of "multiple attachments." Yet when she teamed up with Bowlby, she seems to have reverted to the Western assumption that mother-centered caretaking is the global norm. For more information, see Seymour (2004), 542.

24. Chisholm (1983), 184 and 185, shortened and edited.

25. As you will learn in Chapter 2, among the Aka Pygmies, infants and young children have the attention of multiple caregivers to the point where all their physical and emotional needs are constantly and quickly met. They are *never alone*! Two Aka researchers wrote that if they were to conduct a Strange Situation assessment with Aka infants, it likely would be literally the only time in their lives that they were completely alone, and therefore a very stressful experience. Meehan & Hawkes, 107.

26. Weisner & Gallimore (2008), 267; italics in the original.

27. Williams (1969), 71. As quoted in Weisner & Gallimore (2008), 266; italics added.

28. Everett (2008), 89–90.

29. In some societies there are no adult-designed, mass-produced educational toys. Lancy (2017), 153, explains that "The very young play mostly with found objects, such as tools and utensils. These may include sharp knives and other 'dangerous' items. The assumption is that that the child will only learn to use the object by actually using it." For an account of youngsters learning through creative play with rocks, branches, and so forth, see Bolin (2006), 62–67 (also discussed in Chapter 3 of this book).

30. Lancy (2017), 149.

31. Lancy (2017), 153–154. There are accounts of adults making small-scale tools for their children, such as bow-and-arrow sets, when their boys show an interest in learning to use them.

32. Have you ever asked yourself why Americans keep children rigorously apart from many aspects of adult life? If you have a convincing answer, let me know via the contact page of this book's website.

33. How children learn complex skills through observation, that is, in the absence of instruction, is a subfield within anthropology of childhood. Its leading light is Barbara Rogoff of the University of California.

34. Lancy (2017), 151. Lancy notes that exceptions to this pattern may be found in hunting societies in which very young children may be unwelcome on hunting expeditions.

35. Ochs & Izquierdo (2009).

CHAPTER 2

1. The opening paragraphs were inspired by Duffy, vii.

2. Boyette (2016a), 759; Hewlett, Bonnie (1991), 157, 171. The claim that current hunter-gatherers live much as humans did a million years ago is common, but I have not seen it attributed to any source.

3. I say "almost-perfect 'state of nature'" because current hunter-gatherers have some modern items, for example, metal pots and clothing, and in some regions they have limited access to health care and other services, and even schools. Many must contend with human-caused loss of their habitat.

4. Among other hunter-gatherer (or forager) groups are the Bofi, Efe, Hadza, and !Kung of Africa; the Nayaka of India; the Batek of Malaysia; the Inuits of Canada; and several U.S.-based Indian tribes such as the Crow, Blackfoot, Delaware, and Comanche. Lew-Levy et al. (2018), 13–14, Table 1. For more details about hunter-gatherers, see Robert Kelly (2013), *The Lifeways of Hunter-Gatherers: The Foraging Spectrum*, Cambridge.

5. These characteristics are based on Hewlett & Hewlett, 78, Table 4.1.

Notes

6. Harari, passages recombined from 49 and 79. As evidence that the size of sapiens' brains has *decreased* since the time of ancient foragers, Harari cites four studies on 418, note 5.

7. Hewlett, Barry (1991), 11–12.

8. Konga, quoted by Hewlett, Bonnie (2013a), 73.

9. Hewlett, Barry (1991), 25. He adds that *banda* is when men flush game and women kill it, whereas *mbembo* is when women flush game and men kill it. See also Bacirongo & Nest, 29–30.

10. Boyette (2013), 48; Hewlett, Bonnie (2013a), 45; and Hewlett, Barry (1991), 25. The *eru* plant, properly termed *Gnetum africanum*, is popular throughout Central Africa; its leaves are eaten raw or cooked, and it has other uses including to ease childbirth. The Aka use the term *kôkô* to refer to a dish made of shredded *eru* leaves. See pfaf.org/user/Plant.aspx?LatinName=Gnetum+africanum.

11. A study of Aka infant and child health during the late 1980s found that they were "healthier than most of their peers in the developing world." Measures included "weight for height," head circumference, and hemoglobin levels. Hewlett, Barry, et al. (1998), 660; cited in turn is Cordes & Hewlett (1990).

12. Konga, quoted by Hewlett, Bonnie (2013a), 53, edited and shortened.

13. This account of the Aka–Ngandu relationship is based on Takeuchi, 11–19. Also see Hewlett, Bonnie (2013a), 45, 49, 218; Hewlett, Barry (1991), 14, 16–17, 24, 29; Boyette (2013), 45–47, 56–59; and Boyette (2019), 482.

14. Manioc, also called cassava, is a draught-tolerant plant with an edible root, somewhat similar to the potato, that is popular throughout the tropics.

15. The Ngandu claim that the Aka are unpunctual, slovenly, irrational, smelly, and full of procreative power; see Takeuchi, 18–19. However, a few Ngandu are kind and sympathetic toward the Aka; see Boyette (2013), 59.

16. Fouts, 296. She adds that, in the forest, Aka camps are a one- to four-hour walk from each other; 307.

17. Bacirongo & Nest, 24–25, 32–33, edited and shortened. Isaac Bacirongo spent the early years of his life as a BaTembo Pygmy in Central Africa. He is one of very few hunter-gatherers to ever choose to live in Western society. Note that, among the Aka, the wife constructs the hut, not the couple together.

18. Hewlett, Bonnie (2013a), 24, edited and shortened.

19. Hewlett, Bonnie (2013a), 43, edited and shortened.

20. Hewlett, Bonnie (2013a), 43–44, and Hewlett, Barry (1991), 32, and (2014), 248. For a photo taken to show how a four-member family sleeps in a twig bed, see Hewlett, Barry, et al. (2019), 45, Figure 3.1.

21. The Aka could easily increase their living space, but they prefer to be physically close. Hewlett et al. (2019), 54.

22. Demographically, the Aka are classed as high fertility (four to six live births per woman) and high child mortality (20% up to 12 months of age, 35–45% up to 15 years of age). Accidental and violent deaths among the Aka are infrequent compared with other hunter-gatherers. Hewlett, Barry (1991), 18–19, 32; and Hewlett, Bonnie (2013a), 39.

23. Hewlett, Bonnie (2013a), 43–44. She adds that "if a wife wants to live elsewhere for a while and her husband does not, she simply leaves. In a few weeks the family's hut begins to leak, then falls apart, and soon the reluctant husband goes to live with his wife."

24. All accounts imply that husband and wife always come from different camps, never the same camp.

25. Hewlett, Barry (1991), 38, 40–43, 173. Also see Hewlett, Barry (2014), 247.

26. Hewlett, Barry (1991), 139, reports that Aka husbands and wives are within sight of each other during 46% of daylight hours, more than any other known society; this percentage increases in the evenings.

27. Wives can become extremely angry if they learn that their husband has been sleeping with other women. Their typical response is to tear down the family hut, which men are not skilled in building. Hewlett, Barry (1991), 41.

28. Hewlett, Barry (1991), 27. Surprisingly, he notes that the Ngandu defer to a *kombeti*—greeting him first, giving him extra cigarettes, and so forth—but the Aka do not. See also Hewlett, Bonnie (2013a), 40.

29. Hewlett, Bonnie (2013a), 41–42, 65; Hewlett, Barry (1991), 28, 39; and Boyette (2013), 49. See also Boyette (2019), 484–86, Tables 3–5.

30. A detailed description of sharing practices is provided by Kitanishi, 17–18, 24. See also Hewlett, Barry (1991), 39; and Boyette (2019), 491.

31. Barry Hewlett (1991), 28, writes that the expectation of sharing on demand is one reason why the Aka have not taken up farming because "an Aka who spends three or four months raising crops must give nearly everything away at harvest time when all the relatives show up to visit and request food."

32. This paragraph largely follows Hewlett, Bonnie (2013a), 42–43.

33. Hewlett, Bonnie (2013a), 10, edited and shortened; see also 133–34.

34. Information about people who assist mothers—called "alloparents" by anthropologists—is from Hewlett, Barry (1991), 34, and (2014), 254. For more detail about Aka alloparenting, consult Meehan (2005), 66, 70; Meehan (2009), 389; and Meehan & Hawks, 96–99, especially 97, Table 3.2. David Lancy reports asking Courtney Meehan, "Who orchestrates the highly fluid pattern of Aka alloparental care? The mother?" "No," replied Meehan. "It's the child." Lancy (2022), 125, note 8.

35. The reputation of Aka fathers is due to research findings by anthropologist Barry S. Hewlett of Washington State University, whose book, *Intimate Fathers*, was published in 1991.

36. Available research enables comparisons to be made with traditional forager and farmer populations in Australia, Mexico, Philippines, Japan, Nepal, Micronesia, Belize, India, and Samoa as well as several other locations in Africa. Hewlett, Barry (1991), 133–36, including Tables 41, 42.

37. Hewlett, Barry (1991), 103–04, edited and shortened. This is one of four such descriptions there.

38. Hewlett, Barry (1991), 94–95, 97–98 including Figure 6, 89–90 including Table 27, 138–39, 144–46.

39. Bullet points are drawn from Hewlett, Barry (1991) ["HB91"] unless otherwise attributed. In order of listing, bullet points are from HB91 101–02 including Table 32; HB91, 89; HB91, 126; HB91, 77–83; Meehan (2005), 72–80; and Fouts, 303, 306.

40. One research study found that young children infrequently sought attention from their fathers. But the researchers showed no indication of being aware of the difference between the father's home camp and the mother's home camp. Meehan & Hawks, 97, including Table 3.2.

41. Hewlett, Barry (1991), 134–35, including Tables 41, 42.

42. Boyette (2010), 6; Hewlett, Barry (1991), 34, and (2014), 450–52; and Hewlett, Bonnie (2013a), 65–66.

43. Boyette (2010), 11, 15.

44. Hewlett, Barry (1991), 34. The article by Hewlett & Roulette (the principal basis for this chapter's "Formal Learning" section) reveals that it is *not* accurate to portray Aka adults as ignoring small children's use of sharp tools. "Aka teaching episodes regularly involved infants learning how to use sharp knives, machetes, and digging sticks," 12. There are references to similar learning topics on 6, Table 1, and 8, Table 3.

45. Hewlett, Barry (1991), 36, and (2014), 252–55; Hewlett, Bonnie (2013a), 66–67; Boyette (2010), 5–6, (2016a), 766, and (2016b), 166–67.

46. An exception is that the adults and children participate together in communal dancing.

47. Another term is "work-themed pretense play." Boyette (2016a), 764.

48. Bacirongo & Nest, 29, edited and shortened.

49. Hewlett et al. (2011), 1174–75, edited and shortened. While researching East Asian students' learning, I found that a common practice there is for an adult to physically grasp a child's hand and guide it through the necessary movements. For details, see Chapter 6 of *The Drive to Learn*, especially page 55.

50. Hewlett, Barry (1991), 35, and Hewlett, Bonnie (2013a), 90.

51. The first quote was reported by Boyette (2016b), 162, edited and shortened, italics added. The second quote is from Hewlett, Bonnie (2013a), 67, edited and shortened, italics added.

52. Hewlett, Barry, et al. (2000), 294–95; see also Boyette (2016a), 760–61.

53. Hewlett, Bonnie (2013a), 54, 66; Hewlett, Barry (1991), 35; and Boyette (2010), 5. Among the Aka, hitting a child is sufficient grounds for divorce.

54. During many months among the Aka, one anthropologist saw an adult strike a child—more of a light tap—three times. One was because of selfishness on the part of the child. One was because the child had carelessly injured another child. One had no discernable reason, but the child was an adolescent and the father was known to be rash. Boyette (2019), 494.

55. This analysis of children's learning depends largely on Hewlett, Barry (2014), 252–53; see also Boyette (2016a), 60; and (2016b), 162; Hewlett, Bonnie (2013a), 65; and Hewlett, Barry (2019), 51. Note that the Aka do *not* trust the Ngandu. The claim that children trust their own worthiness and competence is my contribution.

56. Hewlett, Barry (1991), 33–34.

57. Boyette (2016b), 159, edited and shortened.

58. This third point is from Boyette (2016b), 161; the first two points are largely my own contribution.

59. Hewlett & Cavalli-Sforza, 931; they estimate that 70% of all crucially important skills have been learned by age 10. See also Hewlett, Bonnie (2013a), 68.

60. These are ten of fifty skills listed by Hewlett & Cavalli-Sforza, 924, 928.

61. Hewlett, Bonnie (2001), 27, 29, including the quote; and Boyette (2010), 14, 23 including Table 4.

62. Hewlett, Bonnie (2013a), 67–68, including the quotes; Hewlett, Barry (1991), 37; and Boyette (2010), 8.

63. Hewlett, Barry (2014), 256; and Hewlett & Hewlett, 93. Details of an initiation for BaTempo Pygmy boys are found in Bacirongo & Nest, 37; it features learning to stalk animals. *Ekila* is discussed by Hewlett, Bonnie (2013a), 96, 100, 107.

64. *Ekila* taboos, among other things, prohibit menstruating women from sleeping in a bed with a hunter.

65. Hewlett, Bonnie (2013a), 100; and Hewlett & Hewlett, 86–88, who quote a girl as explaining that "when the breasts start coming out is when girls know to build their own hut."

66. Hewlett, Barry (1991), 37; and Hewlett & Hewlett, 80–81.

67. Hewlett & Hewlett, 88. It's possible that the girl's references to chimpanzees actually meant Ngandu, who do not point their teeth.

68. Hewlett & Hewlett, 86–87, including the first quote, edited and shortened; and Hewlett, Bonnie (2013a), 101–2, including the second quote, edited and shortened.

69. Hewlett & Hewlett, 83–84 including Table 4.3; and Hewlett, Bonnie (2013a), 102. Ages of marriage are approximate, as the Aka do not keep track of birth dates.

70. My meditation on Aka identify-formation is indebted to Hewlett, Bonnie (2001), 28–30; and Hewlett & Hewlett, 76–77, including the quote.

71. Hewlett & Roulette, 12.

72. The first factor is drawn from Boyette & Hewlett, 291; and Boyette (2016a), 765.

73. Hewlett, Bonnie (2013a), 65.

74. Lancy & Grove, 154. Their term "chore curriculum," portrayed as "laid out for all children to observe," was coined to "contrast dramatically with the U.S. 'core curriculum' concealed in classrooms, textbooks, and lessons taught by 'certified' teachers." (The Lancy & Grove article is not specifically about the Aka.) See also David Lancy's 2012 paper, "The Chore Curriculum," available at no charge via Google Scholar.

75. The second factor is drawn from Lew-Levy et al. (2017), 386. I say that there's "*virtually* no separation between work and play" because I'm aware that children sometimes engage in *ndanga*, similar to our "keep away" game.

76. The third factor is drawn from Hewlett et al. (2011), 1173–74, see also 1176; and Berl & Hewlett (not paginated), 9th page. The latter note that the same Aka values condition the children to *not* view adults as founts of authoritative knowledge.

77. Hewlett, Barry et al. (2016), 42–43; Berl & Hewlett (not paginated), 3rd, 4th, 7th, and 8th pages. The research procedure and its findings both were more complex than I report in the text.

78. Hewlett, Barry, et al. (2016), 39. For the findings on the WEIRD children and chimpanzees, cited is Lyons, Derek, et al. (2007), "The Hidden Structure of Over-imitation," available at no charge via Google Scholar. Hewlett says this earlier study was conducted in the United Kingdom, but I am unable to verify that from the Lyons et al. article.

79. Boyette (2019), 490, edited and shortened.

80. Beginning around 2000, opportunities for Aka children to attend school became available due to the efforts of missionaries. Schools are located in the Ngandu villages, so if Aka parents want to send their children—and some do—their camp must be near a village much of the year. Hewlett, Bonnie (2013a), 211, 191.

81. Hewlett & Roulette, 4.

82. Hewlett & Roulette, 6, Table 1; 7, Table 2; 8, Table 3; 10. The authors caution that "teaching" cannot be the byproduct of another activity; if an adult cries "Snake!" a child might learn but "teaching" hasn't occurred, 4. See also Hewlett, Barry, et al. (2016), 36–38.

83. "Baby talk," a.k.a. "motherese" and "parentese," occurs when an adult talks to a young child in a high-pitched voice along with a slower rhythm and exaggerated sing-song tones. Hewlett and his colleagues state that they did not observe Aka parents engaging in baby talk. However, recent research has found that baby talk occurs in a wide variety of societies, including those of hunter-gatherers. For details, visit nytimes.com/2022/07/24/science/parentese-babies-global-language.html.

84. Hewlett, Barry, et al. (2016), 36–38; and Hewlett & Roulette, 6–7; 9, Table 6; 10–12. There was evidence that the 12- to 14-month-old infants were responding to the teaching because they imitated the teacher 41% of the time.

85. The first sentence of this paragraph relies on Boyette (2010), 5. The rest is my contribution.

86. Found in Hewlett, Barry, et al. (2011), 1175. Attributed to Hewlett, Bonnie (in press), *Women of the Forest and Village: Ethnographic Narratives from the Congo Basin*. That manuscript almost certainly was published in 2013 under the title, *Listen, Here Is a Story*.

87. The claim that Aka children trust their own worthiness and capacity is my contribution.

CHAPTER 3

1. These two paragraphs are based on Bolin, 2–5.

2. For a traditional highland community to have access to all the resources necessary for subsistence, it needs access to land at a variety of altitudes, which correspond to ecological niches. Accordingly, households have long been widely dispersed across the mountainsides, rather than concentrated in villages. At the heart of this system was the *ayllu*, a kin-based organization with a decentralized system of governance; ayllu members pooled labor and resources toward the common good. Lane, 112–13.

3. During the span of years when anthropologist Inge Bolin carried out fieldwork in the ayllu that she was studying (resulting in *Growing Up in a Culture of Respect*),

there was no way to arrive at that ayllu other than to hike mile after mile up a narrow path from Cusipata, a town in the Vilcanota Valley southeast of Cuzco.

4. "Men and women are quite strong and have tremendous stamina. They can easily travel up to forty kilometers a day, even while carrying loads of forty or fifty kilograms. When traveling with them, one sees the ease with which they climb hills, showing no great fatigue even when children are along." Flores-Ochoa, 31, edited.

5. These three paragraphs are based on Dougherty, 18, 125–127, 142–144. For a thorough review of what is known about the Inca, see Kevin Lane (2022), *The Inca* (200 pages, illustrated).

6. Dougherty, 126–127, edited and shortened. A fascinating, 40-minute documentary discussing the Incas' precise stonework with multi-ton boulders is "The Living Stones of Sacsayhuamán," on YouTube.

7. Lane, 85–87. Lane, 63, describes *quipu* as a "mnemonic 'writing' device on knotted strings that seems to have been unsuitable for long, elaborate narratives, instead coding short messages and tabulating amounts." To this day, scholars have not fully cracked the *quipu* code.

8. These two paragraphs are based on Flores-Ochoa, 18; and Bolin, 11–12.

9. Flores-Ochoa, 41, 94–108. A web search will reveal that you and I can easily purchase edible clay.

10. Bolin, 55–56, and 168, note 18. Lane, 107, describes the "desired end product as being lightweight, desiccated, and pebble-like," and provides a color photo on the facing page.

11. Flores-Ochoa, 7–8, quotes this definition of pastoralism: "An economy that derives the bulk of the food supply from domesticated animals. Pastoralists usually do not eat plant products, except those obtained by trading or gathering. They often travel or migrate to get good pastures. Their animals provide milk, meat, transport, hides, and hair." Cited is Charles Winick (1961), *Dictionary of Anthropology*, 403.

12. Lane, 110, notes that dried meat was called *charqui*, one of the only Quechua words to make its way into English as "jerky."

13. Bolin, 6; Winterhalder et al., abstract.

14. These two paragraphs are based on Bolin, 6, 34–35; and Flores-Ochoa, 93.

15. These three paragraphs are based on Salas Carreño, 815, 821–822, 825.

16. Lane, 65, explains that this way of making sense of the world is known as animism, the belief that all things are alive. Animism is a belief in "the interaction or relatedness between people and animals, or environments, emphasizing the real or imagined life force that animates them. Animism opposes the separation that exists between the physical and the metaphysical in many Western religions."

17. Bolin, 126.

18. In the Quechua mind, both the time when an activity occurs and the natural and social environment where it occurs are embraced by the single concept, *pacha*. (García, 146, note.) A friend of mine who has visited areas where the Quechua live reports that, "The Quechua we spent time with always talked about Pachamama with great reverence"; Willa Hallowell, personal communication. The Constitution of Ecuador includes this provision in Article 71: "Nature, or Pacha Mama, where life is reproduced and occurs, has the right to integral respect for its existence and for the

maintenance and regeneration of its life cycles, structure, functions, and evolutionary processes." I could not find any similar provision in the Constitution of Peru.

19. Salas Carreño, 827; Bolin, 139.

20. Bolin, 42–43.

21. Details about the division of labor between men and women is from Bolin, 53, 79, 139.

22. Bolin, x, edited and shortened.

23. Anthropologist Inge Bolin (based at Malaspina University College in British Columbia, Canada) lived in the high-altitude ayllu named Chillihuani during portions of 1988, 1990, 1991, 1992, 1994, 1996, 1997, 1998, 1999, 2000, 2001, 2002, and 2004. Bolin, 9.

24. Bolin, xi, 2.

25. Bolin, 47, edited and shortened.

26. Bolin, 43, edited and shortened.

27. Bolin, 116, attributes this pithy evaluation of coca chewing to the historian and film producer Alan Ereira, in his 1991 film, *From the Heart of the World*.

28. The scientific name of coca is *erythroxylum coca*. The ash chewed with it is generally made from the burnt stalks of the quinoa or similar plant. The ashes are mixed with water and solidify into blocks, from which a small bite is taken after one begins to chew coca leaves. The ash acts as a catalyst to release the active substances in the leaves. Flores-Ochoa, 44, note. See also Lane, 104.

29. These two paragraphs are based on Allen, 159–160.

30. The hallpay account is based primarily on Allen (1981), 159–160, supplemented by an extended discussion of hallpay by Salas Carreño, 822. The resulting account has also undergone my editing in order to shorten it and enhance its clarity.

31. Meyerson, Chapter 11 (Nook version, not paginated), my paraphrase.

32. Bolin, 21, 30. Bolin discusses one hospital delivery, that of Luisita, who was profoundly disabled due to asphyxia during birth. Luisita never became able to feed herself, sit up unaided, or talk. Luisita was born in Cuzco because her father was working in construction there. See pages 57–58, including a photo of Luisita. Bolin witnessed births that ended in the deaths of both mother and child. At some point during Bolin's years-long association with the Chillihuani ayllu, it acquired a health station staffed by a nurse, who sometimes assisted with births. Inge Bolin, personal communication, April 2021.

33. This paragraph and the next four are based on Bolin, 19, 16–32, 36–39; and Flores-Ochoa, 60.

34. Inge Bolin, personal communication.

35. This paragraph and the next are based on Bolin, 27–28, 48–49, 50–52, and 168, note 15.

36. Bolin, 40–42.

37. Bolin, 39–40, edited and shortened.

38. Bolin, 38–39, edited and shortened; italics added. See also Flores-Ochoa, 61.

39. This section is based on Flores-Ochoa, 61; and on Bolin, 33, 43, 45–46.

40. This section is based on Flores-Ochoa, 61; and on Bolin, 37, 43, 60, 153.

41. Bolin, 37.

42. This section is based primarily on Bolin, 36, 39, 46–47. The detail about *wawa* is from Ames, 146. See also Flores-Ochoa, 51–52, who notes that, in some cases, little girls wear red clothing, while little boys wear white. Treating boy and girl children similarly reflects the almost complete equality that exists between male and female adults; Lancy (2022), 92.

43. This section is based on Bolin, 67–69.

44. Flores-Ochoa, 60–61; Bolin, 73. *Runa hina kay* can be translated into Spanish as *pórtate como gente*, and into English as "behave like a human being." Researcher Fernando García, a native Quechua, adds that he often heard such admonishments when parents corrected their children for breaking community norms. García, 140, especially note 2.

45. Ames, 153, mentions this research, which used the Human Relations Area Files data base; she cites Rogoff, Barbara, et al. (1975), Age of assignment of roles and responsibilities to children: A cross-cultural survey, *Human Development*, *18*, 353–369.

46. Ames, 149, shortened and edited.

47. Ames, 150, shortened and edited.

48. Ames, 152, drawing from two sentences.

49. Bolin, 33, edited and shortened. A photo of the "charming hostess," Anali, appears on page 34.

50. Rogoff (2014), 70. On that page, Rogoff includes the same photo of Anali and tells the same story, adding that she gained this information via a personal communication with Bolin in November 2013.

51. Flores-Ochoa, 51–52.

52. This paragraph and the next three are based on Bolin, 70, 73–77, 79, 155; and Flores-Ochoa, 69, 103.

53. I believe that for eight-year-old children in *any* society, the answer is "yes." Why do we parents in the United States (except on farms) give our children almost no responsibility? I take up this matter in Chapter 7.

54. This paragraph is based on Flores-Ochoa, 102–109.

55. Lane, 25 & 126, notes that the llama was the Incas' main beast of burden. The outer limits of the Inca Empire's expansion coincided rather neatly with the natural range of the llama.

56. Flores-Ochoa, 108, edited and shortened.

57. Details about adolescent romance and marriage are from Bolin, 136, 142.

58. Details about community organizations are from Bolin, 144–49.

59. Overviews of the *cargo* system and *Rondas Campesinas* are available on Wikipedia.

60. Garcia-Rivera, 90, edited and shortened.

61. This paragraph and the next three are based on Bolin, 62–64, 153, 155.

62. Bolin, 63–65; edited and shortened; "found objects" is my contribution. A photograph of these children constructing their mini-homestead appears on page 64.

63. This paragraph and the next are based on Bolin, 65.

64. Some anthropologists maintain that, in the case of children in traditional societies, it doesn't make sense for us to distinguish between "play" and "work"; the children themselves don't make this distinction.

65. Flores-Ochoa, 100.

66. Bolin, 72; the resulting photograph is on that page.

67. Bolin, 86, quotes two teachers identified as "Teacher Yanet" and "Teacher Marcial." The latter added that the Quechua children "have not yet attained a distorted worldview by watching television." The second quote, from page x, appears to be Bolin's own summary of several teachers' views.

68. Bolin, 85–86.

69. Bolin, 90; the middle school principal's quote is on page ix and is attributed to Aníbal Durán.

70. Bolin, 91.

71. This section is based on Bolin, 94.

72. Based on Bolin, 94.

73. Based on Bolin, 98–104. Across those seven pages, Bolin goes into considerable detail about weaving and braiding.

74. Flores-Ochoa, 100–101, edited and shortened. He also describes the three other pattern categories.

75. Bolin, 62.

76. Bolin, 72.

77. The main international comparative test is the Program for International Student Assessment (PISA), which is administered by the Organization for Economic Cooperation and Development (OECD).

78. Researcher Fernando García (a native Quechua) writes that "parents demand the support of schools so that children learn competencies for other realities outside of their community." García, 147.

79. The term "communitarian" designates a group-oriented system of values that is sharply different from the "individualistic" system of values that animates much everyday behavior among Americans.

80. García, 149. See also 141.

CHAPTER 4

1. The Navajo prefer to be known as *Diné*, which translated into English means "[The] People."

2. Anthropologists' views of the Navajo are based on Kluckhohn & Leighton, 303–04; Leighton & Kluckhohn, 109–14; and Chisholm (1983), 48–49. Chisholm reports that many researchers agree that a dimension of the Navajo personality is "morbid melancholia" and "endemic uneasiness." The quote is from Kluckhohn & Leighton, 303.

3. Historical details are from Kluckhohn & Leighton, 37, 40–43; Chisholm (1983), 45–46; and Lamphere, 3. A few details come from Wikipedia entries, for example,

"The Long Walk of the Navajo," which includes an account of what happened when a woman needed to give birth during the Walk.

4. Today, Fort Defiance is in extreme eastern Arizona; Fort Sumner is in eastern New Mexico.

5. Dyk, 2, edited and shortened. The autobiography is *Left Handed, Son of Old Man Hat*, recorded by Walter Dyk.

6. The term "Anglo," widely in use at the time, generally referred to anyone who was able to communicate in English and, ethnically, was neither Native American nor Hispanic. Be aware, however, that not all "Anglo" settlers had immigrated from England.

7. Stock reduction details are from Kluckhohn & Leighton, 26, 73–75, 83; Chisholm (1983), 47; Downs (1964), 93; and Dyk, xv. A few details come from the Wikipedia entry on "Navajo Livestock Reduction."

8. Details about the Navajo language rely on Kluckhohn & Leighton, 253–54, 308; see also 297. I have not been able to corroborate Kluckhohn & Leighton's interpretation. One commentator interpreted "Hunger is killing me" as simply being more evocative—painting a picture in the listener's mind—than our bland "I am hungry." Jack Ballard, Jr. (n.d.), Navajo gospel: An overview, which I found on Academia.edu.

9. Information about the Navajos' world comes from Kluckhohn & Leighton, 179–81, 192–93, 199; Leighton & Kluckhohn, 40; Chisholm (1983), 42, 45, 53; Chisholm (2014), 169; Lamphere, 28, 150; and Witherspoon (1975), 16.

10. The second half of this paragraph paraphrases Kluckhohn & Leighton, 180. However, I substituted "secular" where Kluckhohn & Leighton wrote "profane."

11. Paragraphs on ethics are based on Kluckhohn & Leighton, 121–22, 297, 314.

12. Reichard, 155, edited and shortened.

13. Details about the economy are based on Kluckhohn & Leighton, 54–57, 94–95, 102; Chisholm (1983), 44, 53, 57–59, 67–68; Witherspoon (1975), 71–73; Reichard, 138; Downs (1964), 18; and Deyhle & Margonis, 152.

14. Witherspoon (1975), 90, observes that, "There is a myth, especially among conservatives, that all Indians live on the government dole. But Navajo pay all taxes that non-Navajo pay except for property tax, and they get no welfare assistance that other Americans do not. They mostly receive aid to dependent children for women without husbands, and old age pensions through Social Security, which they pay into just like other Americans."

15. Information about desert living is based on Reichard, 138; Chisholm (1983), 44, 53, 57–58, 67–68; Lamphere, 3; and Witherspoon (1975), 75.

16. Deyhle & Margonis, 152.

17. Leighton & Kluckhohn, 3, shortened.

18. McCloskey, 156, edited and shortened.

19. Details about daily life come from Kluckhohn & Leighton, 94–96; Leighton & Kluckhohn, 45; Downs (1964), 87; and Witherspoon (1975), 71–73.

20. Dyk, 5.

21. The paragraph about hogans is based on Kluckhohn & Leighton, 87–91; and on Wikipedia's "Hogan" entry, which includes photographs illustrating the evolution of hogans from small rough mounds to mid-sized log cabins. See also navajopeople.org

/navajo-hogans.htm. The report that hogans were more comfortable than homesteaders' cabins is from Kluckhohn & Leighton, 88.

22. Kluckhohn & Leighton, 114–17. Three pages are needed to discuss names because each Navajo usually ends up with several names, so that "this whole system is to the white man one of the most baffling aspects of the Navajo way of life." The two amusing names that I quote appear to have been acquired somehow by two Navajos who were "candidates for the Marine Corps."

23. Details about birth and early weeks are from Leighton & Kluckhohn, 14–18, 27–28, 31–35; and Phillips & Lobar, 15.

24. During the 1940s, the Navajo infection rate during births was 10.0 per 1000. The Arizona rate was 4.0 per 1000 and the U.S. rate was 2.7 per 1000. Leighton & Kluckhohn, 15.

25. Leighton & Kluckhohn, 14. The quote is Kluckhohn's; his original quote uses "primitive" instead of "traditional."

26. Leighton & Kluckhohn, 15–16, edited and greatly shortened. The much longer account goes into detail about measures that are taken if the delivery is unusually difficult.

27. I have not found a concise account of what infant shaping looks like, although presumably it appears to be a somewhat vigorous massage. I do know it occurs in other societies. I found one book about it: *The Bioarchaeology of Artificial Cranial Modifications: New Approaches to Head Shaping and its Meanings in Pre-Columbian Mesoamerica and Beyond*, by Vera Tiesler (2016).

28. Leighton & Kluckhohn, 35, add the following: "The child is not thoroughly washed each time it soils itself. A little girl of four will scrape out the 'diapers' of her young brother in a perfectly matter-of-fact manner."

29. Details about cradleboards are from Chisholm (1983), 74–78, 172–73, 218; Leighton & Kluckhohn, 22–26; Phillips & Lobar, 17; and Reichard, 45.

30. A major study of Navajo cradleboards and their effect on the mother–infant relationship was carried out during the mid-1970s in Arizona by Ph.D. candidate James S. Chisholm. It was published in 1983 as *Navajo Infancy: An Ethological Study of Child Development*.

31. Chisholm (1983), 218. Chisholm notes that, "Regardless of where they were observed, infants on the cradleboard were significantly more likely ($p < .01$) to be within arm's reach of mother than infants not on the cradleboard. It makes travel with the infant easier and it makes it easier for the mother to watch her child—*and* have the child out from underfoot—while she carried out her various tasks in and around the home."

32. These two paragraphs are based on Chisholm (1983), 68–69, 208–210.

33. The paragraph on the Navajo matriarchy is based on McCloskey, 16; Lamphere, 87; Downs (1964), 68; Witherspoon (1975), 15, 75; and Leighton & Kluckhohn, 97–98. McCloskey, 16, adds this: "When grandmothers were asked, 'How many grandchildren do you have?,' they responded by distinguishing between those grandchildren born to their daughters and those born to their sons."

34. Details about the attention infants receive are from Leighton & Kluckhohn, 27–33; Phillips & Lobar, 17; and Leighton & Kluckhohn, 48. The paragraph on the First Laugh is based on McCloskey, 193; Phillips & Lobar, 17; and Chisholm (2014), 173.

35. Details about molding behavior are from Leighton & Kluckhohn, 51–53; Deyhle & LeCompte, 160; and Phillips & Lobar, 18, who in turn reference Downs (1972), n.p.

36. Leighton & Kluckhohn, 52, write that, "Parents have a propensity for referring the child to what 'people' may say. A mother is unlikely to say, 'If you act like that you'll disgrace me'; rather, she'll say, 'If you act like that people will make fun of you.' So parents do not set themselves up directly as the punisher." (This is why Navajo society has been termed a "shame culture" instead of a "guilt culture.")

37. The basic purposes of the *Yeibichai* initiation ritual are to recognize youngsters as members of the Navajo tribe ("The People") and to introduce them to participation in ceremonial life. The *Yeibichai* initiation is described in detail by Kluckhohn & Leighton, 208–09.

38. Dyk, 27–28, edited and shortened.

39. Dyk, 4, shortened. Before Left Handed's mother scolded him, she had run in the direction the coyote carried the dog and searched for quite a while without success.

40. Details on the handling of dangerous things are based on Reichard, 48; Lee, 13; and Phillips & Lobar, 18. In their discussion of this matter, Phillips & Lobar reference Satz (1982), n.p.

41. On this matter, Left Handed offers a contrary report, though without suggesting how old he might have been at the time: "My mother said, 'No, he never carried a knife around with him. I don't allow him to have a knife because he hasn't enough sense to carry one.'" Dyk, 15.

42. Details about the weaned child are from Leighton & Kluckhohn, 33–37, 40–43; and Chisholm (1983), 68, 208.

43. Leighton & Kluckhohn, 43; shortened and edited. Quoted is Clyde Kluckhohn, who built a towering reputation in the field of anthropology based largely on his extensive work with Navajo people.

44. Details about responsibility are from Leighton & Kluckhohn, 43, 57–59; Kluckhohn & Leighton, 106; Chisholm (2014), 171; and Phillips & Lobar, 18.

45. Dyk, 57; edited and shortened.

46. Lee (1961), 11. She adds that the children eventually "can take their turn at supplying the meat for the family meal, and they can contribute mutton when this is needed for ceremonials or to entertain visitors."

47. Details on gender roles are from Leighton & Kluckhohn, 58–59; and Reichard, 48–49.

48. Phillips & Lobar, 18, write that, "At about 12 years of age, an adult such as the father or uncle will take the boy for a ride, evaluate his behavior on a horse, and if he passes the test, he is considered an adult."

49. Reichard, 10, edited and shortened.

50. Reichard, 33–34, 78, edited and shortened, italics added.

51. WEIRD stands for Western, Educated, Industrialized, Rich, and Democratic. WEIRD is discussed at length in the Introduction to this book.

52. Details about embracing womanhood are from Kluckhohn & Leighton, 102; Leighton & Kluckhohn, 76–77; and Deyhle & Margonis, 137. Leighton & Kluckhohn describe a four-day *Kinaaldá* beginning on page 76. See also navajopeople.org/blog/kinaalda-celebrating-maturity-of-girls-among-the-navajo/.

53. Deyhle & Margonis, 139.

54. McCloskey, 161, edited and shortened.

55. Leighton & Kluchhohn, 54–55.

56. Lamphere, 157–58; Reichard, 51.

57. Kluckhohn & Leighton, 228–29.

58. Dyk, 178, edited and shortened.

59. The discussion of the ethic of noninterference draws upon Leighton & Kluckhohn, 52; Downs (1964), 69–70; and Deyhle & LeCompte, 160. The phrases "nudging to act appropriately" and "ethic of noninterference" both originated with Deyhle & LeCompte.

60. This question is being discussed because it is a central concern to anthropologists who are trying to figure out how traditional children learn.

61. Dyk, 6, shortened. It's not clear whether the man, Red Wife Beater, was already known by Left Handed.

62. Reichard, 48–49, 59.

63. Leighton & Kluckhohn, 59, shortened. The girl was six years old at the time.

64. Chisholm (2014), 167–68, 175–76, 179. Chisholm references Whitherspoon (1977), 186.

65. Chisholm (2014), 180.

66. Details on the cultural roles of grandmothers and fathers are from McCloskey, 182, 195; and Leighton & Kluckhohn, 50, 53.

67. Leighton & Kluckhohn, 54, edited and shortened.

68. Dyk, 55, edited and shortened.

69. McClosky, 180.

70. Leighton & Kluchhohn, 50.

71. The discussion of government schooling is based on Kluckhohn & Leighton, 42, 64, 141–43, 145–46; Deyhle, 281–88; and Chisholm (1983), 55–56.

72. The U.S. Department of the Interior, under its first-ever Native American cabinet secretary, Deb Haaland, launched a probe in 2021 into the history of the boarding schools. The first report emerging from that probe was published in May 2022. It is 106 pages long, includes historical photographs, and concludes that "the United States directly targeted American Indian, Alaska Native, and Native Hawaiian children in the pursuit of a policy of cultural assimilation that coincided with Indian territorial dispossession." You can read this entire report by searching the web for "Federal Indian Boarding School Initiative Investigative Report."

73. Details about parent–teacher culture clashes are from Deyhle, 285–86; Deyhle & LeCompte, 159–60; Deyhle & Margonis, 163.

74. Details about student–teacher culture clashes are from on Kluckhohn & Leighton, 315; Leighton & Kluckhohn, 68; Reichard, 137; and Chisholm (2014), 181–82.

75. Progressive teaching is grounded in "a philosophy of education that promotes active, experiential learning, as opposed to learning solely from books, lectures,

recitation, and practice." Diane Ravitch (2007), *EdSpeak: A Glossary of Educational Terms, Phrases, Buzzwords, and Jargon.*

76. Deyhle & LeCompte, 163, shortened.

77. Details about student–parent culture clashes are from Kluckhohn & Leighton, 144–149.

78. Deyhle, 284, shortened.

79. Leighton & Kluckhohn, 69–70, shortened.

80. Leighton & Kluckhohn, 68, 74, edited, shortened, and combined into one quote. The speaker is Clyde Kluckhohn.

81. These sentences draw on the wording of Chisholm (2014), 180.

CHAPTER 5

1. "Levant" in this book is limited to present-day southeastern Turkey, Syria, Lebanon, Jordan, Israel, Palestine (Gaza Strip), northeastern Egypt, and northwestern Saudi Arabia. (Most of the fieldwork on which this chapter is based was completed in Syria, Lebanon, and Jordan.) "Levant" in its widest historical sense comprises all the countries along the Eastern Mediterranean shores from Greece around to eastern Libya. Levant means "the eastern place, where the sun rises." Scholars use this term because it refers to a geographic region without suggesting political connotations.

2. Jabbur, 2–3, edited and shortened. Jibrail Jabbur (1900–1991) is author of *The Bedouins and the Desert* (1995), an authoritative, 670-page study. Jabbur and another scholar, Dawn Chatty, do not capitalize "bedouin."

3. Al-Naimi, 1–8; assembled from statements on those pages. Ali Al-Naimi (1935–) became the first CEO of Saudi Aramco, then served as Saudi Arabia's Minister of Petroleum (1995–2016). Alan Greenspan quipped that Al-Naimi "is the most important man you never heard of."

4. Jabbur, 29, states the fact about the Koran without specifying passages. But Jabbur, 475–76 and footnotes 3–11, discusses specific Old Testament passages.

5. For details about Isaiah 13:20, visit BibleStudyTools.com/isaiah/13–20.html.

6. In Jabbur's Chapter XIX, "The History of the Bedouins in Northern Arabia," raiding is prominently discussed.

7. Chatty (2010), 23. Chatty argues that pastoralism was an offshoot of agriculture, a "sophisticated adaptation to environmental pressure," but she does not elaborate further.

8. Details on the traditional economy come from Jabbur, 35–38, 40, 222–23, 532; and Chatty (1978), 406.

9. Clarified butter, also known as ghee, is pure milk fat that has been separated from water and milk solids.

10. Details about camels are from Jabbur, 197–99, 219, 221; see also Chatty (1978), 407.

11. Jabbur, 221. Jabbur does not offer details about the nature of the vermin but adds that washing in camel's urine gives hair a reddish hue. Jabbur, 222, contains a

full-page photo of a Bedouin woman holding a receptacle behind a camel, patiently waiting for it to urinate.

12. Details about tents are from Jabbur, 241–43, 247–49, 253–54, 291; Chatty (1978), 401–02, 409; and Katakura, 170.

13. Reem Al Rasheed, who provided input to this chapter, adds that "One rule of Bedouin generosity is that they take care of (i.e., provide food and bedding for) any stranger who comes upon them for three days without asking him where he comes from." Personal communication.

14. Jabbur, 314. Jabbur in turn cites Al-Muqanna' al-Kindī, *Hamāsa, II*, 34.

15. Details about the switch to trucks are from Chatty (1978), 408–10; see also page 414 note 6. Dawn Chatty is the author of the book *From Camel to Truck* (2013).

16. Details about sedentarization are from Jabbur, 524–25, 58, 531, 535; and Chatty (2010), 21, 23, 25–26.

17. Katakura, 47–48, 167–68.

18. Chatty (2010), 25–26. Chatty focuses on Lebanon and suggests that Syria did likewise. She mentions, too, that "Jordan opted for a more laissez-faire policy by encouraging Bedouin settlement rather than coercing it."

19. Marey-Sarwan, et al. (2016a), 105, edited and shortened. Not all Bedouin villages in the Levant are unrecognized. Marey-Sarwan et al. (2017), 176–77, notes that in those villages that are unrecognized, families "are not granted permission to construct any permanent living structures, [the hope being] to resettle them in cities to ensure that they do not hinder the expansion of Jewish settlements. A large number of Bedouin homes are demolished every year by the authorities."

20. At least three anthropologists have emphasized the children's constant social immersion: Williams, 32; Brink (1994), 237; and Granqvist, 123. Their fieldwork occurred, respectively, in Lebanon, Egypt, and Palestine.

21. Details about fathers and mothers are based on Jabbar, 290–93; Lutfiyya, 509; Prothro (1961), 128–29; see also Rugh (1997), 76, 23–24, 223–24.

22. There are plenty of anthropological and historical studies of the nomadic Bedouin, but almost no attention has been paid to their children or their parenting practices. Jibrail Jabbur's 670-page book includes one page headed "Boys and Girls," and Lady Ann Blunt's two-volume travel diary scarcely mentions children. This is why the remainder of this chapter infrequently mentions, specifically, the Bedouin.

23. Williams, 24, edited and shortened. *Fellaheen* are Middle Eastern peasant farmers and agricultural laborers.

24. Details about newborns are from Granqvist, 58–61, 76–77, 79; Williams, 23–24, 26–27; Lutfiyya, 506, 515; Prothro (1961), 57–58; and Katakura, 92–93.

25. Details about the days of rest are from Ammar, 91, 99; Lutfiyya, 517; Williams, 27; and Katakura, 93.

26. van Geldermalsen, 163, edited and shortened.

27. The "evil eye" is a malevolent spirit thought capable of causing injury or death, a superstition that arose in ancient times and spread into the Jewish, Islamic, Buddhist, and Hindu traditions. Britannica.com/topic/evil-eye. I've been informed that the evil eye is not imagined by believers to be animate; rather, it's more like an energy or a curse (Kay Jones, personal communication).

28. These details about the evil eye are from Lutfiyya, 515–16; Ammar, 111; and Beck, 574–75.

29. Abu-Rabia, 22, raised as a nomadic Bedouin, writes that, because boys were highly prized, they were dressed as girls until age four or five in order to avoid the evil eye.

30. van Geldermalsen, 164, edited and shortened.

31. Details about the naming ceremony are from Fernea (1995), 8; Ammar, 91–93; and Katakura, 93.

32. Details about breast-feeding are from Ammar, 99–100; Prothro (1961), 72; see also Lutfiyya, 517, and Katakura, 93–94.

33. Details about toilet-training are mainly from Williams, 31; also from Prothro (1961), 85–86; Fuller, 36; Lutfiyya, 515, 518; and Ammar, 103–04. Apparently in some areas, toilet-training begins in the eighth or ninth month.

34. Details regarding parents' concerns about giving birth to many children are from Beck, 573; Marey-Sarwan (2016a), 113–14; Prothro (1970), 590; and Williams, 21. The account of returning after 14 years is Williams's.

35. Dr. Rugh rented a room in the village, seeking peace to finish a book, but she was drawn into the life of the family. I have greatly shortened and extensively paraphrased this story, based on pages 204–06 of Rugh's excellent book, *Within the Circle* (1997).

36. Rugh (1997), 206–07.

37. This paragraph relies substantially on Rugh (1997), 207.

38. In describing the roles of children, I relied on Haj-Yahia, 433–35; Ammar, 126, 128–9, 141–42; Fuller, 39–40; Patai, 579; Williams, 36–37; and Rugh (1997), 199, 213, 225–26, 239.

39. Details on Arab village children are from Rugh (1997), 173–76, 223; Haj-Yahia, 431; Ammar, 133; Williams, 39–40; and Fernea (1995), 5. See also Jabbur, 287–88.

40. Weaning details are from Prothro (1961), 66, 76–77; Patai, 579; Williams, 29–30; Fernea (1995), 7; and Granqvist, 107–9.

41. Brink (1994), 243–44; and Brink (1995), 89. Brink quotes Whiting & Edwards (1988), *Children of Different Worlds*, 142–44. A similar pattern associated with weaning, believed to yield a similar outcome, has been termed "active dependency." For more information about this, see in Chapter 6 (about Hindu Villagers in India) the last few paragraphs of the section on Informal Learning.

42. Granqvist, 109, notes that "there have been cases where a mother is suckling her child although she is carrying a new life in her womb, but this is condemned by public opinion."

43. Brink (1995), 88; and Ammar, 106, 114. See also Beck, 575; and Fernea (1995), 7.

44. Fuller, 39. But Williams, 61–62, 73, describes male Lebanese youth as responding to "minimal demands" while their sisters are endlessly busy.

45. Ammar, 30–31, provides detailed "duty sheets" for Egyptian boys and girls ages three to seven and seven to twelve.

46. Granqvist, 131–32, edited and shortened.

47. Granqvist, 138, edited and shortened.

48. Rugh (1997), 22–23, edited and shortened.

49. These three paragraphs rely on Rugh (1997), 65–66, 199–200, 203, 237–38.

50. Material from paragraph four to the end of this subsection is drawn from Rugh (1997), 28–29, 181–83, 199–200, 212, 229–31; the quote is from 29. Rugh's grasp of the Arab mindset is impressive.

51. Nydell, 42, paraphrase; see also 44–45. The veiling and secluding of women originated in Persia and Byzantium.

52. Jabbur, 263–66, paraphrase. Jabbur adds, 267, that interest in kinship and descent was common among the Semitic peoples; he points to the Old Testament's frequent recounting of genealogies.

53. Fernea (1995), 7.

54. Fernea (1991), 460.

55. Fernea (1995), 6, paraphrase. A similar view is offered by Ammar, 111. See also Beck, 573; Williams, 33; Lutfiyya, 508; and Prothro (1961), 121.

56. If their first child is a boy, Husayn, the parents' names ever after are "Abu Husayn" and "Um Husayn."

57. Williams, 23.

58. Fuller, 51–52. There are differing accounts of what pre-adolescent and adolescent girls do and may not do; local custom plays a role. See Hamamsy, 595; and Lutfiyya, 509.

59. Regarding male circumcision, see Fernea (1995), 8; and Fuller, 42. For an extended description, see Ammar, 116–20.

60. This observation was expressed by male anthropologists Ammar, 50, and Lutfiyya, 510–12; and by females Chatty (1978), 400, and Rugh, (1997), 222, 233–35.

61. Rugh (1997), 74–75, edited and shortened.

62. Fernea (1995), 7–8; Lutfiyya, 519. Ammar, 133, says that "the main objective of child-rearing is to cultivate a docile and yielding disposition in the child." The private vs. public aspects of *adab* are from Ammar, 130.

63. Details about mothers' and fathers' discipline are from Brink (1994), 243; Brink (1995), 86; Fernea (1995), 8; Williams, 38–39; Lutfiyya, 518–19; Ammar, 133–34; and Lichtenstadter, 607. Katakura, 160, adds that it is not unusual to see a mother chastising her married son.

64. Details on the lazy child are from Ammar, 126; the quote is edited.

65. Details on adult relatives' discipline are from Fernea (1995), 9.

66. Details on child socialization by slightly older children are from Ammar, 128.

67. Jabbar, 297, 393–94; Granqvist, 142.

68. These two paragraphs are based on Jabbur, 391, 530, 535; Lichtenstadter, 613; and Granqvist, 166.

69. Rugh (1984), 257; and Williams, 58.

70. See endnote 23.

71. Williams, 58.

72. Williams, 48, edited and shortened. For a description of a better-equipped school, see Katakura, 63–65.

73. Williams, 49–50.

74. Fernea (1995), 8–9; see also Ammar, 212.

75. Rugh (1997), 27–28, edited and shortened.

76. Rugh (1984), 258, edited and shortened.

77. Ammar, 141, reports that he "seldom noticed grown-ups talking about their childhood, and his informants found it very difficult, even unbecoming, to recall their own childhood days."

78. This insightful thought was shared with me by my editor, Kay Jones, who was raised on a farm and was recalling how her parents dealt with her.

79. Jabbur, 263–267.

80. Rugh (1997), 223. The woman was an Egyptian.

CHAPTER 6

1. Yasir, A4. India's Constitution lists 22 languages, and the last government census in 2011 named 121 "major" languages, (i.e., with 10,000 speakers or more). Currently, an Indian scholar and his large team are trying to document all languages actively in use; so far, they've researched 780 languages, with hundreds more left to be studied. Details at nytimes.com/2022/06/11/world/asia/india-languages-ganesh-devy.html. The anthropologist cited is Susan Seymour, whose fieldwork was completed in the eastern state of Orissa, where Odia is spoken.

2. The meanings of "caste," *varna*, and *jāti* have been the subject of much scholarly debate. I have relied primarily on Mandelbaum, 29, who encourages his readers to use varna instead of caste (which he views as too imprecise); and on my professional colleague Dr. Bidhan Chandra of Empire State College in New York, who has maintained a strong relationship with his native India. Also helpful have been the explanations provided by Wikipedia; see especially its discussion of caste.

3. I am indebted to Dr. Bidhan Chandra for educating me about the ways in which Indians refer to their economically and socially disadvantaged compatriots. They are regarded as belonging to the fourth (lowest) varna, called *Shudra*, which originally designated the cultivators. The term *Dalit* was coined during the late 1940s by the architects of the Indian Constitution. Both *Dalit* and *Harijan* were banned a few years ago, but both—and especially *Dalit*—remain in wide use. In official circles, these severely disadvantaged citizens are said to belong to one of the "Scheduled Castes."

4. See Appendix B, entitled "Sources of Information for the Five Main Chapters," near the end of this book.

5. The Nayars are both matrilineal and matrilocal, the latter term meaning that newlyweds usually live with or near the wife's parents, instead of with the husband's as in the rest of India. See Mencher (1963).

6. Kurtz, 58, italics added.

7. Mandelbaum, 3. The ambassador was named Megasthenes.

8. The scriptures include the Veda, Ramayana, Mahabharata texts. The latter two, especially, have a great deal to say about rules of daily behavior including guidelines for parent–child relationships. Dr. Bidhan Chandra, personal communication.

9. These two paragraphs rely on Isaac et al., 39–40, and on the discussion of the *Vedas* at WorldHistory.org/The_Vedas/.

10. Details about the Raj rely in part on Roland, 18. An anthropologist friend of mine, Laila Williamson, pointed out that during the century of the East India Company's sway over portions of India (1757–1857), its leaders very largely adapted to the ways of life of native Indians. As her source for this information, she cited books on British India by the celebrated British historian, William Dalrymple.

11. A gyroscope is any rapidly spinning wheel, which firmly maintains its orientation in space (a spinning top keeps its balance, and a moving bicycle doesn't topple left or right); thus, a gyroscope is a metaphor for steadiness of internal purpose. Radar is constantly looking outward to determine what is going on in the environment so that its operator can react appropriately; thus, radar is a metaphor for responsiveness to others. This insightful gyroscope/radar metaphor comes from Roland, 252; see also 95–96, 201. The admiration we feel for personal integrity is an excellent example of the Western gyroscope in action.

12. Alexander, 82, reports that in 1997, 73% of the population was rural; cited in turn is World Bank, 2020.

13. Trawick, 87–88, edited and shortened.

14. These thoughts on hierarchy rely in part on Roland, 101; see his note 15. You could say that in the United States, one's social status depends on their role, while in India one's role depends on their social status.

15. The Indian terms are as follows: priests and scholars, *Brahmins* [or *Brahmans*]; warriors and rulers, *Kshatriyas*; tradesmen, *Vaishyas*; and cultivators, *Shudras*. Mandelbaum, 22–25.

16. See the fourth paragraph of this chapter.

17. Details about the *jātis* rely on Minturn & Hitchcock, 8–9, 17, and on Mandelbaum, 14–16.

18. This paragraph relies on Mandelbaum, 27.

19. Minturn & Hitchcock, 25 and 55, edited and shortened.

20. Seymour (1999), 62–63, edited and shortened.

21. The explanation of "joint" is drawn from Sarangapani, 37 note 9.

22. Details about mothers are from Trawick, 93; Seymour (1980), 131–34; and Seymour (1999), 76–78, 297 note 14.

23. Details about fathers are from Chaudhary, 75–77; and Kennedy, 166 including note 11; the "stranger" quote is from Sarangapani, 34.

24. Details about siblings are from Sarangapani, 35; and Mandelbaum, 67–68. For a discussion about the absence of sibling rivalry see Minturn & Hitchcock, 137.

25. Details about uncles and aunts are from Mandelbaum, 71–73.

26. Details about grandparents are from Madan, 84–86; and Chaudhary, 78, 81.

27. These two paragraphs rely on Mandelbaum, 38, 40, and on Chaudhary, 74, 84; the quote is from Chaudhary, 73.

28. Seymour (1999), 63, adds that the younger daughters-in-law also exhibit formal respect in a variety of ways for their mother-in-law, their older brothers-in-law, and their husbands. For example, in the presence of respected elders they keep the end of their long scarfs draped over their heads and their heads bowed so that there can be no eye contact. They also lower themselves to the ground and kiss the feet of their respected elders, including their husbands, as though they were deities. See also

117, 145. Saraswathi & Pai, 84, note that *purdah* began during the Moghul period, 1526–1857, and was an expression of the "excessive concern" with female chastity.

29. Details about the separation of "joint" households are from Mandelbaum, 34–35, and Roland, 92, 209–211. Married adult sons leave their parental household to gain more control over their own lives.

30. This paragraph relies on Seymour (1999), 79, and on Trawick, 157. The 21 kinship terms come from the Tamil language; see Trawick, 120, Fig. 4.

31. A parallel cousin is a cousin from a parent's same-sex sibling, while a cross-cousin is from a parent's opposite-sex sibling. Wikipedia.

32. Details on mystical influences on birth come from Madan, 65–66.

33. One's *karma* is associated with one's deeds in past lives. The motivation for Indians to do good deeds and conform to social norms is so that, through *karma*, they will gain a better station in their next life. Minturn & Hitchcock, 10.

34. This description of giving birth and activities during the next two weeks is based on Minturn & Hitchcock, 100–101, and on Seymour (1999), 71. For more about the ritual pollution associated with giving birth, see Madan, 70–71, and Seymour (1999), 297 note 8. For a short but informative discussion of the general meaning of ritual pollution, visit http://encyclopedia.uia.org/en/problem/153463.

35. This *shransondar* ceremony was described by Madan, 71.

36. This hair-cutting ceremony was described by Minturn & Hitchcock, 104.

37. Seymour (1999), 81, edited and shortened.

38. The discussion of infant excrement is based on Minturn & Hitchcock, 109; and Seymour (1999), 82; see also Narain, 6. The cow-dung remark is my own.

39. See endnote 48.

40. Details about the care of new infants come from Minturn & Hitchcock, 107–08, 111–12; Seymour (1980), 128–31; Seymour (1999), 72–74, 83; and Freed & Freed, 71–73, 75–76.

41. Information about early childhood activities comes from Minturn & Hitchcock, 112–13, 125–28; and Madan, 86.

42. Seymour (1975), is an excellent source for exploring how traditional villagers approach child-rearing (although the concept of intentional "child-rearing" is virtually nonexistent among most villagers).

43. Details about toileting and weaning come from Minturn & Hitchcock, 114; Seymour (1999), 82; and Narain, 6. Madan, 83, reports from the state of Kashmir that weaning usually doesn't occur "until after the child is two years of age." Seymour (1999), 82, reports that there are no words for "to toilet-train" and "to wean" in the Oriya language; I have assumed that this is likely true in at least some other languages of India.

44. These two paragraphs rely on Seymour (1975), 52; Seymour (1980), 148–50; Freed & Freed, 72–73; and Madan, 86. The quote is from Seymour (1980), 134.

45. This paragraph relies on Raj & Raval, 63, 65; Kao & Kinha, 75–77; and Paiva, 194. See also Minturn & Hitchcock, 113, 118–19. For a thoughtful and wide-ranging exploration of these matters, see Roland, 12, 21, 57, 236, 240.

46. Details about gaining compliance come from Mencher, 60–62; Mandelbaum, 120–22; Paiva, 198–201; and Minturn & Hitchcock, 113, 120–23. The quote is from Paiva, 198.

47. This shame–guilt shift was described by Mencher, 54–55, 63–64. Mencher's fieldwork occurred in the state of Kerala among the matrilineal Nayars. Bidhan Chandra tells me that this kind of shame–guilt shift is the opposite of his experience, which is that parents usually warn a child that bad behavior will lower the family's image in the eyes of others (penalty: being shamed by others).

48. This section relies on Seymour (1976), 788–791; Seymour (1980), 141–42; Seymour (1999), 158, 167–69; and Rohner & Chaki-Sircar, 4–5, 87.

49. Rohner & Chaki-Sircar, 30, edited and shortened. Freed & Freed, 113–114, report that making cow-dung cakes was considered a pleasant occupation by girls, for it could be performed while sitting on the ground. Dung was considered a form of wealth; one festival was actually called "Cowdung Wealth." Dr. Bidhan Chandra notes that cow dung is considered holy because it comes from cows, which are venerated in India; personal communication.

50. Freed & Freed, 61, edited and shortened.

51. Rohner & Chaki-Sircar, 88, edited and shortened.

52. This paragraph paraphrases Seymour (1988), 365; see also 369 note 6. I have encountered no discussion of what happens in an economically disadvantaged family when the *firstborn* child turns three; one possible explanation is that older cousins who live nearby play a role.

53. Trawick, 75, shortened; her fieldwork occurred in the state of Tamil Nadu.

54. This paragraph paraphrases Minturn & Hitchcock, 148–49; their fieldwork occurred in the northern region of the northern state of Uttar Pradesh.

55. Minturn & Hitchcock, 150, 153–54, edited and shortened.

56. Edwards, 15; edited.

57. This paragraph draws on Roland, 236.

58. Details about the father–son relationship are from Mandelbaum, 46–47, 60; he attributes the quote to Gough, 836. See also Trawick, 158–59, 163.

59. Details about the mother–son relationship are from Mandelbaum, 62.

60. Ranade, 2–3, 6–7, edited and shortened.

61. This paragraph is based on Seymour (1999), 86–87; and Mandelbaum, 84. Seymour adds that most girls aren't directed to care for younger siblings, they "simply begin to do it."

62. Rohner & Chaki-Sircar, 31, 33, 90–91, edited, shortened, and woven together. Rohner & Chaki-Sircar's book is the best source for accounts of Dalit (untouchable) children's work; see also 29, 89–95. See also Seymour (1980), 142–43.

63. *Mahinder* refers to an economic relationship, often lifelong, between a Dalit male and his high-caste employer. Rohner & Chaki-Sircar, 197.

64. Rohner & Chaki-Sircar, 23–24, 88–89, edited, shortened, and woven together. In the 1980s, a *mahinder* boy's monthly salary had a U.S. dollar equivalent to $0.26, while that of an adult equaled $2.60.

65. These paragraphs are based on Madan, 67–68, 90, 95, 217; and Seymour (1999), 213. Trawick, 108, notes that dowries were outlawed at one point; however, the law proved unenforceable.

66. Seymour (1999), 59, 93–94, italics added.

67. This explanation is based on Seymour (1999), 85.

68. If you are familiar with the Netflix series, *Indian Matchmaking*, you might think the information in this paragraph is erroneous. Note, however, that the families involved are among the most elite and wealthy in India, and the twenty-somethings all have attained bachelors and/or masters degrees in the United States, the United Kingdom, or Western Europe. *Indian Matchmaking* is not at all representative of India in general.

69. Mandelbaum, 84; the quote is attributed to Morris Opler (1958), 561.

70. The first account of a bride's reception is from the state of Kashmir; Madan, 114–15; see also 109, 118–19. The second account is from the state of Uttar Pradesh; Minturn & Hitchcock, 59–60.

71. These paragraphs are based on Mandelbaum, 86–88. See also Seymour (1999), 55–57.

72. These paragraphs are based on Minturn & Hitchcock, 29.

73. These paragraphs are based on Seymour (1975), 52–54; Freed & Freed, 66, 111–13; Roland, 216; and Kennedy, 172.

74. Kennedy, 172, note 23; second quote is shortened.

75. Freed & Freed, 112. The Freeds add, "These small tasks were not thought of as work," but do not elaborate.

76. Details about use of the hands is based on Freed & Freed, 60–64.

77. Seymour (1975), 47–48; see also 53–54.

78. Minturn & Hitchcock, 129–30; edited and shortened.

79. The first quote is from Seymour (1975), 53, shortened. The second is from Seymour (1999), 76, edited and shortened.

80. Mencher, 56–58, a combination of sentences from across those pages.

81. A similar pattern associated with nursing/weaning, also thought to lead to expectations of interdependency, has been termed "inconsistent nurturance." For more insight, see in Chapter 5 (about Village Arabs in the Levant) the discussion of "dethronement" near the end of the section entitled Learning to Be Arab: The Early Childhood Years.

82. These paragraphs are based on Freed & Freed, 108–10, 123–27; Seymour (1999), 170; Madan, 86; and Sarangapani, 28–29, 62–63. Sarangapani adds that the disinclination to send girls to school began to change in the 1980s.

83. These paragraphs are based on Minturn & Hitchcock, 91–92; Sarangapani, 164–65; and Mencher, 57.

84. Sarangapani, 166–67. The alleged distinction between memorization and rote is recognized beyond India. See pages 11–14 of my book, *The Drive to Learn*. Also see Ference Marton et al. (1996), Memorizing and understanding: The keys to the paradox, in *The Chinese Learner: Cultural, Psychological, and Contextual Influences*. This analysis by Marton and his colleagues is summarized at thedrivetolearn .info/annotated-bibliography/#annotations.

85. This explanation of maturity is from Raj & Raval, 64.

CHAPTER 7

1. Insights and research findings for this section come from, among others, Gaskins & Paradise, 85–87, 91, 107–08; Maynard & Tovote, 198–99; Boyette (2016), 264–65; Lancy & Grove, 150, 154–56, 163; Chick, 119; Lew-Levy et al. (2017), 386; Boyette & Hewlett, 291; Hewlett et al. (2016), 43; and Hewlett et al. (2019), 51–52.

2. High mortality among infants and young children is due largely to infectious and parasitic diseases, malnutrition, and a variety of other illnesses; accidents are rarely the cause. Lancy (2015), 15, 104–11.

3. This traditional set of values also has been termed "pediatric" because of its preoccupying concern with the survival and health of the infant during the early years of life. LeVine et al. (1994), 249.

4. My private editor, Kay Jones, grew up on a dairy farm. She says that farm children have opportunities every day to contribute to their family's economy—so long as the farm raises livestock such as cows, pigs, chickens, and so forth.

5. This modern set of values also has been termed "pedagogic" because of its preoccupying concern with the growing child's learning and behavioral competencies. LeVine et al. (1994), 249.

6. Smith, 190. Harriet J. Smith is a clinical psychologist who formerly was a research primatologist. Her 2005 book, *Parenting for Primates*, is a history of the evolution of parenting behavior in human and nonhuman primates, written to help human parents understand the evolutionary basis of parenting behavior. It is conceivable that Smith picked up the insight that *modern parents give while traditional parents receive* from Robert A. LeVine, who was discussing it in 1988, 6–7, and possibly earlier. Almost the same insight is stated by Ochs & Izquierdo, 400, in their outstanding 2009 article, "Responsibility in Childhood."

7. Discussed in these paragraphs is the "demographic transition," long known to social scientists: Traditional societies are characterized by high birth rates, in part to compensate for high death rates and in part because children genuinely are needed. As traditional societies begin transitioning to modern ones with schooling for children and industrial labor for adults, the death rate declines, largely due to improved nutrition and medical care. After some years pass, the birth rate declines. Why? Major factors include (a) increased family income, but at the expense of an absent parent; (b) increased education and status of women, which tends to draw their interests away from the family; and (c) reduced opportunities for children to work due to school attendance, decline of subsistence tasks, and prohibitions against children in most workplaces. (Child labor, poorly paid, is an exception.) Parents' values shift in favor of smaller broods. Note that the demographic transition was observed prior to the availability of contraceptives. For more information, search the Internet for "demographic transition."

8. The six examples are drawn from Chapter 7, the Chore Curriculum, of Lancy (3rd Edition, 2022). Many of the same examples can be found in the same numbered/named chapter of Lancy (2nd Edition, 2015).

9. Gaimster, 127.

10. Heywood, 123, edited.

11. Lancy (1996), 156.

12. Lancy (1983), 121–22, edited.

13. Mead, 633, shortened.

14. Nerlove et al., 276, edited and shortened.

15. Ames, 152, edited and shortened.

16. Wenger, 290, edited and shortened.

17. Gaskins, 287, edited and shortened.

18. Matsigenka society in the Peruvian Amazon, and Samoan society in Upolu, Samoa.

19. Ochs & Izquierdo, 399, shortened and edited. I highly recommend this insightful article.

20. Lancy (2017), 128–28, paraphrased.

21. As discussed in the Introduction, WEIRD stands for Western, Educated, Industrialized, Rich, Democratic. (WEIRD societies also are Urbanized: WEIRDU.)

22. Fasulo, et al., 28.

23. Lancy (2017), 132, shortened.

24. Rheingold, entire article, especially 117–121. The research was more complex, and the findings were richer, than I am suggesting in the text. This research probably occurred in or near Chapel Hill, North Carolina.

25. Rheingold, 116.

26. In discussing responsibility, I have consistently used examples of tasks that benefit the entire group (the family) to which the child belongs, usually tasks repeated on a daily or weekly basis. I am aware that many parents also treat as "responsibilities" (a) personal care tasks such as brushing teeth, getting dressed, and taking a bath; (b) politeness rules such as sharing toys, showing respect, and saying please; and (c) school-related tasks such as doing homework and preparing for special school events.

CHAPTER 8

1. Montgomery, 29.

2. As discussed in the Introduction, WEIRD stands for Western, Educated, Industrialized, Rich, Democratic. (WEIRD societies also are Urbanized: WEIRDU.)

3. Lew-Levy et al. (2017), 386.

4. This sentence paraphrases Lancy & Grove, 154. Lancy originated "chore curriculum" to stand in contrast to educators' term "core curriculum."

5. Sometimes adults fashion a child-size replica for youngsters' practice, for example, a small bow and arrow set.

6. There is reason to believe that inculcating manners, morals, myths, and symbols is a key objective of most initiation rites for children in traditional societies.

7. The Navajo are an exception. As described in Chapter 4, adults take great interest in each youngster's progress in learning to talk, and especially encourage the learning of kinship terms.

8. Insights and research findings for this section come from, among others, Freed & Freed, 117–18; Ullrich, 235–37, 241; Packer, 377–78, 382–83, 435–37; Gaskins & Paradise, 101–3; Lancy & Grove, 153, 166; Harkness & Super, 67; Hewlett & Mac-Farlan, 430; Montgomery, 152; Anderson-Levitt, 999.

9. I am referring to cuneiform writing, consisting of wedge-shaped impressions in soft clay. The Wikipedia entry for cuneiform includes many clear, close-up photographs of cuneiform tablets.

10. An exception is the initiation rituals that occur in many traditional societies, which are largely for the purpose of sharing the group's wisdom with its youth. Recall the *Kinaaldá* ritual for Navajo girls.

11. When attempts have been made to create settings in which children are to learn didactic or factual information through the informal means practiced in the village, the results are disastrous. Researchers report that "informal learning environments have no greater claim on solid, conceptually accurate, deeply meaningful interpretations than any other form of learning." Lancy (2022), 156, note 36. Lancy cites Gaea Leinhardt & Karen Knutson (2004), *Listening in on Museum Conversations*, 7.

12. Be aware that considerable research has been done on memorization. The findings might surprise you. A good short introduction to this topic is in my 2017 book, *The Drive to Learn*, 11–14.

13. This sentence is closely modeled on Maynard & Tovote, 183.

14. For the ideas in this paragraph, I am indebted to the prompting of Ames, 153.

15. Gray, 454. Gray is discussing "play," whereas I am striving to avoid the word "play" because I believe that, for most Americans, it carries connotations of frivolity and lack of purpose other than fun.

16. Packer, 229.

17. As I know from experience, boarding a bus together with many others is a totally different experience in the United Kingdom and in China. In the United Kingdom we all politely "queue." In China we all energetically compete.

18. "In ancient Rome, elite *pueri* [boys] imitated the actions of their fathers and other adult males by pretending that they were magistrates wearing togas, carrying *fasces* [bound bundle of wooden rods with an axe], and passing judgment from tribunals." Lancy (2022), 234; Lancy cites Janette McWilliam (2013), "The socialization of Roman children," *The Oxford Handbook of Childhood and Education in the Classical World*, 178.

19. In Germany and France today, state-sanctioned apprenticeship systems continue to thrive. Search the Internet for "German apprenticeship system" and "French apprenticeship system."

20. Gaskins & Paradise, 98–100, 102. The leading light in the study of children's learning via observation, imitation, and pitching in is Barbara Rogoff of the University of California. For more insight into "open attention," see Chapter 6 of my 2017 book, *The Drive to Learn*.

21. I realize that it's never collective alignment (harmony) all the time. See, in the Introduction, the subsection entitled "About the Apparent Tendency to Idealize."

22. Smith, 183, 190; Packer, 384–85.

23. One of my readers, Willa Hallowell, points out that an unfortunate exception is gang membership.

24. This sentence paraphrases Gray, 444; Gray is discussing the views of historian Howard Chudacoff, as set forth in Chudacoff's 2007 book, *Children at Play: An American History*. The "high plateau" began in the early 1900s because it was during that period that child labor was restricted by law.

25. Gray, 447–49. Gray cites too many studies to list here. A key one is Jean M. Twenge et al. (2010), Birth cohort increases in psychopathology among young Americans, 1938–2007: A cross-temporal meta-analysis of the MMPI, *Clinical Psychology Review, 30*, 145–54. Gray's suicide statistics come from the Centers for Disease Control and two other sources.

26. An exception is the BaMbuti Pygmies of the Ituri Forest in Africa. Their children always have their own playground, called *bopi*, a few yards from the main camp. There is no reason to imagine that BaMbuti parents in any sense "curate" this area. Colin M. Turnbull, *The Forest People*, Simon & Schuster, 128.

27. Reference is to the book about Aka dads, *Intimate Fathers*, by Barry Hewlett.

28. The original term for this value constellation was "collectivist." Concern arose that this term conjured up Communism in some people's minds. "Communitarian" has come into use more recently. For a useful comparative discussion of the communitarian and individualistic (or "independent") models of the family, see Packer, 313–14.

29. *Wall Street Journal*, 20–21 August 2022, A3: "According to a Brookings Institution estimate, a married, middle-income couple with two children would spend $310,605 to raise their younger child born in 2015 through age 17."

30. I describe child-centeredness in education as a "supposed virtue" because of what I learned about preschool and primary school education in East Asia when I wrote my 2020 book, *A Mirror for Americans: What the East Asian Experience Tells Us about Teaching Students Who Excel*.

31. This paragraph is influenced by Lancy (2022), 414.

32. "Bread and circuses" is attributed to the Roman poet Juvenal (active around 100 AD). He was referring to the Roman government's practice of providing free wheat and entertaining extravaganzas to keep the poorer citizens contented and to retain their political allegiance. For more detailed information, consult the discussions in Wikipedia, The Free Dictionary, and other sources.

33. Thank you to my editor, Kay Jones, for supplying me with the idea that generated this paragraph.

34. I write of "family farms that raise livestock" because that is my experience during childhood summers, and that of my friend and editor, Kay Jones, who was raised on a family farm. Kay doubts that similar opportunities exist for children on larger mechanized farms, or on farms that raise only fruit or crops.

35. On the day I wrote this sentence, this news item appeared: "Colorado has passed a law making it explicitly legal for a child to play or walk outside without

parental supervision, after a rash of unwarranted reports of child abuse or neglect. Under a previous law, parents could be accused of neglect if they left kids in an environment 'injurious to the child's health or welfare.' That invited 221,000 calls to the state's child abuse hotline last year, many of them reporting that a kid was simply playing outside or walking to school alone." *The Week*, 15 April 2022, p. 6.

36. Young people have started to respond with their own banned books club: bannedbooksclub.com.

37. Lenore Skenazy (2021), *Free-Range Kids: How Parents and Teachers Can Let Go and Let Grow, 2nd Ed.* William Stixrud & Ned Johnson (2018), *The Self-Driven Child: The Science and Sense of Giving Your Kids More Control Over Their Lives.*

38. From 2018 to 2021, an estimated 50,000 high school referees quit, most often because of parents' behavior. Hundreds of games are being cancelled due to a lack of referees. "As parents spend more time and money on children's sports, families are coming to these sporting events with professional-level expectations. A 2019 Harris Poll found that one in four parents reported spending about $500 per month on youth sports." nytimes.com/2022/04/21/sports/referee-shortage-youth-sports.html.

39. Anthropologists take a dim view of experts, many of whom believe children are genetically driven. In turn, that would mean that childhood has universal characteristics, leading further to the belief that there's one best way to parent: what the expert recommends. LeVine & New, 5; Lancy (2017), 150.

40. "The traditional sequence of childcare apprenticeship followed by parenting is reversed in WEIRD societies. We marry and establish our household first, then get on-the-job childcare training. Both mothers and fathers are likely to be in the same boat, and both are likely to doubt their abilities as parents when parenting doesn't 'come naturally.'" Smith, 104, edited.

41. The age of girls' menarche in WEIRD societies has been declining gradually, relative to the age of girls' menarche in traditional societies. Even within the same society, the age of urban and suburban girls' menarche tends to decline relative to that of rural and village girls. The determinants of the age of menarche are thought to include genetics, socioeconomics, general health, nutrition, exercise, and even family size. For details, search the Internet for "age of menarche." See also Lancy (2022), 309.

42. The Aka present an extreme case in that, as soon as they are weaned, children pretty much do whatever they wish.

43. In Chapter 6, about village Indians, we also saw that even fully grown sons can be prevented from making significant decisions so long as their fathers are living and sentient.

44. H. L. Mencken (1880–1956) came up with this definition: Puritanism is the haunting fear that someone, somewhere, may be happy.

APPENDIX A

1. Appendix A, Table 1 generalizes the range of differences that anthropologists view as significant in the characteristic background and context in which traditional

and American children are raised; anticipate exceptions. The American middle-class column assumes urban or suburban home locations (not rural or farm). Principal source is Lancy (2017), 144–58. Other sources include Lancy & Grove, 154–56, 163; Hewlett & MacFarlan, 429; Hewlett et al. (2016), 43; Hewlett & Hewlett, 94, 98; Boyette & Hewlett, 291; Boyette (2016), 264–65; Smith, 183, 190; and Packer, 313–14.

2. Appendix A, Table 2 broadly generalizes what anthropologists have concluded about traditional rural-agrarian societies and modern (mainly Western) urban-industrial societies; anticipate exceptions. This table is not intended as a summary of Chapters 2 through 6. Sources include Sharma & LeVine (1998), 56; Montgomery, 30–31; LeVine et al. (1994), 249; LeVine (1988), 6–7; Packer, 313–14; Hewlett & MacFarlan, 429; Smith, 171; Wenger, 290; Benedict, 43–44; Kağıtçıbaşı, entire article.

3. Appendix A, Table 3 generalizes what anthropologists have found about traditional and modern middle-class societies; anticipate exceptions. This table is not a summary of Chapters 2 through 6. The American middle-class column assumes urban or suburban home locations (not rural or farm). Main source is Lancy (2017), 144–58. Others include Seymour (1975), 52–56; Seymour (1999), 85; Deyhle (1994), 158; Lancy (2010), 86–91; Kennedy, 162–74; and these Figures in Packer: 4.15 on p. 141, 4.16 on p. 142, and 5.9 on p. 170; all of which are based on Keller (2003) and (2019).

4. Appendix A, Table 4 generalizes what anthropologists have found about traditional and modern middle-class societies; anticipate exceptions. This table is not a summary of Chapters 2 through 6. The American middle-class column assumes urban or suburban home locations (not rural or farm). Main source is Lancy (2017), 144–58. Others include Seymour (1975), 52–56; Seymour (1999), 85; Deyhle (1994), 158; Lancy (2010), 86–91; Kennedy, 162–74; and these Figures in Packer: 4.15 on p. 141, 4.16 on p. 142, and 5.9 on p. 170; all of which are based on Keller (2003) and (2019).

5. Appendix A, Table 5 broadly generalizes what anthropologists have found about learning in unschooled and recently schooled traditional and village societies; anticipate exceptions. The American middle-class column assumes urban or suburban locations (not rural or farm). This table is not intended as a summary of Chapters 2 through 6. Sources include Freed & Freed, 117–18; Hewlett & MacFarlan, 430; Anderson-Levitt, 999; Montgomery, 152; Packer 435–37, 377–78, 382–83; Lancy (2010), 90, 98; Lancy & A. Grove, 153, 166; Harkness & Super, 67; Gaskins & Paradise, 101–03; Ullrich, 235–37, 241. For East–West contrasts in schooling, see C. Grove (2017a) and C. Grove (2020).

APPENDIX B

1. I soon realized that if the word "style" or "styles" is in a title, the reported research almost always is the result of a survey by psychologists, and therefore of little or no interest to me.

2. The books.google.com website catalogues thousands upon thousands of books but is inconsistent in the information it makes available about each one. In some

cases, very little information is provided. In others, excerpts are provided from random locations within the book, sometimes not even including the table of contents. Without at least a book's table of contents, random excerpts are not useful to me.

3. To gain access to a journal article, one usually needs to pay between $25 and $50. A few articles are available at no charge, as explained in the text.

4. Researchers using quantitative methods usually count the occurrence of certain types of behavior. An example is the number of times that a specific relative (e.g., a grandmother or a sibling) feeds food other than breast milk to children aged two to four. In the case of this example, the findings showed that public health campaigns about child feeding needed to be directed toward all relatives, not just mothers. Fouts & Brookshire, entire article.

5. The participant observation method is discussed in both the Introduction and Chapter 1.

6. Witherspoon, ix.

7. Here is a list of regions linked with researchers. *Kashmir*: Madan (1989). *Punjab*: Gideon (1962). *Uttar Pradesh*: Minturn & Hitchcock (1966), Whiting & Whiting (1975), and Whiting & Edwards (1988). *Gujarat*: Keller et al. (2005). *Karnataka*: Kennedy (1954). *Kerala*: Mencher (1963). *Tamil Nadu*: Trawick (1992). *West Bengal*: Rohner & Chaki-Sircar (1988). *Orissa*: Seymour (multiple years between 1975 and 2013). In the vicinity of *Delhi*, one village was studied by Freed & Freed (1981) and, later, by Sharma & LeVine (1998), and another by Sarangapani (2003). These are not the only anthropological studies of children and parenting in India.

8. See Seymour (2013) for an excellent overview of her longitudinal research in Orissa.

9. The biggest difference I encountered was that, among a group called the Nayars in the southern state of Kerala, descent is traced through the mother's side, not the father's. However, this made little difference in child-rearing practices.

10. Examples include Chaudhary (2012), Isaac et al. (2014), Paiva (2008), Raj & Raval (2003), Sharma & LeVine (1988), Tuli (2012), and Mandelbaum (1970).

11. Kurtz, 58.

Bibliography

Citations for the Introduction, Chapters 1, 7, and 8, and Appendices A and B

Ames, Patricia. (2013). Learning to be responsible: Young children transitions outside school. *Learning, Culture, and Social Interaction, 2,* 143–154.

Anderson-Levitt, Kathryn M. (2005). The schoolyard gate: Schooling and childhood in global perspective. *Journal of Social History, 38* (4), 987–1006.

Benedict, Ruth. (2008). Continuities and discontinuities in cultural conditioning. *Anthropology and Child Development: A Cross-Cultural Reader,* Robert LeVine & Rebecca New, eds. Wiley-Blackwell, 42–48.

Blum, Susan D. (2017). Unseen WEIRD assumptions: The so-called language gap discourse and ideologies of language, childhood, and learning. *International Multilingual Research Journal, 11* (1), 23–38.

Blunt, Lady Anne. (1879). *Bedouin Tribes of the Euphrates, Vol. I.* John Murray. This volume contains no information about who republished it.

Blunt, Lady Anne. (1879). *Bedouin Tribes of the Euphrates, Vol. II.* John Murray. Republished by Franklin Classics, an imprint of Creative Media Partners.

Boyette, Adam H. (2016). Children's play and culture learning in an egalitarian foraging society. *Child Development, 87* (3), 759–769.

Boyette, Adam H., & Barry S. Hewlett. (2017). Autonomy, equality, and teaching among Aka foragers and Ngandu farmers of the Congo Basin. *Human Nature, 28,* 289–322.

Bruner, Jerome S. (1996). *The culture of education.* Harvard University Press.

Chick, Garry. (2010). Work, play, and learning. *The Anthropology of Learning in Childhood,* David Lancy et al., eds. Rowman & Littlefield, 119–143.

Deyhle, Donna. (1994). Cultural differences in child development: Navajo adolescents in middle schools. *Theory into Practice, 33* (3), 156–166.

Everett, Daniel L. (2008). *Don't sleep, there are snakes: Life and language in the Amazonian Jungle.* Pantheon.

Fasulo, Alessandra, Heather Loyd, & Vincent Padiglione. (2007). Children's socialization into cleaning practices: A cross-cultural perspective. *Discourse & Society, 18* (1), 11–33.

Freed, Ruth S., & Stanley A. Freed. (1981). Enculturation and education in Shanti Nagar. *Anthropological Papers of The American Museum of Natural History, Vol. 57* (2): 49–156.

Gaimster, David. (1997). Stoneware production in medieval and early modern Germany. *Pottery in the Making: World Ceramic Traditions*, Ian Freestone & David Gaimster, eds. British Museum Press, 122–133.

Gaskins, Suzanne. (2008). Children's daily lives among the Yucatec Maya. *Anthropology and Child Development: A Cross-Cultural Reader*, Robert LeVine & Rebecca New, eds. Wiley-Blackwell, 280–88.

Gaskins, Suzanne, & Ruth Paradise. (2010). Learning through observation in daily life. *The Anthropology of Learning in Childhood*, David Lancy et al., eds. Rowman & Littlefield, 85–117.

Goody, Esther. (1982). *Parenthood and social reproduction: Fostering and occupational roles in West Africa.* Cambridge University Press.

Gray, Peter. (2011). The decline of play and the rise of psychopathology in children and adolescents. *American Journal of Play, 3* (4), 443–463.

Grove, Cornelius. (2013). *The Aptitude myth: How an ancient belief came to undermine children's learning today.* Rowman & Littlefield.

Grove, Cornelius. (2017a). *The Drive to learn: What the East Asian experience tells us about raising students who excel.* Rowman & Littlefield.

Grove, Cornelius. (2017b). Pedagogy across cultures. *International Encyclopedia of Intercultural Communication.* Wiley-Blackwell, 2017.

Grove, Cornelius. (2020). *A mirror for Americans: What the East Asian experience tells us about teaching students who excel.* Rowman & Littlefield.

Hall, G. Stanley. (1904). *Adolescence: Its psychology and its relations to physiology, anthropology, sociology, sex, crime, religion, and education.* Appleton; now published by Hesperides Press.

Harkness, Sara, Charles M. Super, & colleagues. (2010). Parental ethnotheories of children's learning. *The Anthropology of Learning in Childhood*, David Lancy et al., eds. Rowman & Littlefield, 65–81.

Hewlett, Barry S. (1991). *Intimate fathers: The nature and context of Aka Pygmy paternal infant care.* University of Michigan Press.

Hewlett, Barry S., & Shane J. MacFarlan. (2010). Fathers' roles in hunter-gatherer and other small-scale cultures. *The Role of the Father in Child Development, 5th Ed.*, Michael E. Lamb, ed. Wiley, 413–434.

Hewlett, Barry S., Richard E. W. Berl, & Casey J. Roulette. (2016). Teaching and overimitation among Aka hunter-gatherers. *Social Learning and Innovation in Contemporary Hunter-Gatherers*, Hideaki Terashima & Barry S. Hewlett, eds. Springer Japan, 35–45.

Hewlett, Barry S., Jean Hudson, Adam H. Boyette, & Hillary N. Fouts. (2019). Intimate living: Sharing space among Aka and other hunter-gatherers. *Towards a Broader View of Hunter-Gatherer Sharing*, Noa Lavi & David E. Friesem, eds. Cambridge University Press, 39–56.

Hewlett, Bonnie L., & Barry S. Hewlett. (2012). Hunter-gatherer adolescence. *Adolescent Identity: Evolutionary, Cultural, and Developmental Perspectives*, Bonnie L. Hewlett, ed. Routledge, 73–101.

Hewlett, Bonnie L. (2013). *Listen, here is a story: Ethnographic life narratives from Aka and Ngandu women of the Congo Basin.* Oxford University Press.

Heywood, Colin. (1988). *Childhood in nineteenth century France: Work, health, and education among the "Classes Populaires."* Cambridge University Press.

Honwana, Alcinda. (2005). The pain of agency: The agency of pain. *Makers and Breakers: Children and Youth in Post-Colonial Africa*, Alcinda Honwana & Filip de Boeck, eds. Africa World Press, 31–52.

Kağıtçıbaşı, Çiğdem. (2005). Autonomy and relatedness in cultural context: Implications for self and family. *Journal of Cross-Cultural Psychology*, *36* (4), 403–422.

Keller, Heide. (2003). Socialization for competence: Cultural models of infancy. *Human Development*, *46* (5), 288–311.

Keller, Heide, R. Yovsi, J. Borke, J. Kärtner, H. Jensen, & Z. Papaligoura. (2004). Developmental consequences of early parenting experiences: Self-recognition and self-regulation in three cultural communities. *Child Development*, *75* (6), 1745–1760.

Keller, Heidi, M. Abels, B. Lamm, R. Yovsi, S. Voelker, & A. Lakhani. (2005). Ecocultural effects on early infant care: A study in Cameroon, India, and Germany. *Ethos*, *33* (4), 512–541.

Keller, Heidi. (2019). The role of emotions in socialization processes across cultures: Implications for theory and practice. *The Handbook of Culture and Psychology, 2nd Ed.*, David Matsumoto & Hyisung Hwang, eds. Oxford University Press.

Kennedy, Beth C. (1954). Rural–urban contrasts in parent-child relations in India. *Indian Journal of Social Work*, *15*, 162–174.

King, Charles. (2019). *Gods of the upper air: How a circle of renegade anthropologists reinvented race, sex, and gender in the twentieth century.* Doubleday.

Kluckhohn, Clyde, & Henry A. Murray, eds. (1948). *Personality in nature, society, and culture.* Knopf.

Kroeber, Alfred L., & Clyde Kluckhohn. (1963). *Culture: A critical review of concepts and definitions.* Vintage Books.

Kurtz, Stanley N. (1992). *All the mothers are one: Hindu India and the cultural reshaping of psychoanalysis.* Columbia University Press.

Ladd, John. (1957). *The structure of a moral code: A philosophical analysis of ethical discourse applied to the ethics of the Navaho Indians.* Harvard University Press.

Lancy, David F. (1983). *Cross-cultural studies in cognition and mathematics.* Academic Press.

Lancy, David F. (1996). *Playing on the mother ground: Cultural routines for children's development.* Guilford Press.

Lancy, David F. (2007). Accounting for variability in mother-child play. *American Anthropologist*, *109* (2), 273–284.

Lancy, David F., & M. Annette Grove. (2010). The role of adults in children's learning. *The Anthropology of Learning in Childhood*, David Lancy et al., eds. Rowman & Littlefield, 145–179.

Lancy, David F. (2010). Learning "from nobody": The limited role of teaching in folk models of children's development. *Childhood in the Past, 3*, 79–106.

Lancy, David F. (2015). *The anthropology of childhood: Cherubs, chattel, changelings, 2nd Ed.* Cambridge University Press.

Lancy, David F. (2017). *Raising children: Surprising insights from other cultures.* Cambridge University Press.

Lancy, David F. (2022). *The anthropology of childhood: Cherubs, chattel, changelings, 3rd Ed.* Cambridge University Press.

LeVine, Robert A. (1977). Child rearing as cultural adaptation. *Culture and Infancy: Variations in the Human Experience*, P. H. Leiderman et al., eds. Academic Press.

LeVine, Robert A. (1988). Human parental care: Universal goals, cultural strategies, individual behavior. *Parental Behavior in Diverse Societies*, R. A. LeVine et al., eds. New Directions for Child Development, No. 40. Jossey-Bass.

LeVine, Robert, Suzanne Dixon, Sarah LeVine, Amy Richman, P. Herbert Leidermann, Constance Keefer, & T. Berry Brazelton. (1994). *Child care and culture: Lessons from Africa.* Cambridge University Press.

LeVine, Robert A. (2007). Ethnographic studies of childhood: A historical overview. *American Anthropologist, 109* (2), 247–260.

LeVine, Robert A., & Karin Norman. (2008). Attachment in anthropological perspective. *Anthropology and Child Development: A Cross-Cultural Reader*, Robert LeVine & Rebecca New, eds. Wiley-Blackwell, 127–142.

LeVine, Robert A., & Rebecca S. New. (2008). Introduction. *Anthropology and Child Development: A Cross-Cultural Reader*, Robert LeVine & Rebecca New, eds. Wiley-Blackwell, 1–7.

LeVine, Robert A. (2021a). My life in psychological anthropology and future research on its history. *The Cultural Psyche: The Selected Papers of Robert A. LeVine on Psychosocial Science*, Dinesh Sharma, ed. Information Age Publishing, 17–36.

LeVine, Robert A. (2021b). Properties of culture: An ethnographic view. *The Cultural Psyche: The Selected Papers of Robert A. LeVine on Psychosocial Science*, Dinesh Sharma, ed. Information Age Publishing, 83–102.

Marey-Sarwan, Ibtisam, Heidi Keller, & Hiltrud Otto. (2016). Stay close to me: Stranger anxiety and maternal beliefs about children's socio-emotional development among Bedouins in the unrecognized villages in the Naqab. *Journal of Cross-Cultural Psychology, 47* (3), 319–332.

Maynard, Ashley E., & Katrin E. Tovote. (2010). Learning from other children. *The Anthropology of Learning in Childhood*, David Lancy et al., eds. Rowman & Littlefield, 181–205.

Mead, Margaret. (1928). *Coming of age in Samoa: A psychological study of primitive youth for Western civilization.* Blue Ribbon Books; now available from Perennial Classics, New American Library, and other publishers.

Meehan, Courtney L., & Sean Hawks. (2013). Cooperative breeding and attachment among the Aka foragers. *Attachment Reconsidered: Cultural Perspectives on a*

Western Theory, Naomi Quinn & Jennifer M. Mageo, eds. Palgrave Macmillan, 85–113.

Montgomery, Heather. (2009). *An introduction to childhood: Anthropological perspectives on children's lives*. Wiley-Blackwell.

Nerlove, Sarah B., John Roberts, Robert Klein, Charles Yarbrough, & Jean-Pierre Habicht. (1974). Natural indicators of cognitive development: An observational study on rural Guatemalan children. *Ethos*, *2*, 265–295.

Ochs, Elinor, & Carolina Izquierdo. (2009). Responsibility in childhood: Three developmental trajectories. *Ethos*, *37* (4), 391–413.

Packer, Martin J. (2021). *Child development: Understanding a cultural perspective, 2nd Ed.* Sage.

Rheingold, Harriet L. (1982). Little children's participation in the work of adults, a nascent prosocial behavior. *Child Development*, *53* (1), 114–125.

Rogoff, Barbara, Martha J. Sellers, Sergio Pirotta, Nathan Fox, & Sheldon H. White. (2008). Age and responsibility. *Anthropology and Child Development: A Cross-Cultural Reader*, Robert LeVine & Rebecca New, eds. Wiley-Blackwell, 251–69.

Rogoff, Barbara. (2014). Learning by observing and pitching in to family and community endeavors: An orientation. *Human Development*, *57*, 69–81.

Seymour, Susan. (1975). Child rearing in India: A case study in change and modernization. *Socialization and Communication in Primary Groups*, Thomas Williams, ed. Mouton.

Seymour, Susan C. (1999). *Women, family, and child care in India*. Cambridge University Press.

Seymour, Susan. (2004). Multiple caretaking of infants and young children: An area in critical need of a feminist psychological anthropology. *Ethos*, *32* (4), 538–556.

Seymour, Susan C. (2013). The Harvard–Bhubaneswar, India project. *The Asian Man*, *7* (1–2), 1–8.

Sharma, Dinesh, & Robert A. LeVine. (1998). Child care in India: A comparative developmental view of infant social environments. *New Directions for Child Development*, *81* (Fall), 45–67.

Smith, Harriet J. (2005). *Parenting for primates*. Harvard University Press.

Ullrich, Helen E. (2017). Conclusion: Transition in Totagadde from 1964 to 2011. *The Women of Totagadde: Broken Silence*, Helen Ullrich, ed. Palgrave Macmillan, 227–242.

Weisner, Thomas S., and Ronald Gallimore. (2008). Child and sibling caregiving. *Anthropology and Child Development: A Cross-Cultural Reader*, Robert LeVine & Rebecca New, eds. Wiley-Blackwell, 265–269.

Weisner, Thomas S. (1982). Sibling interdependence and child caretaking: a cross-cultural view. *Sibling Relationships*, Michael Lamb & Brian Sutton-Smith, eds. Erlbaum, 303–27.

Wenger, Martha. (2008). Children's work, play, and relationships among the Giriama of Kenya. *Anthropology and Child Development: A Cross-Cultural Reader*, Robert LeVine & Rebecca New, eds. Wiley-Blackwell, 289–306.

Whiting, Beatrice B., & Carolyn P. Edwards. (1988). *Children of different worlds: The formation of social behavior*. Harvard University Press.
Williams, Thomas R. (1969). *A Borneo childhood*. Holt, Rinehart, and Winston.
Winick, Charles. (1961). *Dictionary of anthropology*. Littlefield-Adams.

About the Author

After attaining a master of arts in teaching at Johns Hopkins University, Cornelius N. Grove taught high school history, worked in educational publishing, traveled extensively in Europe and Africa, and completed a doctorate in education (Ed.D.) at Columbia University. He then served for 11 years as director of research for AFS, the student exchange organization, simultaneously holding adjunct teaching posts at Columbia and New School Universities. In 1986, he taught at Beijing Foreign Studies University, after which he co-authored *Encountering the Chinese: A Modern Country, An Ancient Culture* (3rd Ed. 2010).

During the 2000s, he became curious about the belief of many Americans that inborn ability is the main determinant of a child's academic performance. This led his penning *The Aptitude Myth: How an Ancient Belief Came to Undermine Children's Learning Today* (2013). He then decided to figure out why East Asian students consistently outperform U.S. students on international comparative tests (such as PISA) and wrote two books on his findings. The first addresses differences in parenting: *The Drive to Learn: What the East Asian Experience Tells Us about Raising Students Who Excel* (2017). The second explores contrasting approaches to classroom teaching in pre- and primary schools: *A Mirror for Americans: What the East Asian Experience Tells Us about Teaching Students Who Excel* (2020).

Dr. Grove retired in 2020 after 31 years as managing partner of GROVEWELL LLC, a global business leadership consultancy. He and his wife have three sons and five grandchildren.